Body codes used within this publication

Type of vehicle

A	Articulated vehicle
B	Single-deck vehicle
C	Single-deck coach
CO	Convertible open-top vehicle
DP	Coach-seated bus
DPH	Coach-seated double-deck bus
H	Double-deck vehicle
M	Minibus (16 seats of less)
O	Open-top vehicle
PO	Partial open-top vehicle

Vehicle type is then followed by seating capacity and then door position and addition equipment; in the instance of double-deck vehicles, upstairs is shown "over" lower deck.

Door position

D	Dual-door vehicle
C	Central-fitted door
F	Front (single-door) vehicle
R	Rear entrance vehicle
T	Triple-door vehicle

Additional equipment

T	Toilet
L	Wheelchair lift

For example, a vehicle shown as H45/31F is a double-deck vehicle, seating 45 upstairs and 31 downstairs; DPH47/25F is a double-deck bus fitted with coach seating, with 47 seats upstairs and 25 downstairs

Our thanks go to Kevin Cooper, for his assistance with the rail section, including supply of photographs, to Ian Attenborough for various regular updates from across the country which have contributed towards this publication, to Peter Hulse for updates for Go North East, and to Malcolm Adcock for his assistance proof reading this publication.

Unless otherwise stated, all photography in this publication is by Brian Cheyney, who also helped to compile, produce and proof read this publication.

First edition 2018

This publication is up to date as at the end of May 2018. While every effort is also made to ensure maximum accuracy, unfortunately 100% accuracy cannot be guaranteed. The authors hold no responsibility for any inconvenience caused by any errors contained within this publication.

Written by Andrew Woolhouse, owner of Woolybus,

211 Marlborough Road, Dagenham, Essex

Printed by Book Printing UK

Front cover: Plymouth Citybus 251, pictured in Plymouth while on route 12A heading to Downgate

Back cover: Thamesdown 145, preserved by Go South Coast, pictured in Warminster as part of a running day

2

Contents

* - also includes Gatwick Express operation

Brighton & Hove

Garage

CS	Hove - Conway Street, Hove, BN3 3LT
LR	Lewes Road - Lewes Road, Brighton, BN2 4AE
NH	Newhaven - Newhaven Workshops, Beach Close, Newhaven, BN9 0BY
WK	Whitehawk Road - Whitehawk Road – Whitehawk Road, Brighton, BN2 5NS

51-57		Scania CK230UB			Scania OmniLink				B43F	
51	YN58BCE	LR	54	YN58BCO	LR	57	YN58BCY	CS
52	YN58BCF	LR	55	YN58BCU	LR			
53	YN58BCK	LR	56	YN58BCV	LR			

Other than coaches and a batch of ex-London Mercedes-Benz Citaros, the Brighton & Hove fleet is predominantly all double-deck. However, a batch of seven Scania Omnilinks form part of the fleet. 52 is seen here in Brighton City Centre while on route 18 heading to Queens Park

105-130		Mercedes-Benz O530G			Mercedes-Benz Citaro G 18.0m * - AB46D			AB53D	
105*	BD57WDC	LR	113*	BD57WDS	LR	125	BL57OXJ	u
106*	BD57WDE	LR	114*	BD57WDT	LR	126	BL57OXP	u
107*	BD57WDK	LR	119	BL57OXK	LR	127	BP57UYK	LR
108*	BD57WDL	LR	120	BP57UYE	LR	128	BP57UYL	LR
109*	BD57WDM	LR	121	BP57UYF	LR	129	BL57OXN	LR
110*	BD57WDN	LR	122	BP57UYG	LR	130	BL57OXM	LR
111*	BD57WDP	LR	123	BP57UYH	LR			
112*	BD57WDR	LR	124	BP57UYJ	LR			

401-421		Volvo B9TL			Wright Eclipse Gemini 2 10.4m			H43/28F	
401	BJ11XHA	CS	403	BJ11XHC	CS	405	BJ11XHE	CS
402	BJ11XHB	CS	404	BJ11XHD	CS	406	BJ11XHF	CS

Brighton & Hove operate a number of ex-London Mercedes-Benz Citaro artics, which can most commonly be found on route 25 and its express version, route 25X. 109, showing the striking "Happies not Hippies" wrap, is seen at the bottom of North Street while on route 25X heading to Sussex University

407	BJ11XHG	LR	412	BJ11XHN	CS	417	BJ11XHT	CS
408	BJ11XHH	LR	413	BJ11XHO	LR	418	BJ11XHU	LR
409	BJ11XHK	LR	414	BJ11XHP	LR	419	BJ11XHV	LR
410	BJ11XHL	LR	415	BJ11XHR	LR	420	BJ11XHW	CS
411	BJ11XHM	CS	416	BJ11XHS	CS	421	BJ11XHX	LR

422-439		Volvo B9TL		Wright Eclipse Gemini 2 10.5m			H43/28F	
422	BF12KYX	LR	428	BF12KXC	LR	434	BF12KXK	LR
423	BF12KYY	LR	429	BF12KXH	LR	435	BF12KXN	LR
424	BF12KXB	LR	430	BF12KXJ	LR	436	BF12KXO	LR
425	BF12KWZ	LR	431	BF12KXG	LR	437	BF12KXM	LR
426	BF12KXA	LR	432	BF12KXE	LR	438	BF12KXR	LR
427	BF12KXD	LR	433	BF12KXL	LR	439	BF12KXS	LR

440	BK10MGV	Volvo B5LH		Wright Eclipse Gemini 2 10.4m			H41/23F	CS
441	BG61SXS	Volvo B5LH		Wright Eclipse Gemini 2 10.4m			H41/23F	CS

442-452		Volvo B5LH		Wright Eclipse Gemini 2 10.5m			H41/25F	
442	BF62UXH	CS	446	BF62UXM	CS	450	BF62UXR	CS
443	BF62UXJ	CS	447	BF62UXN	CS	451	BF62UXS	CS
444	BF62UXK	CS	448	BF62UXO	CS	452	BF62UXT	CS
445	BF62UXL	CS	449	BF62UXP	CS			

453-490		Volvo B9TL		Wright Eclipse Gemini 2 10.5m			H43/28F	
453	BK13NZV	CS	456	BK13NZY	CS	459	BK13OAB	CS
454	BK13NZW	CS	457	BK13NZZ	CS	460	BK13OAC	CS
455	BK13NZX	CS	458	BK13OAA	CS	461	BK13OAD	CS

Routes 28 and 29 in Brighton are branded as The Regency Routes, with buses carrying this striking maroon and cream livery. 431 is seen turning into Old Steine while heading to Lewes and Ringmer on route 28

462	BK13OAE	CS	472	BK13OAU	CS	482	BJ63UJL	CS
463	BK13OAG	CS	473	BJ63UJA	CS	483	BJ63UJM	WK
464	BK13OAH	CS	474	BJ63UJB	CS	484	BJ63UJN	WK
465	BK13OAJ	CS	475	BJ63UJC	CS	485	BJ63UJO	WK
466	BK13OAL	CS	476	BJ63UJD	CS	486	BJ63UJP	NH
467	BK13OAM	CS	477	BJ63UJE	CS	487	BJ63UJR	NH
468	BK13OAN	CS	478	BJ63UJF	WK	488	BJ63UJS	NH
469	BK13OAO	CS	479	BJ63UJG	WK	489	BJ63UJT	NH
470	BK13OAP	CS	480	BJ63UJH	WK	490	BJ63UJU	CS
471	BK13OAS	CS	481	BJ63UJK	CS			

500	BV66GYJ	Mercedes-Benz City 45	Mercedes-Benz	B17F	CS
502	HF08UHT	Scania K340EB4	Irizar Century	C49FT	CS
503	YR58RUH	Scania K340EB4	Irizar Century	C49FT	CS
504	YR58RUU	Scania K340EB4	Irizar Century	C49FT	CS
505	UK59BCL	Scania K340EB4	Irizar Century	C49FT	CS
550	BF12KXP	Volvo B9TL	Wright Eclipse Gemini 2 10.5m	DPH43/29F	CS
551	BF12KXT	Volvo B9TL	Wright Eclipse Gemini 2 10.5m	DPH43/29F	CS

616-670		Scania N94UD	East Lancs Omnidekka 10.6m	H47/32F
			* - O47/33F

616*	GX03SSV	CS	634	YN04GKG	WK	641	YN04AOT	WK
623	YN04GJK	WK	635	YN04GKJ	WK	642	YN04AOU	WK
629	YN04GKC	WK	636	YN04GKK	NH	643	YN04AOV	WK
630	YN04GKD	WK	637	YN04AOM	NH	644	YN04AOW	WK
631	YN04GJX	WK	638	YN04AOO	NH	645	YN04AOX	WK
632	YN04GKE	WK	639	YN04AOP	NH	646	YN04AOY	WK
633	YN04GKF	CS	640	YN04AOR	NH	647	YN05GZK	WK

Above: *Spiritbus is the fleet name used for the coach operation part of Brighton & Hove. 550 is seen here in Brighton City Centre while on a private hire duty*

Below: *Showing its First World War Centenary livery is 662, pictured here in Brighton City Centre while on route 5B heading to Hollingbury*

648	YN05GZM	WK	656	YN55NFO	CS	662	YN55NFJ	CS
649	YN05GZH	CS	657	YN55NFH	CS	663	YN55NFA	NH
650	YN05GZJ	CS	658	YN55NFK	LR	665	YN55NFD	CS
652	YN05GZO	CS	659	YN55NFL	LR	666	YN55NFG	NH
655	YN55NFF	CS	660	YN55NFM	LR			
667	YN06SZW	NH	669	YN06SZY	CS			
668	YN06SZX	NH	670	YN06SZZ	LR			

671-688		Scania N270UD		East Lancs Omnidekka 10.6m			H47/28F	
671	YN07UOT	LR	677	YN57FYA	LR	683	YN57FYE	LR
672	YN07UOU	LR	678	YN57FYJ	LR	684	YN57FYO	LR
673	YN07UOF	LR	679	YN57FYB	LR	685	YN57FYP	LR
674	YN07UOG	LR	680	YN57FYK	LR	686	YN57FYF	LR
675	YN57FYC	u	681	YN57FYL	LR	687	YN57FYG	LR
676	YN57FYD	LR	682	YN57FYM	LR	688	YN57FYH	LR

Brighton & Hove have more recently been taking Wright Streetdecks into stock as their standard double-deck vehicle, to low height configuration. 803 is seen here in Brighton City Centre, pictured while on route 1 heading to Whitehawk

801-855		Wright Streetdeck		Wright Streetdeck 10.6m			H45/25D	
801	SK16GWC	WK	811	SK16GWP	WK	821	SK16GXD	u
802	SK16GWD	WK	812	SK16GWU	WK	822	SK16GXE	WK
803	SK16GWE	WK	813	SK16GWV	WK	823	SK16GXF	WK
804	SK16GWF	WK	814	SK16GWW	WK	824	SK16GXG	WK
805	SK16GWG	WK	815	SK16GWX	WK	825	SK17HJA	WK
806	SK16GWJ	WK	816	SK16GWY	WK	826	SK17HJC	WK
807	SK16GWL	WK	817	SK16GWZ	WK	827	SK17HJD	WK
808	SK16GWM	WK	818	SK16GXA	WK	828	SK17HJE	WK
809	SK16GWN	WK	819	SK16GXB	WK	829	SK67FJJ	WK
810	SK16GWO	WK	820	SK16GXC	WK	830	SK67FJN	WK

831	SK67FJO	WK	840	SK67FKV	CS	849	SK67FLN	LR
832	SK67FJP	CS	841	SK67FKW	LR	850	SK67FLP	LR
833	SK67FJU	CS	842	SK67FKX	LR	851	SK67FLR	LR
834	SK67FJV	CS	843	SK67FKY	LR	852	SK67FLV	LR
835	SK67FJX	CS	844	SK67FKZ	LR	853	SK67FLW	LR
836	SK67FJY	CS	845	SK67FLA	LR	854	SK67FLX	LR
837	SK67FJZ	CS	846	SK67FLJ	LR	855	SK67FLZ	LR
838	SK67FKT	CS	847	SK67FLL	LR			
839	SK67FKU	CS	848	SK67FLM	LR			

Showing the full-height version of the Wright Streetdeck in the Brighton & Hove is 827, pictured here near the Royal Pavilion while heading to Brighton Marina on route 7

901-920		Scania N94UD		East Lancs Omnidekka			H51/37F	
				* - O49/35F				
901	YN56FFA	LR	908	YN56FFJ	LR	915	YN56FFS	LR
902	YN56FFB	LR	909	YN56FFK	LR	916	YN56FFT	LR
903	YN56FFC	LR	910	YN56FFL	LR	917	YN56FFU	LR
904	YN56FFD	LR	911	YN56FFM	LR	918	YN56FFV	LR
905	YN56FFE	LR	912	YN56FFO	LR	919*	YN06NYK	CS
906	YN56FFG	LR	913	YN56FFP	LR	920*	YN06NYL	CS
907	YN56FFH	LR	914	YN56FFR	LR			

921-947		Wright Streetdeck		Wright Streetdeck 11.5m			H47/34F	
921	BX15OMT	NH	928	BX15ONC	NH	935	BX15ONM	NH
922	BX15OMU	NH	929	BX15ONF	NH	936	BX15ONN	NH
923	BX15OMV	NH	930	BX15ONG	NH	937	BX15ONO	NH
924	BX15OMW	NH	931	BX15ONH	NH	938	BX15ONP	NH
925	BX15OMY	NH	932	BX15ONJ	NH	939	BX15ONR	NH
926	BX15ONA	NH	933	BX15ONK	NH	940	BX15ONS	NH
927	BX15ONB	NH	934	BX15ONL	NH	941	BX15ONT	NH

| 942 | BX15ONU | NH | 944 | BX15ONW | NH | 946 | SK67FJE | NH |
| 943 | BX15ONV | NH | 945 | SK67FJD | NH | 947 | SK67FJF | NH |

Route 12 , linking Brighton with Eastbourne, is branded as the Coaster, complete with a batch of dedicated long-wheelbase Wright Streetdecks in this eye-catching green and blue livery. 944 is seen here in Brighton City Centre while on a short working to Seaford Library

7221	R221HCD	Volvo B10BLE	Wright Renown 12.0m	B46F	CSt
7236	R236HCD	Volvo B10BLE	Wright Renown 12.0m	B39F	LRt
7548	YN05HCD	Scania CN94UB	Scania OmniCity	B24D	LRt
7549	YN05HCE	Scania CN94UB	Scania OmniCity	B24D	LRt
7951	PL51LDK	Volvo B7TL	Plaxton President 10.0m	DPH41/20D	LRt
7952	PL51LDN	Volvo B7TL	Plaxton President 10.0m	DPH41/20D	LRt
RML2317	CUV317C	AEC Routemaster	Park Royal 30ft	H40/32R	LR

Liveries
Unless stated below, all vehicles in this fleet carry standard fleet livery;

Science Bus: 106, 107
Happies Not Hippies: 109
Music Bus: 130
Paddle Round The Pier: 418
Regency: 422-437
Spirit of Sussex: 500, 503-505, 530, 550, 551
City Sightseeing: 616, 919, 920
World War I Centenary: 662
Coaster: 921-944
Allover orange: 7236
Brighton & Hove Training: 7548, 7549, 7951, 7952
Tilling: RML2317

Carousel

Garage
WY   High Wycombe - Unit 2, Hughenden Avenue, High Wycombe, HP13 5SG

214-222		Scania N230UD		Alexander Enviro 400 10.9m			H51/29F	
214	CF10OXF	WY	217	FF10OXF	WY	220	JF10OXF	WY
215	DF10OXF	WY	218	GF10OXF	WY	221	KF10OXF	WY
216	EF10OXF	WY	219	HF10OXF	WY	222	LF10OXF	WY

A batch of 9 Alexander Enviro 400-bodied Scania double-deckers were cascaded to the Carousel operation in 2016. 218 is seen here arriving in High Wycombe while on route 36

401-409		Wright Streetlite Max		Wright Streetlite 11.5m			B45F	
401	SM15HWC	WY	404	SM65LNF	WY	407	SK16GXX	WY
402	SM15HWD	WY	405	SM65LNG	WY	408	SK16GXY	WY
403	SM65LNE	WY	406	SK16GXL	WY	409	SK16GXZ	WY

418	AE59AWH	MAN 14.240	MCV Evolution 11.3m	B44F	WY
419	AE59AWJ	MAN 14.240	MCV Evolution 11.3m	B44F	WY

420-424		MAN 14.240		Alexander Enviro 200 10.9m			B38F	
420	RX60DLY	WY	422	RX60DME	WY	424	RX60FKF	WY
421	RX60DLZ	WY	423	RX60DMF	WY			

502	OU57FGV	Dennis E200Dart SFD111	Alexander Enviro 200 8.9m	B29F	WY
503	OU57FGX	Dennis E200Dart SFD111	Alexander Enviro 200 8.9m	B29F	WY
551	C1WYC	Dennis E200Dart SFD333	MCV Evolution 10.8m	B40F	WY
552	C2WYC	Dennis E200Dart SFD321	Alexander Enviro 200 10.8m	B38F	WY
553	C3WYC	Dennis E200Dart SFD333	MCV Evolution 10.8m	B40F	WY

Seen here in High Wycombe Bus Station is 419, pictured while heading to Chesham on route 1A

709-713			Optare Solo M950		Optare Solo 9.5m			B32F	
709	MX08MYV	WY		711	MX58AAF	WY	713	MX58AAN	WY
710	MX08MYY	WY		712	MX58AAJ	WY			

805	YJ56WUE	Optare Tempo X1260	Optare Tempo 12.6m	B47F	w
873	AE61EWO	Mercedes-Benz OC500U	MCV Evolution 12.0m	B43F	WY
874	AE61EWP	Mercedes-Benz OC500U	MCV Evolution 12.0m	B43F	WY
875	AE61EWR	Mercedes-Benz OC500U	MCV Evolution 12.0m	B43F	WY
876	BD09ZRC	Mercedes-Benz O530	Mercedes-Benz Citaro 12.0m	B40F	WY
877	BT09GOH	Mercedes-Benz O530	Mercedes-Benz Citaro 12.0m	B40F	WY
878	BT09GOJ	Mercedes-Benz O530	Mercedes-Benz Citaro 12.0m	B40F	WY
914	OU08HGO	Scania CN230UD	Scania OmniCity 10.8m	H45/30F	WY
	BN17JXY	Mercedes-Benz 516CDi	Mercedes-Benz	B21F	WY

Previous registrations

551	AJ58PZS		553	AE59AWM
552	OU57FKB			

Liveries
Unless stated below, all vehicles in this fleet carry standard fleet livery;

Wycombe Park & Ride: 407-409
Allover white: 502, 503
Thames Travel: 709, 914
Allover silver: BN17JXY

Chambers

Garage
SY   Sudbury - Meekings Road, Chilton Industrial Estate, Sudbury, CO10 6XE

1	BX55FYH	Mercedes-Benz 1836RL		Mercedes-Benz Touro			C49FT	SY
2	BX55FYJ	Mercedes-Benz 1836RL		Mercedes-Benz Touro			C49FT	SY
3	M655KVU	Volvo B10M-60		Van Hool Alizee			C49FT	SY
10	S291TVW	Volvo B10M-62		Plaxton Premiere 320 12.0m			C53F	SY
252	EU03BZK	Dennis Dart SLF SFD3CA		Alexander Pointer 2 10.7m			B37F	SY
261	EY57FZE	Dennis E200Dart SFD321		Alexander Enviro 200 10.8m			B37F	SY

564-572		Volvo B7TL			Plaxton President 10.0m		H45/22F	
564	W409WGH	SY	567	W457WGH	SY	570	W487WGH	SY
566	W428WGH	SY	568	W458WGH	SY	572	W489WGH	SY

724	W824NNJ	Dennis Trident SFD321			East Lancs Lolyne 10.5m		H47/31F	u

800-811		Scania N94UD			East Lancs OmniDekka 10.6m		H45/29F	
800	YN53RYP	SY	804	YN55PZF	SY	808	YN55PZL	SY
801	YN55PZC	SY	805	YN55PZG	SY	809	YN55PZM	SY
802	YN55PZD	SY	806	YN55PZH	SY	810	YN55PZO	SY
803	YN55PZE	SY	807	YN55PZJ	SY	811	YN55PZP	SY

Liveries
Unless stated below, all vehicles in this fleet carry standard fleet livery;

Old Hedingham & District: 10
KonectBus: 724
Anglian Bus: 804

808, new to Metrobus before cascading to Chambers in 2015, is seen here arriving in Colchester on route 84

Go North East

Garages

CK	Crook - Unit 1, Virginia Buildings, Prospect Road, Crook, DL15 8JN
CR	Chester-Le-Street - Picktree Lane, Chester-le-street, DH3 3SW
DE	Deptford - Deptford Terrace, Deptford, Sunderland, SR4 6DD
GR	Gateshead - Mandela Way, Gateshead, NE11 9DH
HM	Hexham - Burn Lane, Hexham, NE46 3HN
PE	Peterlee - 3 Cook Way, North West Industrial Estate, Peterlee, SR8 2HY
PM	Percy Main - Rothbury Terrace, North Shields, NE29 7AP
SY	Stanley - High Street, Stanley, DH9 0TE
WA	Washington - Industrial Road, Washington, NE37 2SD

557	NK53TKY	Dennis Dart SLF SFD6BA	Alexander Pointer 2 8.8m	B29F	w
618	NK55RUV	Dennis Dart SLF SFD6BA	Alexander Pointer 2 8.8m	B29F	HM
619	NK55RUW	Dennis Dart SLF SFD6BA	Alexander Pointer 2 8.8m	B29F	HM

625-636   Optare Solo SR M880   Optare Solo SR 8.8m   B27F

625	NK11HBB	PM	629	NK61EFY	DE	633	NK61FEX	GR
626	NK61DBX	HM	630	NK61EGY	DE	634	NK61FJO	GR
627	NK61DBY	PM	631	NK61FEU	PM	635	NK61FJP	HM
628	NK61DBZ	GR	632	NK61FEV	PM	636	NK61FMD	HM

The Go North East fleet is host to a very wide variety of liveries. Shown here carrying the lime green-based Sunderland Connect livery is 630, it is in Sunderland town centre while on route 700 heading to Roker Beach

637-652   Optare Solo SR M900   Optare Solo SR 9.0m   B29F
                                              * - B30F

637*	NK12HCD	DE	640*	NK62DWY	DE	643	NL63XZP	SY
638*	NK12HCE	DE	641	NL63YBA	SY	644	NL63XZR	SY
639*	NK12HCF	DE	642	NL63XZO	SY	645	NL63XZS	SY

646	NL63XZT	SY	649	NL63XZW	PM	652	NL63XZZ	PM
647	NL63XZU	SY	650	NL63XZX	PM			
648	NL63XZV	PM	651	NL63XZY	PM			

A batch of Optare Solo SRs also operate on the Venture routes in Stanley. Seen here parked in Consett Bus Station is 641, showing the special Venture livery

653-690		Optare Solo SR M9250		Optare Solo SR 9.25m			B30F	
				* - B29F				
653	NK15GDE	PM	666	NK15EMJ	PE	679	NK16BXX	PM
654	NK15GDF	PM	667*	NK16BXH	HM	680	NK16BXY	PM
655	NK15GDJ	PE	668*	NK16BXJ	HM	681	NK66CWW	DE
656	NK15GDO	PE	669*	NK16BXL	HM	682	NK66CWX	WA
657	NK15GEY	PE	670*	NK16BXM	HM	683	NK66CWY	WA
658	NK15GFA	PE	671*	NK16BXN	HM	684	NK66CWZ	WA
659	NK15GFE	PE	672	NK16BXO	PM	685	NK66CXA	WA
660	NK15GFG	PE	673	NK16BXP	PM	686	NK66CXB	WA
661	NK15GFJ	PE	674	NK16BXR	PM	687	NK66CXC	WA
662	NK15GFO	PE	675	NK16BXS	PM	688	NK66CXD	WA
663	NK15GFU	PE	676	NK16BXU	PM	689	NK66CXE	DE
664	NK15GFV	PE	677	NK16BXV	PM	690	NK66CXF	DE
665	NK15GFX	PE	678	NK16BXW	PM			

691-696		Optare Solo SR M890		Optare Solo SR 8.9m			B29F	
691	YJ13HNW	PE	693	YJ13HNY	PE	695	YJ13HOA	CR
692	YJ13HNX	PE	694	YJ13HNZ	PE	696	YJ13HOH	DE

697-705		Optare Solo M880		Optare Solo 8.8m			B29F	
697	YJ59NNH	DE	699	YJ10MFP	DE	701	YJ10MFA	WA
698	YJ10MFO	DE	700	YJ10MFU	DE	702	YJ10MFE	WA

703	YJ10MFF	WA	704	YJ10MFK	WA	705	YJ10MFN	CR

706-709		Optare Solo M710SE		Optare Solo 7.1m			DP23F	
706	WK58EAE	CR	708	WK58EAG	CR			
707	WK58EAF	CR	709	WK58EAJ	PM			

710-714		Optare Solo M920		Optare Solo 9.2m			B33F	
710	WK59CWU	GR	712	WK59CWX	GR	714	WK59CWZ	DE
711	WK59CWW	GR	713	WK59CWY	DE			

3818	S818OFT	Volvo Olympian		NC Palatine 2			H47/30F	w
3819	S819OFT	Volvo Olympian		NC Palatine 2			H47/30F	GR
3832	S832OFT	Volvo Olympian		NC Palatine 2			H43/22F	w

3941-3965		Volvo B7TL		Wright Eclipse Gemini 10.6m			H45/29F	
3941	NK05GZO	WA	3962	JCN822	CR	3965	574CPT	CR
3942	NK05GZP	WA	3963	NK06JXD	CR			
3943	FCU190	WA	3964	NK06JXC	CR			

Go North East have a fair number of vehicles bodied by Wrightbus, both single-deckers and double-deckers. 3963 is seen about to enter Gateshead Bus Station while on route 97 heading to the Metrocentre

3967-3983		Volvo B7TL		East Lancs Myllennium Vyking 11.0m H45/20D				
3967	PN02XCL	GR	3973	PJ02PYZ	GR	3977	PJ02PZD	GR
3968	PJ02PYU	GR	3974	PJ02PZA	GR	3983	PJ02PZL	GR
3970	PJ02PYW	DE	3975	PJ02PZB	GR			
3971	PJ02PYX	GR	3976	PJ02PZC	GR			

3995	GX03SSZ	Scania N94UD		East Lancs Omnidekka 10.6m			CO47/32F	PM
3996	GX03STZ	Scania N94UD		East Lancs Omnidekka 10.6m			CO47/32F	PM

4899	V989ETN		Volvo B10BLE		Wright Renown 12.0m		B43F	GR

4926-4976			Scania L94UB		Wright Solar * - B39F		B42F	
4926	Y926ERG	w	4945	NK51OLJ	w	4964*	NL52WVV	GRt
4929	Y929ERG	w	4947	NK51OLN	GR	4965*	NL52WVW	GRt
4930	Y493ETN	w	4948	NK51OLO	GR	4966	NL52WVX	GR
4932	Y932ERG	GR	4949	NK51OLP	GR	4967	NK53UNT	GR
4933	Y933ERG	GR	4956	NL52WVM	w	4969	NK53UNV	DE
4934	Y934ERG	w	4957	NL52WVN	w	4971	NK53UNX	w
4937	NK51OKW	w	4958	NL52WVO	CR	4973	NK53UNZ	w
4938	NK51OKX	GR	4959	NL52WVP	w	4974	NK53UOA	w
4940	NK51OLB	GR	4960	NL52WVR	CR	4975	NK53UOB	w
4941	NK51OLC	GR	4961*	NL52WVS	GRt	4976	NK53UOC	DE
4942	NK51OLE	CR	4962*	NL52WVT	GRt			
4944	NK51OLH	GR	4963*	NL52WVU	GRt			

4978-4982			Volvo B7RLE		Wright Eclipse Urban 12.0m		B43F	
4978	NK54NUH	PM	4980	NK54NUM	PM	4982	NK54NUP	PM
4979	NK54NUJ	PM	4981	NK54NUO	PM			

4989-5232			Scania L94UB		Wright Solar * - B40F		B43F	
4989	YN51MKV	DE	5201	NK54NUU	CR	5205	NK54NUY	PE
4990	YN51MKX	DE	5202*	NK54NUV	GRt	5206	NK54NVA	PE
4991	YR02ZYK	w	5203	NK54NUW	w	5207	NK54NVB	DE
4992	YR02ZYM	DE	5204	NK54NUX	PE	5208	NK54NVC	DE

Another livery carried in the Go North East fleet is this green-based Highwayman livery, dedicated to route 98.
Seen in Newcastle town centre while covering a working on route 97 to the Metrocentre is 5218

5209	NK54NVD	DE	5217	NK54NVN	GR	5225	NK54NVY	GR
5210*	NK54NVE	GRt	5218	NK54NVO	GR	5226	NK54NVZ	GR
5211	NK54NVF	DE	5219	NK54NVP	GR	5227	NK54NWA	GR
5212	NK54NVG	DE	5220	NK54NVT	GR	5228	NK54NWB	GR
5213	NK54NVH	DE	5221	NK54NVU	GR	5229	NK55OLG	CR
5214	NK54NVJ	DE	5222	NK54NVV	GR	5230	NK55OLH	CR
5215	NK54NVL	DE	5223	NK54NVW	GR	5231	NK55OLJ	CR
5216	NK54NVM	GR	5224	NK54NVX	GR	5232	NK55OLM	CR

5234-5274		Scania CN230UB		Scania OmniCity 12.0m		B41F		
5234	NK56KHB	SY	5249	NK56KHV	SY	5263	NK56KJY	WA
5235	NK56KHC	SY	5250	NK56KHW	SY	5264	NK56KJZ	PM
5236	NK56KHD	DE	5251	NK56KHX	DE	5265	NK56KKA	PM
5237	NK56KHE	DE	5252	NK56KHY	SY	5266	NK56KKB	PM
5238	NK56KHF	SY	5253	NK56KHZ	SY	5267	NK56KKC	PM
5239	NK56KHG	SY	5254	NK56KJA	WA	5268	NK56KKD	PM
5240	NK56KHH	SY	5255	NK56KJE	WA	5269	NK56KKE	PM
5241	NK56KHJ	SY	5256	NK56KJF	WA	5270	NK56KKF	PM
5242	NK56KHL	SY	5257	NK56KJJ	WA	5271	NK56KKG	PM
5243	NK56KHM	WA	5258	NK56KJN	WA	5272	NK56KKH	PM
5244	NK56KHO	WA	5259	NK56KJO	WA	5273	NK56KKJ	PM
5245	NK56KHP	WA	5260	NK56KJU	WA	5274	NK56KKL	PM
5246	NK56KHR	WA	5261	NK56KJV	WA			
5247	NK56KHT	WA	5262	NK56KJX	WA			

Another of the wide variety of liveries covered by vehicles in the Go North East fleet is the Toon Link. 5236 is seen here while on route 31 arriving in Newcastle

5275-5368			Mercedes-Benz O530			Mercedes-Benz Citaro 12.0m * - B39F		B40F		
5275	NK07KPG	GR	5300	NK08CHF	HM	5325	NK58DWC	GR		
5276	NK07KPJ	GR	5301	NK08CHG	HM	5326	NK58DWD	DE		
5277	NK07KPL	WA	5302	NK08CHH	HM	5327	NK58DWE	DE		
5278	NK07KPN	GR	5303	NK08CHJ	HM	5328	BJ10VUN	DE		
5279	NK07KPO	GR	5304	NK08CHL	HM	5329	BJ10VUO	DE		
5280	NK07KPP	GR	5305	NK08CHN	GR	5330	BJ10VUP	DE		
5281	NK07KPR	GR	5306	NK08CHO	GR	5331	BJ10VUR	DE		
5282	NK07KPT	GR	5307	NK08CHV	GR	5332	BJ10VUS	DE		
5283	NK07KPU	GR	5308	NK08CHX	GR	5333	BJ10VUT	DE		
5284	NK08CFP	GR	5309	NK08CHY	GR	5334	BJ10VUU	DE		
5285	NK08CFU	DE	5310	NK08MXY	GR	5335	BJ10VUV	DE		
5286	NK08CFV	DE	5311	NK08MXZ	GR	5336	BJ10VUW	DE		
5287	NK08CFX	DE	5312	NK08MYA	GR	5337*	HF06FUA	DE		
5288	NK08CFZ	DE	5313	NK08MYB	GR	5338*	HF06FUB	DE		
5289	NK08CGE	DE	5314	NK08MYC	GR	5358	BX63BCK	WA		
5290	NK08CGF	DE	5315	NK08MYD	GR	5359	BX63BCO	WA		
5291	NK08CGG	DE	5316	NK08MYF	GR	5360	BX63BCU	WA		
5292	NK08CGO	DE	5317	NK08MYG	GR	5361	BX63BCV	WA		
5293	NK08CGU	GR	5318	NK08MZV	GR	5362	BX63BCY	WA		
5294	NK08CGV	GR	5319	NK08MZW	w	5363	BX63BCZ	WA		
5295	NK08CGX	GR	5320	NK58DVW	GR	5364	BX63BDE	WA		
5296	NK08CGY	GR	5321	N21GNE	GR	5365	BX63BDF	WA		
5297	NK08CGZ	GR	5322	NK58DVY	GR	5366	BX63BDO	WA		
5298	NK08CHC	DE	5323	NK58DVZ	GR	5367	BX63BDU	WA		
5299	NK08CHD	HM	5324	NK58DWA	GR	5368	BX63BDV	WA		

The Mercedes-Benz Citaro also features in the Go North East in some number. 5306 is seen in Sunderland while on route 36 heading for Chester-le-Street, showing the debranded Goldlink livery that this vehicle used to carry; it has since been refurbished and repainted into Crusader livery

5369-5376 — Wright Streetlite Max / Wright Streetlite 11.5m — B45F

Fleet	Reg		Fleet	Reg		Fleet	Reg	
5369	NL63XAZ	DE	5372	NL63XBC	DE	5375	NL63XBF	DE
5370	NL63XBA	DE	5373	NL63XBD	DE	5376	NL63XBG	DE
5371	NL63XBB	DE	5374	NL63XBE	DE			

5377-5390 — Optare Versa V1170 / Optare Versa 11.7m — B43F

Fleet	Reg		Fleet	Reg		Fleet	Reg	
5377	NL63YAA	GR	5382	NL63YAH	GR	5387	NL63YAV	GR
5378	NL63YAD	GR	5383	NL63YAJ	GR	5388	NL63YAW	GR
5379	NL63YAE	GR	5384	NL63YAK	GR	5389	NL63YAX	GR
5380	NL63YAF	GR	5385	NL63YAO	GR	5390	NL63YAY	GR
5381	NL63YAG	GR	5386	NL63YAU	GR			

5391-5480 — Wright Streetlite Max / Wright Streetlite 11.5m — B45F

Fleet	Reg		Fleet	Reg		Fleet	Reg	
5391	NK15EMV	GR	5404	NK15ENT	CR	5417	NK15EOH	SY
5392	NK15EMX	GR	5405	NK15ENU	CR	5418	NK15EOJ	SY
5393	NK15ENC	GR	5406	NK15ENV	CR	5419	NK15EOL	SY
5394	NK15ENE	GR	5407	NK15ENW	CR	5420	NK16BYA	DE
5395	NK15ENF	CR	5408	NK15ENX	CR	5421	NK16BYB	DE
5396	NK15ENH	CR	5409	NK15ENY	SY	5422	NK16BYC	DE
5397	NK15ENJ	CR	5410	NK15EOA	SY	5423	NK16BYD	DE
5398	NK15ENL	CR	5411	NK15EOB	SY	5424	NK16BYF	DE
5399	NK15ENM	CR	5412	NK15EOC	SY	5425	NK16BYG	DE
5400	NK15ENN	CR	5413	NK15EOD	SY	5426	NK16BYH	r
5401	NK15ENO	SY	5414	NK15EOE	SY	5427	NK16BYJ	DE
5402	NK15ENP	CR	5415	NK15EOF	SY	5428	NK16BYL	DE
5403	NK15ENR	CR	5416	NK15EOG	SY	5429	NK16BYM	DE

There are well over 100 Wright Streetlites in the Go North East fleet, including nearly 100 of the "Max" long-wheelbase variety. 5412 is seen in Consett bus station while on route 45 heading to Newcastle City Centre, showing the Red Kite livery carried by this vehicle

5430	NK16BYN	DE	5447	NK66EVH	SY	5464	NK17GHU	DE
5431	NK16BYO	DE	5448	NK66EVJ	SY	5465	NK17GHV	DE
5432	NK16BYP	DE	5449	NK66EVL	SY	5466	NK17GHX	DE
5433	NK16BYR	DE	5450	NK66EVM	SY	5467	NK17GHY	DE
5434	NK16BYS	DE	5451	NK66EVN	SY	5468	NK17GHZ	DE
5435	NK16BYT	DE	5452	NK66EWA	GR	5469	NK17GJE	DE
5436	NK16BXZ	DE	5453	NK66EWB	GR	5470	NK17GJF	DE
5437	NK16BWY	DE	5454	NK66EWC	GR	5471	NK17GJG	DE
5438	NK16BWZ	DE	5455	NK66EWD	GR	5472	NK17GJJ	DE
5439	NK16AZU	DE	5456	NK66EWE	GR	5473	NK17GJO	DE
5440	NK16AZV	DE	5457	NK66EWF	GR	5474	NK17GJU	DE
5441	NK16AZW	DE	5458	NK66EWH	GR	5475	NK17GJV	DE
5442	NK66EVB	SY	5459	NK66EWJ	GR	5476	NK17GJX	DE
5443	NK66EVC	SY	5460	NK66EWL	GR	5477	NK17GJY	DE
5444	NK66EVD	SY	5461	NK66EWM	GR	5478	NK17GJZ	DE
5445	NK66EVF	SY	5462	NK66EWN	GR	5479	NK17GKA	DE
5446	NK66EVG	SY	5463	NK17GHO	DE	5480	NK17GKC	DE

6001-6007		Volvo B9TL		Wright Eclipse Gemini 2 10.4m			H43/28F	
6001	NK11BGZ	WA	6004	NK11BHE	WA	6007	NK11BHL	WA
6002	NK11BHA	WA	6005	NK11BHF	WA			
6003	NK11BHD	WA	6006	NK11BHJ	WA			

6009-6039		Volvo B7TL		Plaxton President 10.0m			H43/22F	
6009	V209LGC	w	6018	V218LGC	w	6030	V330LGC	CR
6010	V310LGC	PM	6019	V319LGC	w	6031	V331LGC	w
6015	V315LGC	w	6020	V220LGC	w	6033	V233LGC	GR
6016	V816KGF	w	6023	V923KGF	PM	6039	V302LGC	w
6017	V317LGC	w	6025	V325LGC	w			

Previous Page: *In 2011, a batch of Plaxton President-bodied Volvo B7TLs were cascaded from London to the North East to replace older vehicles. 6019 is seen here in Durham while running out of service. This vehicle has recently been withdrawn from service*

6043-6055		Volvo B9TL			Wright Eclipse Gemini 2 10.5m			H43/28F	
6043	NK12GCO	GR	6048	NK12GCZ	HM	6053	NK12GDO	WA
6044	NK12GCU	GR	6049	NK12GDA	WA	6054	NK62EKD	WA
6045	NK12GCV	GR	6050	NK12GDE	WA	6055	NK62EJF	WA
6046	NK12GCX	GR	6051	NK12GDF	WA			
6047	NK12GCY	HM	6052	NK12GDJ	WA			

6056-6070		Volvo B5LH			Wright Eclipse Gemini 2 10.5m			H41/25F	
6056	NK62CBV	PM	6061	NK62CJE	PM	6066	NK62CYC	PM
6057	NK62CCV	PM	6062	NK62CJJ	PM	6067	NK62CYE	PM
6058	NK62CCY	PM	6063	NK62CKC	PM	6068	NK62CYF	PM
6059	NK62CEN	PM	6064	NK62CLZ	PM	6069	NK62CZA	PM
6060	NK62CFN	PM	6065	NK62CME	PM	6070	NK62CZL	PM

The Angel of the North is a monument that Newcastle take a lot of pride in, including using it as branding on buses. 6058 is seen here entering Gateshead Bus Station while on route 21 heading to Newcastle

6071-6121		Volvo B9TL			Wright Eclipse Gemini 2 10.5m			H43/28F	
					* - H45/28F				
6071	NK62FAA	GR	6079	NK62FHY	HM	6087	NL63YHP	DE
6072	NK62FBA	GR	6080	NK62FJE	HM	6088	NL63YHR	DE
6073	NK62FCC	GR	6081	NK62FKG	GR	6089	NL63YHS	DE
6074	NK62FDM	GR	6082	NK62FLF	GR	6090	NL63YHT	DE
6075	NK62FDN	HM	6083	NK13EJO	GR	6091	NL63YHU	DE
6076	NK62FEU	HM	6084	NL63XBS	GR	6092	NL63YHV	DE
6077	NK62FGJ	HM	6085	NL63YHN	DE	6093	NL63YHW	DE
6078	NK62FHE	HM	6086	NL63YHO	DE	6094	NL63YHX	DE

6095	NL63YHY	DE	6104	NL63YJG	PM	6113	NL63XBX	PM
6096	NL63YHZ	DE	6105	NL63YJH	PM	6114	NL63XBY	PM
6097	NL63YJA	DE	6106	NL63YCJ	PM	6115	NL63XBZ	PM
6098	NL63YJB	DE	6107	NL63YCK	PM	6116	NL63XCA	PM
6099	NL63YJC	DE	6108	NL63YCM	PM	6117	NL63XCB	PM
6100	NL63YJD	DE	6109	NL63YCN	PM	6118*	BG15RNF	SY
6101	NL63YJE	PM	6110	NL63YCO	PM	6119*	BG15RNJ	SY
6102	NL63YJF	PM	6111	NL63XBV	PM	6120*	BG15RNN	SY
6103	NL63XBT	PM	6112	NL63XBW	PM	6121*	BG15RNO	SY

The standard fleet livery is allover red with Go North East logos, as shown here by 6084, pictured at Consett Bus Station while on route X9 heading to Newcastle

6122-6148		Scania N94UD		East Lancs Omnidekka 10.6m			H47/32F	
				* - H47/25F				
6122	GX03SSU	SY	6131	YN04GJE	SY	6140	YN04GJJ	CR
6123	GX03SUH	SY	6132	YN04GJF	PM	6141	YN04GJY	CR
6124	GX03SUU	SY	6133	YN04GJG	SY	6142	YN04GJZ	CR
6125	GX03SUV	SY	6134	YN04GJU	PM	6143	YN04GKA	SY
6126	GX03SUY	GR	6135	YN04GJV	PM	6144*	340GUP	u
6127	GX03SVA	GR	6136	GX03SUA	PM	6145*	YN55NFC	PM
6128	GX03SVC	SY	6137	GX03SVF	SY	6146	X21GNE	CK
6129	GX03SVD	GR	6138	GX03SVG	SY	6147	CU6860	PM
6130	GX03SVE	w	6139	GX03SVJ	SY	6148	CU7661	PM

6149-6161		Volvo B9TL		Wright Eclipse Gemini 2 10.5m			H39/28F	
6149	LJ62KBY	DE	6154	LJ62KLS	DE	6159	LJ62KYG	DE
6150	LJ62KCU	DE	6155	LJ62KOX	DE	6160	LJ62KZD	DE
6151	LJ62KDV	DE	6156	LJ62KXX	DE	6161	LJ62KZP	DE
6152	LJ62KDZ	DE	6157	LJ62KXZ	DE			
6153	LJ62KLC	DE	6158	LJ62KYA	DE			

6301-6307		Wright Streetdeck		Wright Streetdeck 10.6m			H39/29F	
6301	NK16BXA	CK	6304	NK16BXD	CK	6307	NK16BXG	CK
6302	NK16BXB	CK	6305	NK16BXE	CK			
6303	NK16BXC	CK	6306	NK16BXF	CK			

6308-6314		Volvo B5TL		Wright Gemini 3 10.6m			H43/34F	
6308	NK67ECD	CK	6311	NK67EBD	GR	6314	NK67EBJ	GR
6309	NK67ECE	GR	6312	NK67EBF	GR			
6310	NK67EBC	GR	6313	NK67EBG	GR			

6315-6333		Wright Streetdeck		Wright Streetdeck 10.6m			H39/29F	
6315	NK67GMG	CR	6322	NK67GNF	CR	6329	NK67GNX	CR
6316	NK67GMO	CR	6323	NK67GNJ	CR	6330	NK67GNY	CR
6317	NK67GMU	CR	6324	NK67GNN	CR	6331	NK67GNZ	CR
6318	NK67GMV	CR	6325	NK67GNO	CR	6332	NK67GOA	CR
6319	NK67GMX	CR	6326	NK67GNP	CR	6333	NK67GOC	CR
6320	NK67GMY	CR	6327	NK67GNU	CR			
6321	NK67GMZ	CR	6328	NK67GNV	CR			

7077	S977ABR	Volvo B10M-62	Plaxton Premiere 350 12.0m	C44FT	GRt
7092	LA55WWN	Volvo B12B	Plaxton Paragon 12.0m	C49FT	GRt
7093	K3VOY	Volvo B12B	Plaxton Paragon 12.0m	C8FT	GRt

Go North East is another subsidiary of the Go-Ahead Group, alongside Go South Coast, who operate National Express services. 7110 is seen here in Nuneaton while on National Express route 460 heading to London

7094-7102 — Scania K340EB6 — Caetano Levante 14.2m * - C69FL — C53FTL

7094	FJ08KLF	w	7097	FJ08KLX	r	7100*	FJ08KMV	HM
7095	FJ08KLS	w	7098	FJ08KLZ	GRt	7101*	FJ08KNV	HM
7096	FJ08KLU	w	7099	FJ08KMU	HM	7102*	FJ08KNW	HM

7103-7117 — Volvo B9R — Caetano Levante 12.6m — C48FTL

7103	FJ61GZC	CR	7108	BF63ZPZ	CR	7113	FJ60EGY	CR
7104	FJ61GZD	CR	7109	BF63ZRA	CR	7114	FJ60HXW	GR
7105	BF63ZPV	CR	7110	BF63ZRC	CR	7115	FJ60HYB	CR
7106	BF63ZPW	CR	7111	BF63ZRY	CR	7116	FJ60KVM	GR
7107	BF63ZPY	CR	7112	BF63ZRZ	CR	7117	FJ60KVO	GR

7120-7137 — Volvo B11RT — Caetano Levante 14.2m — C56FTL

7120	BX65WDA	CR	7126	BX16CKJ	CR	7132	BX16CLU	CR
7121	BX65WDC	CR	7127	BX16CKK	CR	7133	BV17GVD	CR
7122	BX65WDD	CR	7128	BX16CKL	CR	7134	BV17GVE	CR
7123	BX65WDE	CR	7129	BX16CKO	CR	7135	BV17GVF	CR
7124	BD65JDZ	CR	7130	BX16CKP	CR	7136	BV17GVG	CR
7125	BX16CKG	CR	7131	BX16CLO	CR	7137	BV17GVJ	CR

8294-8338 — Optare Versa V1110 — Optare Versa 11.1m * - B38F — B39F

8294	NK09FUP	CR	8298	NK09FUW	CR	8302	NK09FVC	CR
8295	NK09FUT	GR	8299	NK09FUY	CR	8304	NK09FVE	CR
8296	NK09FUU	CR	8300	NK09FVA	CR	8305	NK09FVF	CR
8297	NK09FUV	CR	8301	NK09FVB	CR	8306	NK09FVG	GR

The Optare Versa also features in the fleet. 8321, showing the purple-based SimpliCity livery, is seen in South Shields while on route 2A heading to Washington

8307	NK09FVH	CK	8318	NK10GOU	GR	8329*	NK11HDN	SY
8308	NK09FVJ	GR	8319*	NK11FXB	CR	8330*	NK11HDO	GR
8309	NK09FVL	GR	8320*	NK11FXC	CR	8331*	NK11HJX	GR
8310	NK10GNY	GR	8321*	NK11FXD	CR	8332*	NK11HJC	GR
8311	NK10GNZ	GR	8322*	NK11FXE	CR	8333*	NK11HJV	GR
8312	NK10GOA	GR	8323*	NK11FXF	CR	8334*	NK11HJE	GR
8313	NK10GOC	GR	8324*	NK11FXG	CR	8335*	NK11HJF	GR
8314	NK10GOE	GR	8325*	NK11FXH	CR	8336*	NK11HJG	GR
8315	NK10GOH	GR	8326*	NK11GWX	CR	8337*	NK11HKP	GR
8316	NK10GOJ	GR	8327*	NK11GWY	GR	8338*	NK11HKT	GR
8317	NK10GOP	GR	8328*	NK11HBC	GR			

8339-8346			Wright Streetlite DF			Wright Streetlite 10.8m		B38F
8339	NL63XBH	GR	8342	NL63XBM	GR	8345	NL63XBP	GR
8340	NL63XBJ	GR	8343	NL63XBN	GR	8346	NL63XBR	GR
8341	NL63XBK	GR	8344	NL63XBO	GR			

Route 53 links Newcastle City Centre with Gateshead and Saltwell Park. For this route, this special green-based livery has been adopted, as seen here on 8345 passing Gateshead Bus Station while heading for Newcastle

9083	YJ65EPU	Optare MetroDecker MD1114	Optare MetroDecker 11.1m	H51/33F	PM
9084	YJ64DZM	Optare Versa V1170H	Optare Versa 11.7m	B44F	GR

Previous registrations

3943	NK05GZR		6147	YN05GZP
3962	NK06JXE		6148	YN05GZR
3965	NK06JXB		7092	K2VOY
5321	NK58DVX		7103	FJ61GZC, JCN822
6144	YN05GZL		7104	FJ61GZD, 574CPT
6146	YN55NFE			

Liveries
Unless stated below, all vehicles in this fleet carry standard fleet livery;

Tynedale Links: 618, 619, 667-671, 5298-5303
IndiGo: 625, 627, 631, 632, 653-666, 672-680, 682-688, 701-705
New Go North East (red with blue rear): 626, 628, 633, 634, 637-639, 647-651, 695, 696, 706-709, 3858, 3962-3965, 3995, 3996, 4932, 4933, 4966, 4989, 5201, 5204-5211, 5214-5217, 5229-5232, 5249, 5251, 5252, 5261-5264, 5283, 5304, 5323-5338, 5439, 5451-5462, 5479, 5480, 6043, 6044, 6048, 6084, 6122, 6123, 6128, 6132, 6134-6142, 6146, 6155-6161, 8294, 8296-8301, 8306-8309, 8325-8328, 9084
Sunderland Connect: 629, 630, 640
Hadrians Wall Bus: 635, 636
Venture: 641-646, 652
Black Cats: 681, 689, 690, 698-700, 4969, 4976, 4990-4992, 5212, 5213, 5463-5478
Heyfordian: 697
MetroCentre: 710-714, 5391-5394
Bargain Bus: 3818
Allover yellow: 3832
Route X1: 3943, 6001, 6003-6007, 6049-6055
Green Arrows: 4938, 4940, 4941, 4944, 4947, 4948, 5218, 5227, 5228
Waggonway: 4956-4960
Highwayman: 4967
Blue Arrows: 4971, 4973-4975, 5203, 5266-5273
Toon Link: 4982, 5234-5242, 5250, 5253, 6124-6127, 6129-6131, 6149-6154
Loop: 5219-5226
Whay-Aye Five-O: 5243-5247, 5254-5260
Coaster: 5265, 6056-6068, 6070
Blaydon Racers: 5275, 5276, 5278, 5279, 5282
Citylink: 5277, 5281, 5293-5297
Allover blue: 5280
Durham Diamond: 5284, 5442-5450
Wear Xpress: 691-694, 5285-5291
Pride and Diversity: 5292
Crusader: 5305-5322
Connections 4: 5358-5368
Drifter: 5369-5376, 8305
Quaylink: 5385-5388, 8310-8318, 8329-8338
Coast & Country: 5395-5400, 5402-5408
Red Kite: 5409-5418, 6118-6121
Prince Bishops: 5420-5437, 5440, 5441
Red Arrows: 6002
Ten Valley Ten: 6045-6047, 6071-6083
Angel: 6069, 6315-6331
Fab 56: 6086-6098
Cobalt Connect: 6101-6114
Allover silver: 6115, 9083
DFDS: 6144, 6145, 6147, 6148
Castles Express: 6301-6307
Routes X9/X10: 6308-6314
Go North East Training: 7077, 7092
Allover white: 7093, 7097, 7098, 7100-7102, 7114, 7116, 7117
National Express: 7094-7096, 7099, 7103-7113, 7115, 7120-7137
South Tyne: 8295
Lambton Worm: 8302, 8304
See It, Do It, Sunderland: 8319-8324
Saltwell Park: 8339-8346

Hedingham & District

Garages

CN	Clacton - Stephenson Road, Gorse Lane Industrial Estate, Clacton-on-Sea, CO15 4XA	
HD	Hedingham - Wethersfield Road, Sible Hedingham, Halstead, CO9 3LB	
KN	Kelvedon - Kelvedon – 215-217 High Street, Kelvedon, Colchester, CO5 9JT	

4	M571XKY	Volvo B10M-62	Plaxton Premiere 350 12.0m	C53F	w
5	N664THO	Volvo B10M-62	Plaxton Premiere 320 12.0m	C53F	HD
6	N667THO	Volvo B10M-62	Plaxton Premiere 320 12.0m	C53F	w
7	P530CLJ	Volvo B10M-62	Plaxton Premiere 320 12.0m	C53F	w
8	R453FWT	Volvo B10M-62	Plaxton Premiere 350 12.0m	C53F	CNt
9	S290TVW	Volvo B10M-62	Plaxton Premiere 320 12.0m	C53F	CN
75	S300XHK	Volvo Olympian	Alexander RL	H51/36F	w
90	N427JBV	Volvo Olympian	NC Palatine 1	H43/30F	w
93	R273LGH	Volvo Olympian	NC Palatine 1	H43/27F	w
95	R279LGH	Volvo Olympian	NC Palatine 1	H43/31F	w
251	PJ02RHE	Dennis Dart SLF SFD3C2	Alexander Pointer 2 10.7m	B39F	CN
253	EU04BVF	Dennis Dart SLF SFD3CA	Alexander Pointer 2 10.7m	B37F	CN
254	EU05AUR	Dennis Dart SLF SFD2BA	Alexander Pointer 2 10.1m	B34F	u
255	EU05AUT	Dennis Dart SLF SFD2BA	Alexander Pointer 2 10.1m	B34F	CN

256-259		Dennis Dart SLF SFD3CA	Alexander Pointer 2 10.7m	B37F		
256	EU55BWC	CN	258	EU56FLN	HD	
257	EU56FLM	CN	259	EU56FLP	HD	

262	EU58JCJ	Dennis E200Dart SFD361	Alexander Enviro 200 10.8m	B37F	HD
263	EU59AYM	Dennis E200Dart SFD3B1	Alexander Enviro 200 10.8m	B37F	HD

The Hedingham & District fleet used to be quite varied. However, since the acquisition by Go-Ahead, there has been a growing sense of standardisation across the fleet. 293, an Alexander Enviro 200 is seen here arriving in Colchester while on route 63, showing the original and more traditional livery of the fleet

264	EU59AYP	Dennis E200Dart SFD3B1	Alexander Enviro 200 10.8m	B37F	CN
265	EU10AOX	Dennis E200Dart SFD3B1	Alexander Enviro 200 10.8m	B37F	CN
289	EJ02KYY	Dennis Dart SLF SFD6BA	Alexander Pointer 2 8.8m	B29F	KN
290	EX02RYR	Dennis Dart SLF SFD6B2	Alexander Pointer 2 8.8m	B29F	KN
291	EU06KCX	Dennis Dart SLF SFD6BA	Alexander Pointer 2 8.8m	B29F	KN
292	EU59AFF	Dennis E200Dart SFD151	Alexander Enviro 200 8.9m	B29F	CN
293	EU59AFJ	Dennis E200Dart SFD151	Alexander Enviro 200 8.9m	B29F	CN
295	SN10CCX	Dennis E200Dart SFD1A1	Alexander Enviro 200 8.9m	B29F	HD
296	SN10CCY	Dennis E200Dart SFD1A1	Alexander Enviro 200 8.9m	B29F	HD
470	EU05CLJ	Volvo B7RLE	Wright Eclipse Urban 12.0m	B43F	HD

470 is unique in the Hedingham fleet in being their only Wright Eclipse Urban. It is seen here entering the gates to the Showbus rally at Duxford, pictured prior to the fleet renumbering with its original fleet number of L340

510-514		Volvo B7TL		Wright Eclipse Gemini 10.6m			H43/29F	
510	LB02YWX	HD	512	LB02YXA	HD	514	LB02YXF	HD
511	LB02YWY	HD	513	LB02YXE	HD			

517	LX05EZR	Volvo B7TL		Wright Eclipse Gemini 10.1m			H41/22D	HD

561-581		Volvo B7TL		Plaxton President 10.0m			H45/25F	
				* - H45/22F				
561	V301LGC	CN	573	W491WGH	KN	578	W519WGH	KN
563	V307LGC	HD	574	W506WGH	KN	579	W526WGH	KN
565*	W425WGH	CN	575	W516WGH	KN	580	W527WGH	KN
569	W484WGH	KN	576	W517WGH	KN	581	W956WGH	CN
571*	W488WGH	CN	577	W518WGH	KN			

615	EU07GVY	Dennis Trident SFD45N	Alexander Enviro 400 10.8m	H47/33F	HD
616	SN10CCV	Dennis Trident SFD48S	Alexander Enviro 400 10.8m	H47/33F	HD

In the Hedingham fleet are two Alexander Enviro 400s, bought new prior to the take over by Go-Ahead. 616 is seen here having arrived in Colchester on route 88

701-734		Dennis Trident SFD321		East Lancs Lolyne 10.5m			H47/31F	
701	T801RFG	CN	721	W821NNJ	CN	727	W827NNJ	CN
702	T802RFG	HD	722	W822NNJ	CN	729	W829NNJ	CN
712	T812RFG	CN	723	W823NNJ	HD	734	W834NNJ	CN
717	T817RFG	CN	726	W826NNJ	CN			

737	T107DBW	Dennis Trident SFD323	Alexander ALX400 10.5m	H47/26F	KN
738	T108DBW	Dennis Trident SFD323	Alexander ALX400 10.5m	H47/26F	KN
739	T117DBW	Dennis Trident SFD323	Alexander ALX400 10.5m	H47/26F	w
743	X386NNO	Dennis Trident SFD311	Alexander ALX400 10.5m	H45/23D	KN

812-820		Scania N94UD		East Lancs Omnidekka 10.6m			H45/29F	
812	YN55PZR	CN	815	YN55PZW	CN	818	YN06JYC	CN
813	YN55PZU	CN	816	YN55PZX	CN	819	YN06JYD	CN
814	YN55PZV	CN	817	YN06JYB	CN	820	YN06JYE	CN

852	AO57HCD	Scania CN230UD	Scania OmniCity 10.8m	H47/30F	CN
9000	PL51LGO	Volvo B7TL	E Lancs Myllennium Vyking 11.0m	H45/20D	KNt
9016	YU02GHA	Scania N94UB	East Lancs Myllenium 10.6m	B29D	KNt
9017	YU02GHD	Scania N94UB	East Lancs Myllenium 10.6m	B29D	KNt
	PJ02REU	Volvo B7TL	Plaxton President 10.0m	H41/20D	u

Previous registrations

5	XEL158	90	N427JBV, WLT527
6	XEL24	565	W425WGH, WLT625
7	A13XEL		

Liveries
Unless stated below, all vehicles in this fleet carry standard fleet livery;

Old Hedingham & District: 4-9, 75, 90, 95, 253-259, 262-265, 291-293, 470, 615, 616, 738, 739
Cream and red: 287, 701, 702, 717, 729
Thames Travel: 295
KonectBus: 510, 721-723, 726, 727
Allover red: 517, 9016, 9017, PJ02REU
Anglian Bus: 712, 715, 743, 852
Plymouth Citybus: 9000

During 2015, a number of East Lancs Omnidekka-bodied Scania double-deckers were cascaded from London to the Chambers and Hedingham & District operations. This included a refurbishment and conversion to single-door, and with that, this new striking livery was launched for these operations. 812 is seen here in Colchester while heading to Brightlingsea on route 87

Konectbus

Garage

KB   Dereham – 7 John Goshawk Road, Rashes Green Industrial Estate, Dereham, NR19 1SY

294	OU57FGZ	Dennis E200Dart SFD111	Alexander Enviro 200 8.9m	B29F	KB
297	SN10CCZ	Dennis E200Dart SFD1A1	Alexander Enviro 200 8.9m	B29F	KB
298	OU57FHA	Dennis E200Dart SFD111	Alexander Enviro 200 8.9m	B29F	KB

300-309   Optare Versa V1110   Optare Versa 11.1m   B37F
* - B38F, $ - B40F

300	MX08UZT	KB		304	MX58KYV	KB		307	AU11ESG	KB
302*	AU08DKL	KB		305$	YJ60KGU	KB		308	AU11EPF	KB
303*	AU08DKN	KB		306$	YJ60KGV	KB		309	AU11EPE	KB

404-415   Optare Tempo X1200   Optare Tempo 12.0m   B42F
* - B43F

404	MX05ELH	KB	409*	YJ57EGY	KB	413*	YJ09MHZ	KB
406	MX06YXU	KB	410*	YJ57EGX	KB	414	YJ55BLX	KB
407	YJ56WVA	KB	411*	MX58ABV	KB	415	YJ06FZK	KB
408	YJ56WVB	KB	412*	YJ09MHY	KB			

Pictured here while on layover in Norwich Bus Station after arriving on route 87 is 411

450	YN07LFU	Scania K94IB4	Scania OmnLink	B45F	KB

451-457   Scania CK230UB   Scania OmnLink   B46F
* - B45F

451*	YN07EZB	KB	454	YT11LVF	KB	457	AU61AVK	KB
452*	AU58AUV	KB	455	AN61LAN	KB			
453	YT11LVE	KB	456	AN61BUS	KB			

458-462		Scania CN94UB		Scania OmniCity 12.0m * - B37D			B36F	
458	YN05HFH	KB	460	YN05HFF	KB	462*	YN03WRJ	w
459	YN05HFJ	KB	461	YN05HFG	w			

Showing the former Anglian Bus livery since the merging of the Anglian Bus operation into that of KonectBus is 459, pictured here arriving in Norwich City Centre on route 5C

515-519		Volvo B7TL		Wright Eclipse Gemini 10.1m			H41/22D	
515	LX05EZK	u	518	LX05EZW	u			
516	LX05EZL	u	519	LX05EZZ	KB			

550	AO57EZM	Scania CN230UD	Scania OmniCity 10.8m	H47/30F	KB
551	AO57EZL	Scania CN230UD	Scania OmniCity 10.8m	H47/30F	KB
553	AO57HCC	Scania CN230UD	Scania OmniCity 10.8m	H47/30F	KB

600-604		Dennis Trident SFD48S		Alexander Enviro 400 10.8m			H47/33F	
600	SN10CFD	KB	602	SN10CFF	KB	604	SN10CEX	KB
601	SN10CFE	KB	603	SN10CFG	KB			

605-639		ADL E40D SFD4DS		ADL Enviro 400 10.8m * - H47/32F			H47/31F	
605*	SN61CZV	KB	613*	SN62AVY	KB	623	SN65OAB	KB
606*	SN61CZW	KB	614*	SN62AVZ	KB	624	SN65OAC	KB
607*	SN61CZX	KB	617	SK15HKA	KB	625	SN65OAD	KB
608*	SN61CZY	KB	618	SK15HKB	KB	626	SN65OAE	KB
609*	SN61CZZ	KB	619	SK15HKC	KB	627	SN65OAG	KB
610*	SN62AVG	KB	620	SK15HKD	KB	628	SN65OAH	KB
611*	SN62AVO	KB	621	SK15HKE	KB	629	SN65OAJ	KB
612*	SN62AVR	KB	622	SN65OAA	KB	630	SN65OAL	KB

631	SN65OAM	KB	634	SN65OAS	KB	637	SN65OAW	KB
632	SN65OAO	KB	635	SN65OAU	KB	638	SN65OAX	KB
633	SN65OAP	KB	636	SN65OAV	KB	639	SN65OAY	KB

KonectBus operate a number of ADL Enviro 400s on various services in Norwich. 627 is seen here on route 502, part of the Norwich Park & Ride network, pictured while heading to the Harford Park & Ride site

740	V161MEV	Dennis Trident SFD311		Alexander ALX400 10.5m		H47/23D	w
800	BD57WDA	Mercedes-Benz O530G		Mercedes-Benz Citaro G 18.0m		AB47T	KB
802	BD57WCZ	Mercedes-Benz O530G		Mercedes-Benz Citaro G 18.0m		AB47T	KB

900-906		Optare Solo M920		Optare Solo 9.2m		B33F	
900	VX51RHZ	r	903	MX53FDP	w	906	AU04JKN	w
901	VX51RJZ	KB	904	MX53FDM	w			
902	YN04LWP	w	905	MX53FDO	w			

907	YT51EBF	Optare Solo M850	Optare Solo 8.5m	B28F	w

950-961		Optare Solo M950		Optare Solo 9.5m		B32F	
950	AU07KMM	KB	954	YN57HPU	w	960	AU58AKK	KB
951	AU07KMK	KB	956	YN57HRA	w	961	AU58AKN	KB
952	AO57BDY	KB	957	YN57HPV	w			
953	YN57HPX	KB	959	AU08GLY	KB			

9015	PJ53NKO	Volvo B7TL	Plaxton President 10.0m	H41/23D	KBt
9018	YU02GHN	Scania N94UB	East Lancs Myllenium 10.6m	B29D	KBt
9019	YR52VHK	Scania N94UB	East Lancs Myllenium 10.6m	B29D	KBt

Liveries
Unless stated below, all vehicles in this fleet carry standard fleet livery;

Allover white: 294
Thames Travel: 297
Carousel Buses: 298
Anglian Bus (yellow with blue swirling skirt): 305-309, 450-462, 550, 551, 553, 740, 902, 903, 905-907, 950, 954, 956, 957, 959-961
London red: 515, 516, 518, 519, 9015, 9018, 9019
Norwich Park & Ride: 600, 603, 622-634, 800, 802
KonectExpress: 605-614, 617-621
Green and blue (for route 5): 635-639

Also showing the former Anglian Bus livery is 959, seen in Castle Meadow, Norwich while on route 50A heading to Cringleford

London

Garages

A	Sutton - Bushey Road, Sutton, SM1 1QJ
AF	Putney - Chelverton Road, London, SW15 1RN
AL	Merton - High Street, London, SW19 1DN
BV	Belvedere - Crabtree Motorway North, Belvedere, DA17 6LJ
BX	Bexleyheath - Erith Road, Bexleyheath, DA7 6BX
C	Croydon - 134 Beddington Lane, Beddington, Croydon, CR9 4ND
FK	Folkestone – Caesars Way, Folkestone, CT19 4AL
LU	Luton - 487 Dunstable Road, Luton, LU4 8DS
MB	Green Street Green - Farnborough Hill, Orpington, BR6 6DA
MG	Morden Wharf - Tunnel Avenue, North Greenwich, London SE10
MW	Mandela Way - Mandela Way, London, SE1 5SS
NP	Northumberland Park - Marsh Lane, London, N18 0XB
NX	New Cross - 28 New Cross Road, London, SE14 5UH
PL	Plough Lane - Waterside Way, London, SW17 0HB
PM	Peckham - Blackpool Road, London, SE15 3SU
Q	Camberwell - 2 Warner Road, London, SE5 9JU
RA	Waterloo - Cornwall Road, London, SE1 8TE
RR	Barking - 51-53 River Road, Barking, IG11 0SW
SI	Silvertown - Factory Road, London, E16 2EL
ST	Sittingbourne - Castle Road, Sittingbourne, ME10 3RL
SW	Stockwell - Binfield Road, London, SW4 6ST

142	LT02ZDR	Dennis Dart SLF SFD6B2	Marshall Capital 8.8m	B25F	RR

The Metrobus part of the Go-Ahead London operation has been in charge of the R-route Orpington network for a long while. 185 is seen here in Orpington while on route R1 heading to the garage at Green Street Green

154-162				Dennis E200Dart SFD1D1		Alexander Enviro 200 8.9m		B26F	
154	YX60FTZ	MB	157	YX60FUY	MB	160		YX60FVC	MB
155	YX60FUV	MB	158	YX60FVA	MB	161		YX60FVD	MB
156	YX60FUW	MB	159	YX60FVB	MB	162		YX60FVE	MB

163-192				ADL E20D SFD1D1		ADL Enviro 200 8.9m		B25F	
163	YX61ENC	MB	173	YX61ENP	MB	183		YX62DZN	MB
164	YX61ENE	MB	174	YX61ENR	MB	184		YX62DZU	MB
165	YX61ENF	MB	175	YX61ENT	MB	185		YX13AJO	MB
166	YX61ENH	MB	176	YX61ENU	MB	186		YX13AJU	MB
167	YX61ENJ	MB	177	YX61ENV	MB	187		YX13AJV	MB
168	YX61ENK	MB	178	YX61ENW	MB	188		YX13AJY	MB
169	YX61ENL	MB	179	YX62DYH	MB	189		YY13VKO	C
170	YX61ENM	MB	180	YX62DYN	MB	190		YY13VKP	C
171	YX61ENN	MB	181	YX62DYS	MB	191		YY13VKR	C
172	YX61ENO	MB	182	YX62DZE	MB	192		YY13VKS	C

214	SN03WMG	Dennis Dart SLF SFD3CA	Alexander Pointer 2 10.7m	B33D	C
215	SN03WMK	Dennis Dart SLF SFD3CA	Alexander Pointer 2 10.7m	B33D	MB
230	PO56JFE	Dennis Dart SLF SFD6BA	East Lancs Esteem 9.0m	B24F	SI
231	PO56JFF	Dennis Dart SLF SFD6BA	East Lancs Esteem 9.0m	B24F	RR
232	PO56JFG	Dennis Dart SLF SFD6BA	East Lancs Esteem 9.0m	B24F	RR

232 is a Dennis Dart SLF with East Lancs Esteem body, a combination that is rare. It is seen in Croydon town centre on Route 367. It has since transferred to East London and is now normally found on route 193

256	SN54GRK	Dennis Dart SLF SFD6BA	Alexander Pointer 2 8.8m	B23F	NP
286	SN03YCK	Dennis Dart SLF SFD6BA	Alexander Pointer 2 8.8m	B23F	w

561-567		Scania CN230UB		Scania OmniCity 12.0m			B33D	
561	YN08OAS	C	564	YN08OAW	C	567	YN08OAZ	C
562	YN58BNA	C	565	YN08OAX	C			
563	YN08OAV	C	566	YN08OAY	C			

613	YN06JXT	Scania N94UB	East Lancs Esteem 10.6m	B29D	MB
707	YX58DXC	MAN 14.240	Alexander Enviro 200 10.7m	B34D	MB

709-721		MAN 14.240		MCV Evolution 10.8m			B28D	
709	AE09DHG	MB	717	AJ58WBG	MB	721	AJ58WBK	C
713	AE09DHP	C	718	AE09DHU	C			
715	AE09DHJ	MB	720	AE09DHL	MB			

731	YX11CTE	ADL E20D SFD5D1	ADL Enviro 200 10.2m	B29D	MB
732	YX11CTF	ADL E20D SFD5D1	ADL Enviro 200 10.2m	B29D	MB
733	YX11CTK	ADL E20D SFD5D1	ADL Enviro 200 10.2m	B29D	MB

Covering for a Mercedes-Benz Citaro which usually operate on route 358 is 761, pictured here by Orpington War Memorial while heading for Crystal Palace

740-762		ADL E20D SFD7E1		ADL Enviro 200 10.8m			B31D	
740	YX13AFF	MB	748	YX13AFZ	SI	756	YX13AHD	MB
741	YX13AFJ	SI	749	YX13AGO	SI	757	YX13AHE	MB
742	YX13AFK	MB	750	YX13AGU	SI	758	YX13AHF	MB
743	YX13AFN	MB	751	YX13AGV	SI	759	YX13AHG	MB
744	YX13AFO	SI	752	YX13AGY	MB	760	YX13AHJ	MB
745	YX13AFU	MB	753	YX13AGZ	MB	761	YX13AHK	MB
746	YX13AFV	MB	754	YX13AHA	MB	762	YX13AHL	MB
747	YX13AFY	SI	755	YX13AHC	MB			

870-899		Scania N230UD		East Lancs Olympus 10.8m			H45/23D	
870	PN09EKR	RR	880	PN09ELW	MB	890	PN09ENK	RR
871	PN09EKT	RR	881	PN09ELX	MB	891	PN09ENL	RR
872	PN09EKU	RR	882	PN09EMF	MB	892	PN09ENM	RR
873	PN09EKV	RR	883	PN09EMK	RR	893	PN09ENO	RR
874	PN09EKW	RR	884	PN09EMV	RR	894	PO59KFW	RR
875	PN09EKX	RR	885	PN09EMX	RR	895	PO59KFX	RR
876	PN09EKY	RR	886	PN09ENC	RR	896	PO59KFY	RR
877	PN09ELO	RR	887	PN09ENE	RR	897	PO59KFZ	C
878	PN09ELU	RR	888	PN09ENF	RR	898	PO59KGA	C
879	PN09ELV	MB	889	PN09ENH	RR	899	PO59KGE	MB

935	YN56FDK	Scania N94UD	East Lancs Omnidekka 10.6m	H45/29F	w
945	YN56FEF	Scania N94UD	East Lancs Omnidekka 10.6m	H45/26D	w
946	YN56FEG	Scania N94UD	East Lancs Omnidekka 10.6m	H45/26D	C

947-952		Scania N230UD		East Lancs Omnidekka 10.6m			H45/23D	
947	YN07EXF	SI	949	YN07EXH	C	951	YN07EXM	C
948	YN07EXG	C	950	YN07EXK	C	952	YN07EXO	C

Route 127 is home to a variety of vehicles, including 957, seen having just left Tooting Broadway while heading to Purley

955-973		Scania CN230UD		Scania OmniCity 10.8m			H41/22D	
955	YR58SNY	C	962	YT59DYF	SI	969	YT59DYP	SI
956	YR58SNZ	C	963	YT59DYG	SI	970	YT59DYS	SI
957	YP58UFV	C	964	YT59DYH	SI	971	YT59DYU	SI
958	YT59DYA	SI	965	YT59DYN	SI	972	YT59DYV	SI
959	YT59DYB	SI	966	YT59DYJ	SI	973	YT59DYW	SI
960	YT59DYC	SI	967	YT59DYM	SI			
961	YT59DYD	SI	968	YT59DYO	SI			

DMN1	LT02NUK	Dennis Dart SLF SFD6B2	Marshall Capital 8.8m	B25F	NP
DMN4	LN51DWO	Dennis Dart SLF SFD2B2	Marshall Capital 10.2m	B28D	w

DMN7-18		Dennis Dart SLF SFD6B2	Marshall Capital 8.8m	B25F	

7	LT02NUM	RR	11	LT02NUV	RR	15	LT02NVH	RR
8	LT02NUO	RR	12	LT02NVE	RR	16	LT02NVJ	RR
9	LT02NUP	RR	13	LT52WUP	RR	17	LT52WUM	RR
10	LT02NUU	r	14	LT52WUO	r	18	LT52WUR	RR

GoAhead are shortly to lose the 193 to Stagecoach and when they do this will be the end of the DMN class of Marshall Capital bodied Dart SLFs. DMN14 is seen in the centre of Romford close to its terminus

DOE1-54		Dennis Trident SFD16M	Optare Olympus 10.3m	H43/21D	

1	LX58CWN	A	19	LX58CXJ	A	37	LX58CYG	A
2	LX58CWO	A	20	LX58CXK	A	38	LX09BXG	A
3	LX58CWP	A	21	LX58CXL	A	39	LX09BXH	A
4	LX58CWR	A	22	LX58CXN	A	40	LX09BXJ	A
5	LX58CWT	A	23	LX58CXO	A	41	LX09BXK	A
6	LX58CWU	A	24	LX58CXP	A	42	LX09BXL	A
7	LX58CWV	A	25	LX58CXR	A	43	LX09BXM	A
8	LX58CWW	A	26	LX58CXS	A	44	LX09BXO	A
9	LX58CWY	A	27	LX58CXT	A	45	LX09AXU	A
10	LX58CWZ	A	28	LX58CXU	A	46	LX09AXV	A
11	LX58CXA	A	29	LX58CXV	A	47	LX09AXW	A
12	LX58CXB	A	30	LX58CXW	A	48	LX09AXY	A
13	LX58CXC	A	31	LX58CXY	A	49	LX09AXZ	A
14	LX58CXD	A	32	LX58CXZ	A	50	LX09AYA	A
15	LX58CXE	A	33	LX58CYA	A	51	LX09AYB	A
16	LX58CXF	A	34	LX58CYC	A	52	LX09AYC	A
17	LX58CXG	A	35	LX58CYE	A	53	LX09AYD	A
18	LX58CXH	A	36	LX58CYF	A	54	LX09AYE	A

In 2017, there was a temporary swap of DOE-class Tridents with MHV-class Volvo hybrids due to emissions requirements in Putney. DOE16 is seen near St Georges Circus while on route 63 heading to Honor Oak

| DP201 | EU53PYJ | Dennis Dart SLF SFD3CA | Alexander Pointer 2 10.7m | B33D | FK |

| E1-39 | | Dennis Trident SFD15L | Alexander Enviro 400 10.2m | H41/24D | |
| | | | * - H41/26D | | |

1	SN06BNA	SW	14	SN06BNZ	SW	28	LX06EZC	PM
2	SN06BNB	SW	15	SN06BOF	SW	29	LX06EZD	PM
3	SN06BND	SW	16	LX06EZL	PM	30	LX06EZE	PM
4	SN06BNE	SW	18	LX06EZN	PM	31	LX06EZF	PM
5	SN06BNF	SW	19	LX06EZO	PM	32	LX06EZG	PM
6	SN06BNJ	SW	20	LX06EZP	PM	33	LX06EZH	PM
7	SN06BNK	SW	21	LX06EZR	PM	34	LX06ECT	PM
8	SN06BNL	SW	22	LX06EZS	PM	35*	LX06ECV	PM
9	SN06BNO	SW	23	LX06EZT	PM	36	LX06FKL	PM
10	SN06BNU	SW	24	LX06EYY	PM	37	LX06FKM	PM
11	SN06BNV	SW	25	LX06EYZ	PM	38*	LX06FKN	SW
12	SN06BNX	SW	26	LX06EZA	PM	39	LX06FKO	BX
13	SN06BNY	SW	27	LX06EZB	PM			

| E40-61 | | Dennis Trident SFD15M | Alexander Enviro 400 10.2m | H41/24D | |
| | | | * - H39/25D | | |

40	LX56ETD	BX	48	LX56ETT	BX	56	LX56EUD	BX
41	LX56ETE	BX	49	LX56ETU	BX	57	LX07BYH	AL
42	LX56ETF	BX	50	LX56ETV	BX	58*	LX07BYC	Q
43	LX56ETJ	BX	51	LX56ETY	BX	59*	LX07BYD	Q
44	LX56ETK	BX	52	LX56ETZ	BX	60*	LX07BYF	Q
45	LX56ETL	BX	53	LX56EUA	BX	61*	LX07BYG	AL
46	LX56ETO	BX	54	LX56EUB	BX			
47	LX56ETR	BX	55	LX56EUC	BX			

Putney Heath is the setting for E31 on route 37. The backdrop of trees and country pub make this location feel like on the outskirts of London.

E62-128			Dennis Trident SFD16M		Alexander Enviro 400 10.2m * - H39/25D		H39/24D	
62*	LX57CHV	NX	85	LX57CKU	AL	108	LX09FAO	AL
63*	LX57CHY	NX	86	LX57CKV	AL	109	LX09FAU	AL
64*	LX57CHZ	NX	87	LX57CKY	AL	110	LX09FBA	AL
65*	LX57CJE	NX	88	LX57CLF	AL	111	LX09FBB	AL
66*	LX57CJF	NX	89	LX57CLJ	AL	112	LX09FBC	AL
67*	LX57CJJ	BX	90	LX57CLN	AL	113	LX09FBD	AL
68	LX57CJO	AL	91	LX57CLO	AL	114	LX09FBE	AL
69	LX57CJU	AL	92	LX57CLV	AL	115	LX09FBF	AL
70	LX57CJV	AL	93	LX57CLY	AL	116	LX09FBG	AL
71	LX57CJY	AL	94	LX08EBP	NX	117	LX09FBJ	AL
72	LX57CJZ	AL	95	LX08EBU	NX	118	LX09FBK	AL
73	LX57CKA	AL	96	LX08EBV	NX	119	LX09FBN	AL
74	LX57CKC	AL	97	LX08EBZ	NX	120	LX09FBO	AL
75	LX57CKD	AL	98	LX08ECA	NX	121	LX09FBU	AL
76	LX57CKE	AL	99	LX08ECC	NX	122	LX09FBV	AL
77	LX57CKF	AL	100	LX09EZU	AL	123	LX09FBY	AL
78	LX57CKG	AL	101	LX09EZV	AL	124	LX09FBZ	AL
79	LX57CKJ	AL	102	LX09EZW	AL	125	LX09FCA	AL
80	LX57CKK	AL	103	LX09EZZ	AL	126	LX09FCC	AL
81	LX57CKL	AL	104	LX09FAF	AL	127	LX09FCD	MG
82	LX57CKN	AL	105	LX09FAJ	AL	128	LX09FCE	MG
83	LX57CKO	AL	106	LX09FAK	AL			
84	LX57CKP	AL	107	LX09FAM	AL			

E129-150			Dennis Trident SFD1DS		Alexander Enviro 400 10.2m		H41/26D	
129	SN60BZA	BX	130	SN60BZB	BX	131	SN60BZC	BX

132	SN60BZD	BX		139	SN60BZL	C		146	SN60BZU	C
133	SN60BZE	Q		140	SN60BZM	C		147	SN60BZV	C
134	SN60BZF	Q		141	SN60BZO	C		148	SN60BZW	C
135	SN60BZG	RR		142	SN60BZP	C		149	SN60BZX	C
136	SN60BZH	MB		143	SN60BZR	C		150	SN60BZY	C
137	SN60BZJ	RR		144	SN60BZS	C				
138	SN60BZK	C		145	SN60BZT	C				

Route 12 is usually worked with New Routemasters, affectionately known as "Borismasters". However, other vehicles sometimes appear on the route, as seen here by E201 in Parliament Square turning into Whitehall while heading to Oxford Circus

E151-280		ADL E40D SFD1DS		ADL Enviro 400 10.2m		H41/24D			
				* - H41/26D					
151*	SN11BTY	AL	168	SN61BGX	RR	185	SN61BHY	Q	
152*	SN11BTZ	AF	169	SN61BGY	RR	186	SN61BHZ	MG	
153*	SN11BUA	AF	170	SN61BGZ	RR	187	SN61BJE	A	
154*	SN11BUE	AF	171	SN61BHA	RR	188	SN61BJF	A	
155*	SN11BUF	AF	172	SN61BHD	RR	189	SN61BJJ	Q	
156*	SN11BUH	AF	173	SN61BGE	RR	190	SN61BJK	Q	
157*	SN11BUJ	AF	174	SN61BHE	RR	191	SN61BJO	Q	
158*	SN11BUO	AF	175	SN61BHF	RR	192	SN61BJU	Q	
159*	SN11BUP	AF	176	SN61BHJ	RR	193	SN61BJV	Q	
160*	SN11BUU	AF	177	SN61BHK	RR	194	SN61BJX	Q	
161*	SN11BUV	AF	178	SN61BHL	RR	195	SN61BJY	Q	
162*	SN11BUW	AF	179	SN61BHO	RR	196	SN61BJZ	Q	
163	SN61BGF	RR	180	SN61BHP	RR	197	SN61BKA	Q	
164	SN61BGK	RR	181	SN61BHU	RR	198	SN61BKD	Q	
165	SN61BGO	RR	182	SN61BHV	RR	199	SN61BKE	Q	
166	SN61BGU	RR	183	SN61BHW	RR	200	SN61BKF	Q	
167	SN61BGV	RR	184	SN61BHX	RR	201	SN61BKG	Q	

No.	Reg	Code	No.	Reg	Code	No.	Reg	Code
202	SN61BKJ	RR	229	YX61DSE	BX	256	YX12FPO	NX
203	SN61BKK	RR	230	YX61DSO	BX	257	YX12FPP	NX
204	SN61BKL	RR	231	YX61DSU	BX	258	YX12FPT	NX
205	SN61DCV	RR	232	YX61DSV	BX	259	YX12FPU	NX
206	SN61DCX	RR	233	YX61DSY	BX	260	YX12FPV	NX
207	SN61DCY	NP	234	YX61DSZ	BX	261	SN62DDE	NX
208	SN61DCZ	MB	235	YX61DTF	BX	262	SN62DDO	NX
209	SN61DDA	MB	236	YX61DTK	BX	263	SN62DDX	NX
210	SN61DDE	MB	237	YX61DTN	BX	264	SN62DFL	NX
211	SN61DDF	MB	238	YX61DPF	BX	265	SN62DFX	NX
212	SN61DDJ	MB	239	YX61DPK	BX	266	SN62DGF	NX
213	SN61DDK	MB	240	YX61DPN	BX	267	SN62DGU	NX
214	SN61DDL	MB	241	YX61DPO	BX	268	SN62DHA	NX
215	SN61DDO	C	242	YX61DPU	BX	269	SN62DHK	NX
216	SN61DDU	C	243	YX61DPV	BX	270	SN62DHZ	NX
217	SN61DDV	C	244	YX61DPY	BX	271	SN62DJO	NX
218	SN61DDX	C	245	YX61DPZ	BX	272	SN62DKJ	NX
219	SN61DDY	C	246	YX12FPA	NX	273	SN62DLY	NX
220	SN61DDZ	C	247	YX12FPF	NX	274	SN62DLZ	NX
221	SN61DEU	C	248	YX12FPC	NX	275	SN62DMV	NX
222	SN61DFA	C	249	YX12FPD	NX	276	SN13CJE	NP
223	SN61DFC	C	250	YX12FPE	NX	277	SN13CJF	SW
224	SN61DFD	MB	251	YX12FPG	NX	278	SN13CJJ	SW
225	SN61DFE	MB	252	YX12FPJ	NX	279	SN13CJO	SW
226	SN61DFF	AL	253	YX12FPK	NX	280	SN13CJU	SW
227	SN61DFG	MB	254	YX12FPL	NX			
228	SN61DFJ	NX	255	YX12FPN	NX			

E281	YX14RTV	ADL E40D SFD4DS	ADL Enviro 400 10.8m	H47/32F	NX
E282	YX14RTZ	ADL E40D SFD4DS	ADL Enviro 400 10.8m	H47/32F	C
E283	YX14RUA	ADL E40D SFD4DS	ADL Enviro 400 10.8m	H47/32F	C
E284	SN66WNE	ADL E40D SFD917	ADL Enviro 400MMC 10.9m	H47/33F	A
E285	SN66WNF	ADL E40D SFD917	ADL Enviro 400MMC 10.9m	H47/33F	A
ED15	AE56OUO	Dennis Dart SLF SFD1HF	MCV Evolution 9.2m	B23D	w
ED24	LX07BYP	Dennis E200Dart SFD511	MCV Evolution 10.4m	B29D	RR
ED28	LX07BYU	Dennis E200Dart SFD511	MCV Evolution 10.4m	B29D	RR

EH1-5   Dennis Trident SFD17R   Alexander Enviro 400 10.2m   H37/24D
* - H37/25D

1	LX58DDJ	SW	3	LX58DDL	SW	5	LX58DDO	SW
2*	LX58DDK	SW	4	LX58DDN	SW			

EH6-20   ADL E40H SFD1BU   ADL Enviro 400 10.2m   H37/24D

6	SN61BLJ	NX	11	SN61DAU	NX	16	SN61DBY	MB
7	SN61BLK	NX	12	SN61DBO	NX	17	SN61DBZ	MB
8	SN61BLV	NX	13	SN61DBU	NX	18	SN61DCE	MB
9	SN61DAA	NX	14	SN61DBV	MB	19	SN61DCO	MB
10	SN61DAO	NX	15	SN61DBX	MB	20	SN61DCU	MB

EH21-38   ADL E40H SFD1BZ   ADL Enviro 400 10.2m   H37/24D

21	YX13BJE	SW	27	YX13BJV	SW	33	YX13BKF	SW
22	YX13BJF	SW	28	YX13BJY	SW	34	YX13BKG	SW
23	YX13BJJ	SW	29	YX13BJZ	SW	35	YX13BKJ	SW
24	YX13BJK	SW	30	YX13BKA	SW	36	YX13BKK	SW
25	YX13BJO	SW	31	YX13BKD	SW	37	YX13BKL	SW
26	YX13BJU	SW	32	YX13BKE	SW	38	YX13BKN	SW

Go-Ahead London have a substantial number of ADL Enviro 400 hybrids, with both original Enviro 400 bodywork, and the later Enviro 400MMC bodywork. An example of the former is seen here by way of EH24, pictured in Pall Mall while heading to Camden Town on route 88

EH39-112		ADL E40H SFD823			ADL Enviro 400MMC 10.4m			H41/25D	
39	YX16OBT	Q	64	YX66WHF	PM	89	YY66OYT	AF
40	YX16OBU	Q	65	YX66WHG	PM	90	YY66OYU	AF
41	YX16OBV	Q	66	YX66WHH	PM	91	YY66OYV	AF
42	YX16OBW	Q	67	YX66WHJ	PM	92	YY66OYW	AF
43	YX16OBY	Q	68	YX66WHK	PM	93	YY66OYX	AF
44	YX16OBZ	Q	69	YX66WHL	PM	94	YY66OYZ	AF
45	YX10OCA	Q	70	YX66WHM	PM	95	YY66OZA	AF
46	YX16OCB	Q	71	YX66WHN	PM	96	YY66OZB	AF
47	YX16OCC	Q	72	YX66WHP	PM	97	YY66OZC	AF
48	YX16OCD	Q	73	YX66WHR	PM	98	YY66OZD	AF
49	YX16OCE	Q	74	YY66OYB	r	99	YY66OZE	AF
50	YX16OCF	Q	75	YY66OYC	Q	100	YY66OZF	AF
51	YX16OCG	Q	76	YY66OYE	Q	101	YY66OZG	AF
52	YX16OCH	Q	77	YY66OYF	Q	102	YY66OZH	AF
53	YX16OCJ	Q	78	YY66OYG	Q	103	YY66OZJ	AF
54	YX16OCL	Q	79	YY66OYH	Q	104	YY66OZK	AF
55	YX16OCM	Q	80	YY66OYJ	Q	105	YY66OZL	AF
56	YX16OCN	Q	81	YY66OYK	Q	106	YX66OZM	AF
57	YX16OCO	Q	82	YY66OYL	Q	107	YY66OZO	AF
58	YX16OCP	Q	83	YY66OYM	Q	108	YY66OZP	AF
59	YX16OCR	Q	84	YY66OYN	AF	109	YY66OZR	AF
60	YX16OCS	Q	85	YY66OYO	AF	110	YY66OZS	AF
61	YX66WHC	PM	86	YY66OYP	AF	111	YY66OZT	AF
62	YX66WHD	PM	87	YY66OYR	AF	112	YY66OZU	AF
63	YX66WHE	PM	88	YY66OYS	AF			

For a number of years, route 42 has been operated with single-deck vehicles. However, in 2016 the route received a long overdue upgrade to double-deck operation. EH55 has an overall ad for Michelin Tyres which was mostly red causing some debate. It is seen passing Bricklayers Arms on its way to Liverpool Street

EH113-224			ADL E40H SFD826		ADL Enviro 400MMC 10.4m		H41/25D	
113	SN66WNY	Q	139	YW17JUH	RR	165	YX67VFK	Q
114	SN66WNZ	NX	140	YW17JUJ	RR	166	YX67VFL	Q
115	SN66WOA	NX	141	YW17JUK	RR	167	YX67VFM	Q
116	SN66WOB	Q	142	YW17JUO	RR	168	YX67VFN	Q
117	SN66WOC	Q	143	YW17JUT	RR	169	YX67VFO	Q
118	SN66WOD	Q	144	YW17JUU	RR	170	YX67VFP	Q
119	SN66WOH	Q	145	YW17JUV	RR	171	YY67UPX	NX
120	SN66WOJ	Q	146	YW17JUX	RR	172	YY67UPZ	NX
121	SN66WOM	Q	147	YW17JUY	RR	173	YY67URA	NX
122	SN66WOR	Q	148	YW17JVA	RR	174	YY67URB	NX
123	SN66WOU	Q	149	YW17JVC	RR	175	YY67URC	NX
124	SN66WOV	Q	150	YW17JVD	RR	176	YY67URE	NX
125	SN66WOX	Q	151	YW17JVE	RR	177	YY67URF	NX
126	SN66WOY	Q	152	YW17JVF	RR	178	YY67URG	NX
127	SN66WPA	Q	153	YW17JVG	RR	179	YY67URH	NX
128	SN66WPD	Q	154	YW17JVH	RR	180	YY67URJ	NX
129	SN66WPE	Q	155	YW17JVJ	RR	181	YY67URK	NX
130	SN66WPF	Q	156	YW17JVK	RR	182	YY67URL	NX
131	YW17JTV	RR	157	YW17JVL	RR	183	YY67URM	NX
132	YW17JTX	RR	158	YW17JVM	RR	184	YY67URN	NX
133	YW17JTY	RR	159	YW17JVN	RR	185	YY67URO	NX
134	YW17JTZ	RR	160	YW17JVO	RR	186	YY67URP	NX
135	YW17JUA	RR	161	YW17JVP	RR	187	YY67URR	NX
136	YW17JUC	RR	162	YX67VFG	Q	188	YY67URS	NX
137	YW17JUE	RR	163	YX67VFH	Q	189	YY67URT	NX
138	YW17JUF	RR	164	YX67VFJ	Q	190	YY67URU	NX

191	YY67URV	NX	203	YY67UTB	NX	215	YX18KPA	Q
192	YY67URW	NX	204	YY67UTC	NX	216	YX18KPE	Q
193	YY67URX	NX	205	YY67UTE	NX	217	YX18KPF	Q
194	YY67URZ	NX	206	YY67UTF	NX	218	YX18KPG	Q
195	YY67USS	NX	207	YY67UTG	NX	219	YX18KPJ	Q
196	YY67UST	NX	208	YY67UTH	NX	220	YX18KPK	Q
197	YY67USU	NX	209	YY67UTJ	NX	221	YX18KPL	Q
198	YY67USV	NX	210	YY67UTK	NX	222	YX18KPN	Q
199	YY67USW	NX	211	YY67UTL	NX	223	YX18KPO	Q
200	YY67USX	NX	212	YY67UTM	NX	224	YX18KPP	Q
201	YY67USZ	NX	213	YY67UTN	NX			
202	YY67UTA	NX	214	YY67UTO	NX			

EH226-263   ADL E40H SFD82A   ADL Enviro 400MMC 10.4m   H41/25D

226	YX18KPR	NX	239	YX18KRO	NX	252	YX18KSZ	NX
227	YX18KPT	NX	240	YX18KRU	NX	253	YX18KTA	NX
228	YX18KPU	NX	241	YX18KRV	NX	254	YX18KTC	NX
229	YX18KPV	NX	242	YX18KRZ	NX	255	YX18KTD	NX
230	YX18KPY	NX	243	YX18KSE	NX	256	YX18KTE	NX
231	YX18KPZ	NX	244	YX18KSF	NX	257	YX18KTF	NX
232	YX18KRD	NX	245	YX18KSJ	NX	258	YX18KTG	NX
233	YX18KRE	NX	246	YX18KSK	NX	259	YX18KTJ	NX
234	YX18KRF	NX	247	YX18KSN	NX	260	YX18KTK	NX
235	YX18KRG	NX	248	YX18KSO	NX	261	YX18KTL	NX
236	YX18KRJ	NX	249	YX18KSU	NX	262	YX18KTN	NX
237	YX18KRK	NX	250	YX18KSV	NX	263	YX18KTO	NX
238	YX18KRN	NX	251	YX18KSY	NX			

EH264-310   ADL E40H SFD826   ADL Enviro 400MMC 10.4m   H41/25D

264	SN18KLU	NX	280	SN18KMZ	296	YX18KXJ
265	SN18KLV	NX	281	SN18KNA	297	YX18KXK
266	SN18KLX	NX	282	SN18KNB	298	YX18KXL
267	SN18KLZ	NX	283	SN18KNC	299	YX18KXM
268	SN18KMA	NX	284	SN18KND	300	YX18KXN
269	SN18KME	NX	285	YX18KWW	301	YX18KXO
270	SN18KMF	NX	286	YX18KWY	302	YX18KXP
271	SN18KMG	NX	287	YX18KWZ	303	YX18KXR
272	SN18KMJ	NX	288	YX18KXA	304	YX18KXS
273	SN18KMK	NX	289	YX18KXB	305	YX18KXT
274	SN18KMM		290	YX18KXC	306	YX18KXU
275	SN18KMO		291	YX18KXD	307	YX18KXV
276	SN18KMU		292	YX18KXE	308	YX18KXW
277	SN18KMV		293	YX18KXF	309	YX18KXY
278	SN18KMX		294	YX18KXG	310	YX18KXZ
279	SN18KMY		295	YX18KXH		

EHV1-16   Volvo B5LH   ADL Enviro 400MMC 10.5m   H41/22D

1	BK15AZR	SI	7	BL15HBO	SI	13	BL15HCA	SI
2	BK15AZT	SI	8	BL15HBP	SI	14	BL15HCC	SI
3	BJ15TWL	SI	9	BL15HBU	SI	15	BL15HCD	SI
4	BL15HBK	SI	10	BL15HBX	SI	16	BL15HBN	SI
5	BJ15TWP	SI	11	BL15HBY	SI			
6	BL15HBJ	SI	12	BL15HBZ	SI			

EI1	YP15NLM	Irizar Electric Bus	Irizar 12.0m	B26D	NX
EI2	YP15NLN	Irizar Electric Bus	Irizar 12.0m	B26D	NX

EHV7 is one of the Volvo/ADL hybrids dedicated to Route 135 that operates between Shoreditch and Crossharbour. Due to a closure of the normal terminal in Shoreditch, route 135 was operating via Shoreditch High Street

EN1-24			Dennis Trident SFD16M		Alexander Enviro 400 10.2m		H41/24D	
1	SN58CDY	NP	9	SN58CEV	NP	17	SN58CFJ	NP
2	SN58CDZ	NP	10	SN58CEX	NP	18	LK08FLH	NP
3	SN58CEA	NP	11	SN58CEY	NP	19	LK08FLJ	NP
4	SN58CEF	NP	12	SN58CFA	NP	20	LK08FLL	NP
5	SN58CEJ	NP	13	SN58CFD	NP	21	LK08FLM	NP
6	SN58CEK	NP	14	SN58CFE	NP	22	LK08FLN	NP
7	SN58CEO	NP	15	SN58CFF	NP	23	LK08FLP	NP
8	SN58CEU	NP	16	SN58CFG	NP	24	LK08FLR	NP

EN25	LK57EJN	Dennis Trident SFD15M	Alexander Enviro 400 10.2m		H41/26D	BX
EN26	LK57EJO	Dennis Trident SFD15M	Alexander Enviro 400 10.2m		H41/26D	BX
EN27	LK08FKX	Dennis Trident SFD16M	Alexander Enviro 400 10.2m		H41/26D	BX
LDP35	P735RYL	Dennis Dart SLF SFD212	Plaxton Pointer 10.0m		B--F	RRa
LDP186	Y986TGH	Dennis Dart SLF SFD112	Plaxton Pointer 2 9.3m		B28F	SI

LDP191-206			Dennis Dart SLF SFD2B2		Alexander Pointer 2 10.1m		B27D	
					* - B30D			
191	SN51UAD	RR	198*	SN51UAL	RR	204	SN51UAT	SWt
194*	SN51UAG	BX	200	SN51UAO	PM	206	SN51UAV	BX

LDP264	LX05EYR	Dennis Dart SLF SFD6BA	Alexander Pointer 2 8.8m		B23F	RR

LDP273-280			Dennis Dart SLF SFD2BA		Alexander Pointer 2 10.1m		B28D	
273	LX06EYT	r	275	LX06EYV	r	277	LX06FBD	r
274	LX06EYU	r	276	LX06EYW	r	278	LX06FBE	r

279	LX06FAA	r	292	LX06EZZ	AL	294	LX06EZK	AL
280	LX06FAF	r	293	LX06EZJ	AL			

A dying breed in the Go-Ahead London is the Dennis Dart SLF, now down to a handful after having had over 300 in the fleet at one point. LDP206 is seen in Sutton while on route 413 heading to Morden Station. This vehicle has since transferred to Bexleyheath Garage

LT41-953		Wright NBfL		Wright NBfL 11.3m			H40/22T	
41	LTZ1041	SW	64	LTZ1064	SW	288	LTZ1288	NX
42	LTZ1042	SW	65	LTZ1065	SW	289	LTZ1289	NX
43	LTZ1043	SW	66	LTZ1066	SW	290	LTZ1290	NX
44	LTZ1044	SW	67	LTZ1067	SW	291	LTZ1291	NX
45	LTZ1045	SW	68	LTZ1068	SW	292	LTZ1292	NX
46	LTZ1046	SW	118	LTZ1118	SW	293	LTZ1293	NX
47	LTZ1047	SW	119	LTZ1119	SW	294	LTZ1294	NX
48	LTZ1048	SW	189	LTZ1189	MW	295	LTZ1295	NX
49	LTZ1049	SW	273	LTZ1273	NX	296	LTZ1296	NX
50	LTZ1050	SW	274	LTZ1274	NX	297	LTZ1297	NX
51	LTZ1051	SW	275	LTZ1275	NX	298	LTZ1298	NX
52	LTZ1052	SW	276	LTZ1276	NX	299	LTZ1299	NX
53	LTZ1053	SW	277	LTZ1277	NX	300	LTZ1300	NX
54	LTZ1054	SW	278	LTZ1278	NX	301	LTZ1301	NX
55	LTZ1055	SW	279	LTZ1279	NX	302	LTZ1302	NX
56	LTZ1056	SW	280	LTZ1280	NX	303	LTZ1303	NX
57	LTZ1057	SW	281	LTZ1281	NX	304	LTZ1304	NX
58	LTZ1058	SW	282	LTZ1282	NX	305	LTZ1305	NX
59	LTZ1059	SW	283	LTZ1283	NX	306	LTZ1306	NX
60	LTZ1060	SW	284	LTZ1284	NX	307	LTZ1307	NX
61	LTZ1061	SW	285	LTZ1285	NX	308	LTZ1308	NX
62	LTZ1062	SW	286	LTZ1286	NX	309	LTZ1309	NX
63	LTZ1063	SW	287	LTZ1287	NX	310	LTZ1310	NX

311	LTZ1311	NX	449	LTZ1449	Q	870	LTZ1870	NX
391	LTZ1391	RR	450	LTZ1450	Q	871	LTZ1871	NX
392	LTZ1392	RR	451	LTZ1451	Q	872	LTZ1872	NX
393	LTZ1393	RR	452	LTZ1452	Q	873	LTZ1873	NX
394	LTZ1394	RR	453	LTZ1453	Q	874	LTZ1874	NX
395	LTZ1395	RR	454	LTZ1454	Q	875	LTZ1875	NP
396	LTZ1396	RR	455	LTZ1455	Q	876	LTZ1876	NP
397	LTZ1397	RR	456	LTZ1456	NX	877	LTZ1877	NP
398	LTZ1398	RR	457	LTZ1457	SW	878	LTZ1878	NP
399	LTZ1399	RR	458	LTZ1458	SW	879	LTZ1879	NP
400	LTZ1400	RR	459	LTZ1459	SW	880	LTZ1880	NP
401	LTZ1401	RR	478	LTZ1478	SW	881	LTZ1881	NP
402	LTZ1402	RR	479	LTZ1479	SW	882	LTZ1882	NP
403	LTZ1403	RR	480	LTZ1480	SW	883	LTZ1883	NP
404	LTZ1404	RR	481	LTZ1481	SW	884	LTZ1884	NP
405	LTZ1405	RR	482	LTZ1482	SW	885	LTZ1885	NP
406	LTZ1406	RR	483	LTZ1483	SW	886	LTZ1886	NP
407	LTZ1407	RR	484	LTZ1484	SW	887	LTZ1887	NP
408	LTZ1408	RR	485	LTZ1485	SW	888	LTZ1888	NP
409	LTZ1409	RR	486	LTZ1486	SW	889	LTZ1889	NP
410	LTZ1410	RR	487	LTZ1487	SW	890	LTZ1890	NP
411	LTZ1411	RR	501	LTZ1501	SW	891	LTZ1891	NP
412	LTZ1412	RR	502	LTZ1502	SW	892	LTZ1892	NP
413	LTZ1413	RR	503	LTZ1503	SW	893	LTZ1893	NP
414	LTZ1414	RR	504	LTZ1504	SW	894	LTZ1894	NP
415	LTZ1415	RR	505	LTZ1505	SW	895	LTZ1895	NP
416	LTZ1416	RR	506	LTZ1506	SW	896	LTZ1896	NP
417	LTZ1417	Q	507	LTZ1507	SW	897	LTZ1897	NP
418	LTZ1418	Q	508	LTZ1508	SW	898	LTZ1898	NP
419	LTZ1419	Q	509	LTZ1509	SW	899	LTZ1899	NP
420	LTZ1420	Q	510	LTZ1510	SW	900	LTZ1900	NP
421	LTZ1421	Q	511	LTZ1511	SW	901	LTZ2101	NP
422	LTZ1422	Q	512	LTZ1512	SW	902	LTZ2102	NP
423	LTZ1423	Q	687	LTZ1687	r	903	LTZ2103	RR
424	LTZ1424	Q	845	LTZ1845	NX	904	LTZ2104	RR
425	LTZ1425	Q	846	LTZ1846	NX	905	LTZ2105	RR
426	LTZ1426	Q	847	LTZ1847	NX	906	LTZ2106	RR
427	LTZ1427	Q	848	LTZ1848	NX	907	LTZ2107	RR
428	LTZ1428	Q	849	LTZ1849	NX	908	LTZ2108	RR
429	LTZ1429	Q	850	LTZ1850	NX	909	LTZ2109	RR
430	LTZ1430	Q	851	LTZ1851	NX	910	LTZ2110	RR
431	LTZ1431	Q	852	LTZ1852	NX	911	LTZ2111	RR
432	LTZ1432	Q	853	LTZ1853	NX	912	LTZ2112	RR
433	LTZ1433	Q	854	LTZ1854	NX	913	LTZ2113	RR
434	LTZ1434	Q	855	LTZ1855	NX	914	LTZ2114	RR
435	LTZ1435	Q	856	LTZ1856	NX	915	LTZ2115	RR
436	LTZ1436	Q	857	LTZ1857	NX	916	LTZ2116	RR
437	LTZ1437	Q	858	LTZ1858	NX	917	LTZ2117	RR
438	LTZ1438	Q	859	LTZ1859	NX	918	LTZ2118	RR
439	LTZ1439	Q	860	LTZ1860	NX	919	LTZ2119	RR
440	LTZ1440	Q	861	LTZ1861	NX	920	LTZ2120	RR
441	LTZ1441	Q	862	LTZ1862	NX	921	LTZ2121	RR
442	LTZ1442	Q	863	LTZ1863	NX	922	LTZ2122	RR
443	LTZ1443	Q	864	LTZ1864	NX	923	LTZ2123	RR
444	LTZ1444	Q	865	LTZ1865	NX	924	LTZ2124	RR
445	LTZ1445	Q	866	LTZ1866	NX	925	LTZ2125	RR
446	LTZ1446	Q	867	LTZ1867	NX	926	LTZ2126	RR
447	LTZ1447	Q	868	LTZ1868	NX	927	LTZ2127	RR
448	LTZ1448	Q	869	LTZ1869	NX	928	LTZ2128	RR

Above: *A number of New Routemasters across London carry allover advert liveries. LT300 is seen here crossing Westminster Bridge in Topman advert livery, while on route 453 heading to Deptford Bridge*

Below: *Route 15 was the first New Routemaster route to transfer operators and have the vehicles transfer with it. LT414, new to Stagecoach, is seen here at Trafalgar Square while heading to Blackwall*

No.	Reg	Code		No.	Reg	Code		No.	Reg	Code
929	LTZ2129	RR		938	LTZ2138	RR		947	LTZ2147	RR
930	LTZ2130	RR		939	LTZ2139	RR		948	LTZ2148	RR
931	LTZ2131	RR		940	LTZ2140	RR		949	LTZ2149	RR
932	LTZ2132	RR		941	LTZ2141	RR		950	LTZ2150	RR
933	LTZ2133	RR		942	LTZ2142	RR		951	LTZ2151	RR
934	LTZ2134	RR		943	LTZ2143	RR		952	LTZ2152	RR
935	LTZ2135	RR		944	LTZ2144	RR		953	LTZ2153	RR
936	LTZ2136	RR		945	LTZ2145	RR				
937	LTZ2137	RR		946	LTZ2146	RR				

Code	Reg	Chassis	Body	Seating	Depot
LUT1	T3FCC	Volvo B7LA	Wright Eclipse Fusion	AB56D	LU
LUT2	T4FCC	Volvo B7LA	Wright Eclipse Fusion	AB56D	LU
LUT3	T5FCC	Volvo B7LA	Wright Eclipse Fusion	AB56D	LU
LUT4	T6FCC	Volvo B7LA	Wright Streetcar	AB37D	LU
LUT5	Y186HNH	Volvo B7L	Wright Eclipse	B26D	LU
MD1	YJ17FXX	Optare MetroDecker	Optare MetroDecker	H41/22D	NX
MDL1	YJ60GGE	VDL DE18FSSB180	MCV Evolution 10.3m	B29D	RR

Originally new for the Red Arrow routes in central London, Go-Ahead London have found a number of uses for their Mercedes-Benz Citaros. MEC15 is seen here in the commercial livery while it acts a driver trainer, pictured while passing Bricklayers Arms

MEC1-50		Mercedes-Benz O530		Mercedes-Benz Citaro 12.0m * - B33D		B21D	
1*	BG09JJK	MG	8*	BG09JKE	MG	15	BD09ZPV	Qt
2*	BG09JJL	MG	9*	BG09JKF	MG	16	BD09ZPW	Qt
3*	BG09JJU	MG	10*	BG09JKJ	MG	17	BD09ZPX	Qt
4*	BG09JJV	MG	11	BD09ZPR	Qt	18	BD09ZPY	NPt
5*	BG09JJX	MG	12*	BD09ZPS	MG	19	BD09ZPZ	Qt
6*	BG09JJY	MG	13	BD09ZPT	NPt	20*	BD09ZRA	MG
7*	BG09JJZ	MG	14	BD09ZPU	NPt	22	BD09ZRE	Qt

23	BD09ZRF	Qt	30*	BD09ZVV	MG	37*	BD09ZWC	MG
24	BD09ZRG	Qt	31	BD09ZVW	Qt	38	BD09ZWE	Qt
25	BD09ZRJ	Qt	32*	BD09ZVX	MG	39	BD09ZWF	Q
26	BD09ZRK	Qt	33	BD09ZVY	Qt	40	BD09ZWG	u
27*	BF59NHJ	MG	34	BD09ZVZ	MG	41	BD09ZWH	Qt
28	BD09ZVT	Qt	35	BD09ZWA	NP	46*	BT09GOU	MG
29	BD09ZVU	Qt	36	BD09ZWB	RAt	50*	BT09GPJ	MG

MEC51-69 — Mercedes-Benz O295 — Mercedes-Benz Citaro 12.0m — **B36D**

51	BF65HUJ	MB	58	BF65HUZ	MB	65	BF65HVH	MB
52	BF65HUO	MB	59	BF65HVA	MB	66	BF65HVJ	MB
53	BF65HUK	MB	60	BF65HVB	MB	67	BF65HVK	MB
54	BF65HUP	MB	61	BF65HVC	MB	68	BF65HVL	MB
55	BF65HUU	MB	62	BF65HVD	MB	69	BF65HVM	MB
56	BF65HUV	MB	63	BF65HVE	MB			
57	BF65HUY	MB	64	BF65HVG	MB			

MHV1-99 — Volvo B5LH — MCV EvoSeti 10.5m — **H41/21D**

1	BU16OYJ	Q	11	BU16OYV	Q	21	BV66VKN	PM
2	BU16OYM	Q	12	BU16OYW	Q	22	BV66VKO	PM
3	BU16OYL	Q	13	BU16OYX	Q	23	BV66VKP	PM
4	BU16OYK	Q	14	BU16OYY	Q	24	BG66MHX	PM
5	BU16OYN	Q	15	BU16OYZ	Q	25	BV66VKR	PM
6	BU16OYO	Q	16	BU16OZA	Q	26	BV66VKS	PM
7	BU16OYP	Q	17	BU16OZE	Q	27	BV66VKT	PM
8	BU16OYR	Q	18	BU16OZC	Q	28	BV66VKU	PM
9	BU16OYS	Q	19	BU16OZD	Q	29	BG66MHY	PM
10	BU16OYT	Q	20	BU16OZB	Q	30	BV66VKW	PM

Go-Ahead London have been the largest UK operator of the MCV EvoSeti body, found on Volvo B5LH hybrid chassis. MHV4 is seen in Shoreditch about to start its journey to Clapham Junction on route 35

31	BG66MHZ	PM	54	BT66MPF	Q	77	BV66VGM	Q
32	BV66VKX	PM	55	BT66MPO	Q	78	BV66VGN	Q
33	BV66VKZ	PM	56	BV66VKG	Q	79	BV66VGO	Q
34	BG66MKA	PM	57	BV66VKH	Q	80	BV66VGP	Q
35	BG66MKC	PM	58	BV66VKJ	Q	81	BV66MHV	Q
36	BG66MKD	PM	59	BV66VKK	Q	82	BV66VKM	Q
37	BV66VHG	PM	60	BV66VFT	Q	83	BV66VKC	MG
38	BG66MJE	PM	61	BV66VHE	Q	84	BV66VKD	MG
39	BG66MJF	PM	62	BV66VKL	Q	85	BV66VKF	MG
40	BG66MJJ	PM	63	BV66VFU	Q	86	LF67EWK	AF
41	BG66MJO	PM	64	BV66VFW	Q	87	LF67EWL	AF
42	BV66VHA	PM	65	BV66VFX	Q	88	LF67EWM	AF
43	BG66MJU	PM	66	BV66VFY	Q	89	LF67EWN	AF
44	BG66MJV	PM	67	BV66VFZ	Q	90	LF67EWO	AF
45	BV66VHC	PM	68	BV66VGA	Q	91	LF67EWP	AF
46	BV66VHD	PM	69	BV66VGC	Q	92	LF67EWR	AF
47	BG66MJX	PM	70	BV66VGD	Q	93	LF67EWS	AF
48	BG66MJY	PM	71	BV66VGE	Q	94	LF67EWT	AF
49	BV66VGU	PM	72	BV66VGF	Q	95	LF67EWU	AF
50	BV66VGX	PM	73	BV66VGG	Q	96	LF67EWV	AF
51	BV66VGY	PM	74	BV66VGJ	Q	97	LF67EWW	AF
52	BV66VGZ	PM	75	BV66VGK	Q	98	LF67EWX	AF
53	BT66MPE	PM	76	BV66VGL	Q	99	LF67EWY	AF

PHD271	SN03YBA	Dennis Dart SLF SFD6BA	Alexander Pointer 2 8.8m	B23F	ST

Another dying breed within the Go-Ahead London fleet is the PVL-class. Originally numbering 419, there are now just over 60 left in stock, including a number being used for driving training. Route 77, based at Stockwell, still hosts PVLs as its standard type and PVL401 is seen near its destination of Tooting Station

PVL75-419		Volvo B7TL		Plaxton President 10.0m			H41/20D	
				* - H41/19D, $ - H41/25F, % - PO41/20D, + - DPH41/20D				
80*	W408WGH	Qt	265+	PN02XBO	ST	401	LX54GZN	w
134*	W534WGH	Qt	282	PJ02RCF	AL	402	LX54GZO	w
135*	W435WGH	Qt	284	PJ02RCU	AL	403	LX54GZP	w
136*	W536WGH	Qt	296	PJ02RFE	AL	404	LX54GZR	w
137*	W537WGH	Qt	362	PJ53SOE	w	405	LX54GZT	SW
138*	W538WGH	Qt	363	PJ53SOH	w	406	LX54GYV	SW
139*	W539WGH	Qt	364	PJ53SOU	w	407	LX54GYW	SW
140*	W404WGH	BXt	365	PJ53SPU	r	408	LX54GYY	SW
141*	W541WGH	Qt	366	PJ53SPV	r	409	LX54GYZ	SW
142*	W542WGH	Qt	370	PJ53SRU	BX	410	LX54GZB	SW
143*	W543WGH	Qt	390	LX54HAA	A	411	LX54GZC	SW
148	X548EGK	w	391	LX54HAE	A	412	LX54GZD	SW
218	Y818TGH	Qt	392	LX54HAO	NP	413	LX54GZE	SW
219$	Y819TGH	FK	393	LX54HAU	SW	414	LX54GZF	SW
221$	Y821TGH	ST	394	LX54HBA	SW	415	LX54GZU	SW
222$	Y822TGH	ST	395	LX54HBB	SW	416	LX54GZV	SW
223$	Y823TGH	ST	396	LX54GZG	SW	417	LX54GZW	SW
224%	Y824TGH	NX	397	LX54GZH	Qt	418	LX54GZY	SW
229	Y729TGH	Qt	398	LX54GZK	BX	419	LX54GZZ	SW
248	Y748TGH	FK	399	LX54GZL	AL			
263+	PN02XBL	ST	400	LX54GZM	AL			

RM9	VLT9	AEC Routemaster		Park Royal 27ft 6in		H36/28R	Q

RML2305-2604		AEC Routemaster		Park Royal 30ft		H40/32R	
				* - CO40/32R			
2305	CUV305C	NX	2516	WLT516	NX		
2318*	CUV318C	NX	2604	NML604E	NX		

SE1-17		Dennis E200Dart SFD511		Alexander Enviro 200 10.2m			B29D	
1	LX07BXH	AL	7	LX07BXO	AL	13	LX07BXW	AL
2	LX07BXJ	AL	8	LX07BXP	AL	14	LX07BXY	AL
3	LX07BXK	AL	9	LX07BXR	AL	15	LX07BXZ	AL
4	LX07BXL	AL	10	LX07BXS	AL	16	LX07BYA	AL
5	LX07BXM	AL	11	LX07BXU	AL	17	LX07BYB	RR
6	LX07BXN	AL	12	LX07BXV	AL			

SE18-35		Dennis E200Dart SFD321		Alexander Enviro 200 10.8m			B32D	
18	SK07DZM	A	24	SN57DWL	RR	30	SN57DWW	RR
19	SK07DZN	RR	25	SN57DWM	RR	31	SN57DWX	RR
20	SK07DZO	RR	26	SN57DWO	RR	32	SN57DWY	RR
21	SN57DWG	RR	27	SN57DWP	RR	33	SN57DWZ	RR
22	SN57DWJ	RR	28	SN57DWU	RR	34	SN57DXA	RR
23	SN57DWK	RR	29	SN57DWV	RR	35	SN57DXB	RR

SE36	YN08DMY	Dennis E200Dart SFD361		Alexander Enviro 200 10.8m		B32D	RR

SE38-46		Dennis E200Dart SFD5A1		Alexander Enviro 200 10.2m			B29D	
38	LX10AUR	RR	41	LX10AUV	RR	44	LX10AVB	RR
39	LX10AUT	RR	42	LX10AUW	RR	45	LX10AVC	RR
40	LX10AUU	RR	43	LX10AUY	RR	46	LX10AVD	RR

SE47-54		Dennis E200Dart SFD3E1		Alexander Enviro 200 10.8m			B32D	
47	YX60EOE	SW	48	YX60EOF	SW	49	YX60EOG	SW

New for the Blue Triangle operation within Go-Ahead London, soon after the acquisition of the company, were a batch of Alexander Enviro 200s for route 364 in East London. SE33 is seen here in Ilford while heading for Dagenham East, still showing the original Blue Triangle livery carried by these vehicles

| 50 | YX60EOH | SW | 52 | YX60EOK | SW | 54 | YX60EOO | SW |
| 51 | YX60EOJ | SW | 53 | YX60EOL | SW | | | |

SE55-84			Dennis E200Dart SFD5D1	Alexander Enviro 200 10.2m		B29D		
55	YX60DXT	BX	65	YX60EPU	BX	75	YX60FCE	BX
56	YX60FSN	BX	66	YX60EOP	BX	76	YX60FCF	BX
57	YX60DXU	BX	67	YX60FCZ	BX	77	YX60FCG	BX
58	YX60FSO	BX	68	YX60FDA	BX	78	YX60FCL	BX
59	YX60FSP	BX	69	YX60FBU	BX	79	YX60FCM	BX
60	YX60FSS	BX	70	YX60FBY	BX	80	YX60FCO	BX
61	YX60DXW	BX	71	YX60FBZ	BX	81	YX60FCP	BX
62	YX60EPO	BX	72	YX60FCA	BX	82	YX60FCU	BX
63	YX60FSU	BX	73	YX60FCC	BX	83	YX60FCV	BX
64	YX60EPP	BX	74	YX60FCD	BX	84	YX60FCY	BX

SE85-93			ADL E20D SFD4D1	ADL Enviro 200 9.3m		B24D		
85	YX11CPE	SI	88	YX11CPN	Q	91	YX11CPV	Q
86	YX11CPF	Q	89	YX11CPO	Q	92	YX11CPY	Q
87	YX11CPK	Q	90	YX11CPU	Q	93	YX11CPZ	Q

SE94-141			ADL E20D SFD3E1	ADL Enviro 200 10.8m		B32D		
94	SN11FFZ	A	99	SN61BKU	RR	104	YX61BWA	MG
95	SN11FGA	RR	100	SN61BKV	RR	105	YX61BWB	MG
96	SN11FGC	RR	101	SN61BKX	RR	106	YX61BWC	MG
97	SN11FGD	RR	102	SN61BKY	RR	107	YX61BWD	MG
98	SN61BKO	RR	103	SN61BKZ	RR	108	YX61BWE	SI

109	YX61BYD	MG	120	YX61BWU	A	131	YX61BWG	SI
110	YX61BYF	MG	121	YX61BWV	SI	132	YX61BWH	SI
111	YX61BYG	MG	122	YX61BWW	SI	133	YX61BWJ	SI
112	YX61BXR	MG	123	YX61BWY	SI	134	YX61BWK	SI
113	YX61BXS	SI	124	YX61BWZ	SI	135	YX61BWL	SI
114	YX61BXU	SI	125	YX61BXA	SI	136	YX61BWM	SI
115	YX61BXV	SI	126	YX61BXB	SI	137	YX61BWN	SI
116	YX61BXW	SI	127	YX61BXC	SI	138	YX61BWO	SI
117	YX61BXY	SI	128	YX61BXD	SI	139	YX61BWP	SI
118	YX61BXZ	SI	129	YX61BXE	SI	140	YX61BVY	SI
119	YX61BYA	SI	130	YX61BWF	SI	141	YX61BVZ	SI

Route 276 is operated by long-wheelbase ADL Enviro 200s. SE124 is seen here in Hackney while heading to Newham Hospital

SE142-193			ADL E20D SFD5D1			ADL Enviro 200 10.2m			B29D		
142	YX61BXK	PM	157	YX61DVG	PM	172	YX61EKL	C			
143	YX61BXL	PM	158	YX61DVH	PM	173	YX61EKM	C			
144	YX61BXM	PM	159	YX61DVJ	PM	174	YX61EKN	C			
145	YX61BXN	AL	160	YX61DVK	PM	175	SN12AUM	PL			
146	YX61BXO	AL	161	YX61DVL	PM	176	SN12AVO	PL			
147	YX61BXP	AL	162	YX61DVM	PM	177	SN12AUP	PL			
148	YX61DTO	AL	163	YX61DVN	PM	178	SN12AUR	PL			
149	YX61DTU	AL	164	YX61DVO	PM	179	SN12AUT	PL			
150	YX61DTV	AL	165	YX61DVP	PM	180	SN12AUU	PL			
151	YX61DTY	Q	166	YX61DVR	PM	181	SN12AUV	PL			
152	YX61DTZ	NX	167	YX61EKF	C	182	SN12AUW	PL			
153	YX61DVA	PM	168	YX61EKG	C	183	SN12AUX	PL			
154	YX61DVB	PM	169	YX61EKH	C	184	SN12AUY	PL			
155	YX61DVC	PM	170	YX61EKJ	C	185	SN12AVB	PL			
156	YX61DVF	PM	171	YX61EKK	C	186	SN12AVC	PL			

187	SN12AVD	PL	190	SN12AVG	PL	193	SN12AVL	PL
188	SN12AVE	PL	191	SN12AVJ	PL			
189	SN12AVF	PL	192	SN12AVK	PL			

SE198-212		ADL E20D SFD7L1		ADL Enviro 200 10.8m			B31D	
198	YY14WDT	SW	203	YY14WDZ	SW	208	YY14WEJ	SW
199	YY14WDU	SW	204	YY14WEA	SW	209	YY14WEK	SW
200	YY14WDV	SW	205	YY14WEC	SW	210	YY14WEO	SW
201	YY14WDW	SW	206	YY14WEF	SW	211	YY14WEP	SW
202	YY14WDX	SW	207	YY14WEH	SW	212	YY14WEU	MG

SE213-234		ADL E20D SFD8LB		ADL Enviro 200 9.6m			B25D	
213	YY64GWZ	MB	221	YY64GXJ	SI	229	YY64TXO	SI
214	YY64GXA	MB	222	YY64GXK	SI	230	YY64TXP	SI
215	YY64GXB	MB	223	YY64TXH	SI	231	YY64TXR	SI
216	YY64GXC	MB	224	YY64TXJ	SI	232	YX15XMK	RR
217	YY64GXD	SI	225	YY64TXK	SI	233	YX15XML	RR
218	YY64GXE	SI	226	YY64TXL	SI	234	YX15XMM	RR
219	YY64GXF	RR	227	YY64TXM	SI			
220	YY64GXH	SI	228	YY64TXN	SI			

Route G1 in South London is home to a batch of short-wheelbase ADL Enviro 200s. SE247 is seen near Tooting Broadway while heading for Green Lane in Streatham

SE235-267		ADL E20D SFD1LB		ADL Enviro 200 8.9m			B25F	
235	YY15CNU	SW	240	YY15CNF	SW	245	YY15EYS	SW
236	YY15CNJ	SW	241	YY15CNV	SW	246	YY15EYT	PL
237	YY15CNK	SW	242	YY15CNX	SW	247	YY15EYU	PL
238	YY15CNN	SW	243	YY15EYP	SW	248	YY15EYV	PL
239	YY15CNO	SW	244	YY15EYR	SW	249	YY15EYW	PL

250	YY15HKA	PL	256	YY15HKG	PL	262	YX65RJY	MB
251	YY15HKB	PL	257	YY15HKH	PL	263	YX65RJZ	MB
252	YY15HKC	PL	258	YY15HKJ	PL	264	YX65RKA	MB
253	YY15HKD	PL	259	YY15GDF	PL	265	YX65RKE	MB
254	YY15HKE	PL	260	YY15GDJ	PL	266	YX65RKF	MB
255	YY15HKF	PL	261	YX65RJV	MB	267	YX65RKJ	MB

SE268-287		ADL E20D SFD7LB		ADL Enviro 200 10.8m		B31D	
268	YX65RNY	A	275	YX65RPY	AL	282	YX65RSO	AL
269	YX65RNZ	A	276	YX65RPZ	AL	283	YX65RSU	AL
270	YX65ROH	A	277	YX65RRO	AL	284	YX65RSV	AL
271	YX65ROU	A	278	YX65RRU	AL	285	YX65RSY	AL
272	YX65RPO	A	279	YX65RRV	AL	286	YX65RSZ	AL
273	YX65RPU	A	280	YX65RRY	AL	287	YX65RTO	AL
274	YX65RPV	AL	281	YX65RRZ	AL			

SE288	SN16OLP	ADL E20D SFD1LB	ADL Enviro 200 8.9m	B24F	MB
SE289	SN16OLR	ADL E20D SFD1LB	ADL Enviro 200 8.9m	B24F	MB
SE290	SN16OLT	ADL E20D SFD1LB	ADL Enviro 200 8.9m	B24F	MB
SE291	YX16OCX	ADL E20D SFDALA	ADL Enviro 200MMC 9.3m	B27D	Q
SE292	YX16OCY	ADL E20D SFDALA	ADL Enviro 200MMC 9.3m	B27D	Q

Go-Ahead London were also the first operator of fully electric single-deck buses in London, and can be found on the Red Arrow routes in central London as well as two other routes recently converted. SEe41 is seen crossing Holborn Viaduct while on route 521 heading to London Bridge

SEe1-51		BYD D9UR		ADL Enviro 200MMC 12.0m		B21D	
1	LJ66CJZ	RA	5	LJ16NNK	RA	9	LJ16NNP	RA
2	LJ66GYY	RA	6	LJ16NNL	RA	10	LJ16NNR	RA
3	LJ16NNG	RA	7	LJ16NNM	RA	11	LJ16NNT	RA
4	LJ16NNH	RA	8	LJ16NNO	RA	12	LJ16NNU	RA

13	LJ66CFM	RA	26	LJ66CGO	RA	39	LJ66CHN	RA
14	LJ66CFN	RA	27	LJ66CGU	RA	40	LJ66CHO	RA
15	LJ66CFO	RA	28	LJ66CGV	RA	41	LJ66CHV	RA
16	LJ66CFP	RA	29	LJ66CGX	RA	42	LJ66CHX	RA
17	LJ66CFU	RA	30	LJ66CGY	RA	43	LJ66CHY	RA
18	LJ66CFV	RA	31	LJ66CGZ	RA	44	LJ66CHZ	RA
19	LJ66CFX	RA	32	LJ66CHC	RA	45	LJ66CJE	RA
20	LJ66CFY	RA	33	LJ66CHD	RA	46	LJ66CJF	RA
21	LJ66CFZ	RA	34	LJ66CHF	RA	47	LJ66CJO	RA
22	LJ66CGE	RA	35	LJ66CHG	RA	48	LJ66CJU	RA
23	LJ66CGF	RA	36	LJ66CHH	RA	49	LJ66CJV	RA
24	LJ66CGG	RA	37	LJ66CHK	RA	50	LJ66CJX	RA
25	LJ66CGK	RA	38	LJ66CHL	RA	51	LJ66CJY	RA

SEe52-76 **BYD D8UR** **ADL Enviro 200MMC 10.8m** **B31D**

52	LJ67DJD	Q	61	LJ67DKD	Q	70	LJ67DKY	NP
53	LJ67DJE	Q	62	LJ67DKE	Q	71	LJ67DKY	NP
54	LJ67DJF	Q	63	LJ67DKF	Q	72	LJ67DLD	NP
55	LJ67DJK	Q	64	LJ67DKK	Q	73	LJ67DLE	NP
56	LJ67DJO	Q	65	LJ67DKL	NP	74	LJ67DLF	NP
57	LJ67DJU	Q	66	LJ67DKN	NP	75	LJ67DLK	NP
58	LJ67DJV	Q	67	LJ67DKO	NP	76	LJ67DLN	NP
59	LJ67DJX	Q	68	LJ67DKU	NP			
60	LJ67DKA	Q	69	LJ67DKV	NP			

Route 360 is also a recent conversion to electric bus operation. SEe58 is seen here crossing Vauxhall Bridge while heading for Elephant & Castle

SEN1-12 Dennis E200Dart SFD1D1 Alexander Enviro 200 8.9m B26F

1	YX60FUA	NP	5	YX60FUF	r	9	YX60FUM	r
2	YX60FUB	r	6	YX60FUG	r	10	YX60FUO	r
3	YX60FUD	r	7	YX60FUH	NP	11	YX60FUP	NP
4	YX60FUE	r	8	YX60FUJ	r	12	YX60FUT	NP

SEN13-20 ADL E20D SFD4D1 ADL Enviro 200 9.3m B24D

13	YX11FYS	NP	16	YX11FYV	r	19	YX11FYZ	r
14	YX11FYT	r	17	YX11FYW	r	20	YX11AGU	r
15	YX11FYU	r	18	YX11FYY	r			

As part of the acquisition of the Northumberland Park operation from First London were a batch of 29 Alexander/ADL Enviro 200s which started the SEN-class. SEN14 is seen here at Southgate while on route 299 heading to Muswell Hill. This route has since passed to Sullivan Buses, while the vehicle remains in the fleet prior to refurbishment and redeployment to route 386 later this year

SEN21-29 ADL E20D SFD8D1 ADL Enviro 200 9.6m B25D

21	YX61FYT	MB	24	YX61FYW	MB	27	YX61FZA	MB
22	YX61FYU	MB	25	YX61FYY	MB	28	YX61FZB	MB
23	YX61FYV	MB	26	YX61FYZ	MB	29	YX61FZZ	MB

SEN30-37 ADL E20D SFD7E1 ADL Enviro 200 10.8m B31D

30	YX61FZO	A	33	YX61FZS	A	36	YX61FZV	PL
31	YX61FZP	A	34	YX61FZT	SW	37	YX61FZW	PL
32	YX61FZR	A	35	YX61FZU	PL			

SEN38 SK07HLO Dennis E200Dart SFD111 Alexander Enviro 200 8.9m B26F RR

		Dennis E200Dart SFD151		Alexander Enviro 200 8.9m			B26F	
39	YX09FLP	SW	41	YX09FLZ	SW	43	YX09FMV	SW
40	YX09FLW	SW	42	YX09FMU	SW			

An oddity in the Go-Ahead London fleet is the SOE-class of Optare Esteem-bodied Dennis E200Darts, the chassis most commonly found with Alexander Enviro 200 bodywork. SOE14 is seen here not long after leaving Wimbledon Bus Station while on route 164 and not far from its terminus in Francis Grove

SOE1-40		Dennis E200Dart SFD551		Optare Esteem 10.4m			B29D	
1	LX09AYF	AL	15	LX09AYW	AL	29	LX09AZR	AL
2	LX09AYG	AL	16	LX09AYY	AL	30	LX09AZT	AL
3	LX09AYH	AL	17	LX09AYZ	AL	31	LX09BXP	C
4	LX09AYJ	AL	18	LX09AZA	AL	32	LX09BXR	C
5	LX09AYK	AL	19	LX09AZB	AL	33	LX09BXS	C
6	LX09AYL	AL	20	LX09AZC	AL	34	LX09EVB	C
7	LX09AYM	AL	21	LX09AZD	AL	35	LX09EVC	C
8	LX09AYN	AL	22	LX09AZF	AL	36	LX09EVD	A
9	LX09AYO	AL	23	LX09AZG	RR	37	LX09EVF	A
10	LX09AYP	AL	24	LX09AZJ	RR	38	LX09EVG	A
11	LX09AYS	AL	25	LX09AZL	RR	39	LX09EVH	A
12	LX09AYT	AL	26	LX09AZN	RR	40	LX09EVJ	A
13	LX09AYU	AL	27	LX09AZO	RR			
14	LX09AYV	AL	28	LX09AZP	AL			

VC1	LK53KVY	Volvo B12B	Plaxton Panther 12.0m	C49FT	ST
VC2	LK53KWE	Volvo B12B	Plaxton Panther 12.0m	C49FT	NP
VC3	UK05BCL	Volvo B12B	Plaxton Panther 12.0m	C51FT	LU
VC4	SF05XEC	Volvo B12M	Jonckheere Mistral	C53F	LU
VC5	LK53KVZ	Volvo B12B	Plaxton Panther 12.0m	C49FT	NP
VC6	YN55WSV	Volvo B12B	Plaxton Panther 12.0m	C49FT	NP
VE1	LX58CWK	Volvo B9TL	Alexander Enviro 400 10.4m	H41/24D	A

VE2	LX58CWL	Volvo B9TL	Alexander Enviro 400 10.4m	H41/24D	A
VE3	LX58CWM	Volvo B9TL	Alexander Enviro 400 10.4m	H41/24D	A
VP18	X171FBB	Volvo B7TL	Plaxton President 10.0m	H41/23D	Qt
VP19	X172FBB	Volvo B7TL	Plaxton President 10.0m	H41/23D	Qt
WDL1	LX58CWG	Wright Gemini 2DL	Wright Gemini 2 10.4m	H41/24D	AL
WES1	LJ17THF	Wright Streetair	Wright Streetair	B22D	Q

A unique member of the Go-Ahead London fleet is WDL1, a Wrightbus Gemini integral vehicle. It is seen near Tooting Broadway while on route 270 heading to Mitcham

WHV1-16		Volvo B5LH		Wright Eclipse Gemini 2 10.4m		H39/21D		
1	LJ61GVW	NX	7	LJ61GXE	NX	13	LJ61GXM	NX
2	LJ61GVX	NX	8	LJ61GXF	NX	14	LJ61GXN	NX
3	LJ61GVY	NX	9	LJ61GXG	NX	15	LJ61GXO	NX
4	LJ61GVZ	NX	10	LJ61GXH	NX	16	LJ61GXP	AL
5	LJ61GWA	NX	11	LJ61GXK	NX			
6	LJ61GWC	NX	12	LJ61GXL	NX			

WHV17-41		Volvo B5LH		Wright Eclipse Gemini 2 10.5m		H39/21D		
17	LJ61NVC	AL	26	LJ61NVN	AL	35	LJ62KGF	AF
18	LJ61NVD	AL	27	LJ12CHH	AL	36	LJ62KGG	AF
19	LJ61NVE	AL	28	LJ61NVP	AL	37	LJ62KGN	AF
20	LJ61NVF	AL	29	LJ61NVR	AL	38	LJ62KGY	AF
21	LJ61NVG	AL	30	LJ61NVS	AL	39	LJ62KHF	AF
22	LJ61NVH	AL	31	LJ12CHK	AL	40	LJ62KHV	AF
23	LJ61NVK	AL	32	LJ62KFD	AF	41	LJ62KKP	AF
24	LJ61NVL	AL	33	LJ62KFF	AF			
25	LJ61NVM	AL	34	LJ62KFU	AF			

The early deliveries of the Volvo B5LH/Wright combination were with the Gemini 2 body. WHV29 is about to reach its destination after crossing Battersea Bridge. Route 19 is now operated by Arriva

WHV42-110		Volvo B5LH		Wright Gemini 3 10.6m			H41/21D	
42	BP15OLN	NX	65	BF65WJN	C	88	BD65EVX	SW
43	BP15OLM	NX	66	BF65WJM	C	89	BD65EVY	SW
44	BP15OLO	NX	67	BF65WJJ	C	90	BD65EVW	SW
45	BP15OLV	C	68	BF65WJV	C	91	BD65EWA	SW
46	BP15OLU	C	69	BF65WJU	C	92	BD65EWP	SW
47	BP15OLR	C	70	BF65WJO	C	93	BD65EWO	SW
48	BP15OLT	C	71	BF65WJG	C	94	BD65EWS	SW
49	BP15OLW	C	72	BF65WJX	C	95	BD65EWY	SW
50	BP15OLX	C	73	BF65WKA	C	96	BD65EWZ	SW
51	BP15OMA	C	74	BF65WJY	C	97	BT65JGF	SW
52	BF65WJA	C	75	BF65WKB	C	98	BD65EWV	SW
53	BP15OMC	C	76	BF65WJZ	C	99	BT65JGU	SW
54	BP15OME	C	77	BF65WKG	C	100	BD65EWX	SW
55	BP15OMB	C	78	BF65WKD	C	101	BD65EVV	SW
56	BP15OMK	C	79	BF65WKC	C	102	BD65EWN	SW
57	BP15OMJ	C	80	BF65WKE	C	103	BD65EWR	SW
58	BP15OML	C	81	BD65EVN	SW	104	BD65EWU	AL
59	BP15OMF	C	82	BF65WLH	SW	105	BT65JFZ	A
60	BP15OMD	C	83	BD65EVM	SW	106	BT65JGO	A
61	BF65WJD	C	84	BD65EVR	SW	107	BD65EWW	SW
62	BF65WJE	C	85	BD65EVP	SW	108	BT65JGV	SW
63	BF65WJC	C	86	BD65EVT	SW	109	BD65EXA	A
64	BF65WJK	C	87	BD65EVU	SW	110	BD65EWT	A

WHV111	BX14TJV	Volvo B5LH	Wright Gemini 3 10.5m	H41/21D	MG

Go-Ahead London have standardised on two manufacturers for their hybrid double-deck requirements, ADL and Volvo. Volvo B5LHs in the fleet have been bodied by Egyptian-based MCV, Scottish-based ADL and Northern Ireland-based Wrightbus. An example of the latter is seen here by way of WHV141, a Wright Gemini 3, pictured at Hyde Park Corner while on route 14 heading to Putney Heath

WHV112-196		Volvo B5LH		Wright Gemini 3 10.6m			H41/21D	
112	BV66VHN	Q	137	BV66VLP	AF	162	BT66MSV	AF
113	BV66VHO	Q	138	BV66VLA	AF	163	BT66MSX	AF
114	BV66VHP	Q	139	BV66VHH	AF	164	BT66MPU	AF
115	BV66VHR	AF	140	BV66ZRY	AF	165	BT66MSY	NX
116	BV66VHT	AF	141	BT66MSO	AF	166	BV66VLO	NX
117	BV66VHU	AF	142	BT66MSU	AF	167	BV66VLR	NX
118	BV66VHW	AF	143	BV66VJA	MG	168	LF67EXA	Q
119	BV66VHX	AF	144	BV66VJC	MG	169	LF67EXB	Q
120	BV66VHY	AF	145	BV66VJD	MG	170	LF67EXC	Q
121	BV66VHZ	AF	146	BV66VJE	MG	171	LF67EXD	Q
122	BV66VJN	AF	147	BV66VJF	MG	172	LF67EXE	Q
123	BV66VJO	AF	148	BV66VJG	MG	173	LF67EXG	Q
124	BV66VJP	AF	149	BV66VJJ	MG	174	LF67EXH	Q
125	BV66VJU	AF	150	BV66VJK	MG	175	LF67EXJ	Q
126	BV66VJY	AF	151	BV66VJL	MG	176	LF67EXK	Q
127	BV66VJZ	AF	152	BV66VJM	MG	177	LF67EXL	Q
128	BV66VKB	AF	153	BV66VKA	MG	178	LF67EXM	Q
129	BV66VLE	AF	154	BV66VLC	MG	179	LF67EXX	Q
130	BV66VLM	AF	155	BV66VLD	MG	180	LF67EXO	Q
131	BV66VLK	AF	156	BV66VLJ	Q	181	LF67EXP	Q
132	BV66VLF	AF	157	BV66VLL	Q	182	LF67EXR	Q
133	BV66VLH	AF	158	BV66VLN	AF	183	LF67EXS	Q
134	BV66ZRZ	AF	159	BV66VLG	AF	184	LF67EXT	Q
135	BV66VHJ	AF	160	BV66VHL	AF	185	LF67EXU	Q
136	BV66VHK	AF	161	BV66ZSD	AF	186	LF67EXV	Q

187	LF67EXW	Q	191	LF67EYB	Q	195	LF67EYH	Q
188	LF67EXN	Q	192	LF67EYC	Q	196	LF67EYJ	Q
189	LF67EXZ	Q	193	LF67EYD	Q			
190	LF67EYA	Q	194	LF67EYG	Q			

WHY1-6		Wright Electrocity		Wright Cadet 10.4m			B26D	
1	LX06ECN	w	3	LX55EAE	w	5	LX55EAG	w
2	LX55EAC	w	4	LX55EAF	w	6	LX55EAJ	w

WHY7-13		Wright Electrocity		Wright Cadet 10.3m * - B27D			B25D	
7*	LX57CLZ	w	10	LX11DVC	w	13	LX11DVH	w
8	LX11DVA	w	11	LX11DVF	w			
9	LX11DVB	w	12	LX11DVG	w			

WS1-9		Wright Streetlite WF		Wright Streetlite 8.8m			B28F	
1	LJ12CGF	MB	4	LJ12CGO	MB	7	LJ12CGX	MB
2	LJ12CGG	MB	5	LJ12CGU	MB	8	LJ12CGY	MB
3	LJ12CGK	MB	6	LJ12CGV	MB	9	LJ12CGZ	MB

WS10-20		Wright Streetlite DF		Wright Streetlite 10.8m			B31D	
10	LJ13GJU	AL	14	LJ13GJZ	AL	18	LJ13GKE	AL
11	LJ13GJV	AL	15	LJ13GKA	AL	19	LJ13GKF	AL
12	LJ13GJX	AL	16	LJ13GKC	AL	20	LJ13GKG	AL
13	LJ13GJY	AL	17	LJ13GKD	AL			

Go-Ahead London operate a special contract on behalf of HereEast in the Olympic Park near Stratford in East London. For this contract, three WS-class Wright Streetlites carry special liveries for HereEast. WS36 and WS38 are pictured here outside the HereEast building (photo courtesy of Richard Cains)

WS21-32 — Wright Streetlite DF — Wright Streetlite 10.4m — B29D

21	LJ13GKK	NP	25	LJ13GKP	NP	29	LJ13GKY	NP
22	LJ13GKL	NP	26	LJ13GKU	NP	30	LJ13GKZ	NP
23	LJ13GKN	NP	27	LJ13GKV	NP	31	LJ13GLF	NP
24	LJ13GKO	NP	28	LJ13GKX	NP	32	LJ13GLK	NP

WS35-64 — Wright Streetlite WF — Wright Streetlite 8.8m — B28F

35	SN64CUC	SI	53	SM15HWJ	NP	60	SM15VKE	NP
36	SN64CUG	SI	54	SM15HWK	NP	61	SM15WCK	NP
38	SN64CUJ	SI	55	SM15VJZ	NP	62	SM15WCL	NP
49	SM15HWE	NP	56	SM15VKA	NP	63	SM15WCN	NP
50	SM15HWF	NP	57	SM15VKB	NP	64	SM15WCO	NP
51	SM15HWG	NP	58	SM15VKC	NP			
52	SM15HWH	NP	59	SM15VKD	NP			

WS65 — Wright Streetlite DF — Wright Streetlite 10.4m — B29D — MG

WS65	SL16YPK	

WS66-78 — Wright Streetlite DF — Wright Streetlite 10.8m — B31D

66	SK66HSC	PL	71	SK66HSL	PL	76	SK17HFV	PL
67	SK66HSE	PL	72	SK66HSN	PL	77	SK17HFW	PL
68	SK66HSF	PL	73	SK66HSO	PL	78	SK17HFX	PL
69	SK66HSG	PL	74	SK66HSU	PL			
70	SK66HSJ	PL	75	SK17HFU	PL			

WS79-86 — Wright Streetlite WF — Wright Streetlite 8.8m — B28F

79	SK17HHE	NP	82	SK17HKB	AF	85	SK17HKE	AF
80	SK17HHF	NP	83	SK17HKC	AF	86	SK17HKF	AF
81	SK17HKA	AF	84	SK17HKD	AF			

WS87-117 — Wright Streetlite DF — Wright Streetlite 10.8m — B31D

87	SK17HKG	PL	98	SK67FKL	C	109	SK67FMJ	MG
88	SK17HKH	PL	99	SK67FKM	C	110	SK67FML	MG
89	SK17HKJ	PL	100	SK67FKN	C	111	SK67FMM	MG
90	SK17HKL	PL	101	SK67FKO	C	112	SK67FMO	MG
91	SK67FKA	C	102	SK67FKP	C	113	SK67FMP	MG
92	SK67FKB	C	103	SK67FKS	C	114	SK67FMU	MG
93	SK67FKE	C	104	SK67FMA	MG	115	SK67FMV	MG
94	SK67FKF	C	105	SK67FMC	MG	116	SK67FMX	MG
95	SK67FKG	C	106	SK67FMD	MG	117	SN18XZV	MG
96	SK67FKH	C	107	SK67FME	MG			
97	SK67FKJ	C	108	SK67FMF	MG			

WSD3-23 — Wright Streetdeck — Wright Streetdeck 10.6m — H41/22D

3	SN18XYV	AL	10	SN18XZD	AL	17	SN18XZL	AL
4	SN18XYW	AL	11	SN18XZE	AL	18	SN18XZM	AL
5	SN18XYX	AL	12	SN18XZF	AL	19	SN18XZO	AL
6	SN18XYY	AL	13	SN18XZG	AL	20	SN18XZP	AL
7	SN18XYZ	AL	14	SN18XZH	AL	21	SN18XZR	AL
8	SN18XZB	AL	15	SN18XZJ	AL	22	SN18XZS	AL
9	SN18XZC	AL	16	SN18XZK	AL	23	SN18XZT	AL

The Wright Streetlite is operated in various lengths and forms (door forward & wheel forward). An example of the 10.8-metre doors-forward kind is WS97, seen near Tooting Broadway while on route 355 heading to Mitcham

WVL18-272		Volvo B7TL		Wright Eclipse Gemini 10.1m			H41/21D	
				* - H41/22D, $ - H41/20D, % - H41/23D, + - CO41/22D				
18*	LG02KHT	w	190%	LX05EZV	NP	228	LX06DZL	C
22*	LG02KHX	w	195*	LX05EZM	w	230	LX06DZN	Q
25*	LG02KJA	w	196%	LX05EZN	BX	231	LX06DZO	MB
27$	LG02KJF	w	197%	LX05EZO	BX	232	LX06DZP	C
75%	LF52ZPE	SW	198%	LX05EZP	BX	233	LX06DZR	MB
79%	LF52ZPK	NP	200%	LX05EZS	NP	234	LX06DZS	NX
83+	LF52ZNR	AL	201%	LX05EZT	NP	235	LX06DZT	NX
90%	LF52ZNY	w	202%	LX05EZU	NP	237	LX06DZV	MB
93+	LF52ZNE	C	203%	LX05EYZ	NP	238	LX06DZW	C
94%	LF52ZNG	SW	204%	LX05EZA	NP	239	LX06DZY	C
95%	LF52ZNH	SW	205*	LX05EZB	NP	240	LX06DZZ	C
96%	LF52ZNJ	SW	206*	LX05EZC	AL	241	LX06EAA	MB
102%	LF52ZLZ	AL	207*	LX05EZD	AL	246	LX06EAJ	AL
104%	LF52ZMU	w	208*	LX05EZE	AL	247	LX06EAK	AL
111*	LX03EDV	NP	209*	LX05EZF	AL	248	LX06EAM	AL
114*	LX03EEF	RR	210*	LX05EZG	AL	249	LX06EAO	RR
115*	LX03EEG	RR	211%	LX05EZH	AL	250	LX06EAP	RR
117*	LX03EEJ	RR	212	LX06DYS	C	252	LX06EAY	w
118*	LX03EEM	w	213	LX06DYT	C	253	LX06EBA	w
119*	LX03ECV	AL	216	LX06DYW	MB	254	LX06EBC	w
120*	LX03ECW	AL	217	LX06DYY	MB	255	LX06EBD	w
121*	LX03ECY	AL	219	LX06DZB	MB	256	LX06FBF	w
137*	LX53AZN	Q	222	LX06DZE	SW	257	LX06EBG	w
153*	LX53BGE	w	224	LX06DZG	MB	258	LX06EBJ	w
159*	LX53BAO	w	225	LX06DZH	SW	259	LX06EBK	w
189*	LX05FBC	NP	226	LX06DZJ	SW	260	LX06EBL	w

261	LX06EBM	w	265	LX06EBU	w	269	LX06ECC	w
262	LX06EBN	w	266	LX06EBV	w	270	LX06ECD	w
263	LX06EBO	w	267	LX06EBZ	w	272	LX06ECF	NX
264	LX06EBP	w	268	LX06ECA	w			

Another dying breed within the Go-Ahead London fleet is the Volvo B7TL with first-generation Wright Eclipse Gemini bodywork. WVL266 is seen here deputising for a New Routemaster on route 12, seen here passing Westminster while heading for Oxford Circus. This bus has recently been withdrawn from service

| WVL274-456 | | Volvo B9TL | | Wright Eclipse Gemini 2 10.4m | | H39/23D | |
| | | | | * - H39/17F | | | |

274	LX59CYL	MG	294	LX59CZM	NX	314	LX59DAA	MG
275	LX59CYO	AL	295	LX59CZN	NX	315	LX59DAO	MG
276	LX59CYP	NX	296	LX59CZO	BX	316	LX59DAU	MG
277	LX59CYS	NX	297	LX59CZP	BX	317	LX59DBO	MG
278	LX59CYT	NX	298	LX59CZR	BX	318	LX59DBU	MG
279	LX59CYU	NX	299	LX59CZS	BX	319	LX59DBV	MG
280	LX59CYV	NX	300	LX59CZT	BX	320	LX59DBY	MG
281	LX59CYW	NX	301	LX59CZU	BX	321	LX59DBZ	MG
282	LX59CYY	NX	302	LX59CZV	BX	322	LX59DCE	MG
283	LX59CYZ	NX	303	LX59CYA	BX	323	LX59DCF	MG
284	LX59CZA	NX	304	LX59CYC	BX	324	LX59DCO	MG
285	LX59CZB	NX	305	LX59CYE	BX	325	LX59DCU	MG
286	LX59CZC	NX	306	LX59CYF	BX	326	LX59DCV	MG
287	LX59CZD	NX	307	LX59CYG	BX	327	LX59DCY	MG
288	LX59CZF	NX	308	LX59CYH	BX	328	LX59DCZ	MG
289	LX59CZG	NX	309	LX59CYJ	BX	329	LX59DDA	MG
290	LX59CZH	NX	310	LX59CYK	BX	330	LX59DDE	MG
291	LX59CZJ	NX	311	LX59CZW	BX	331	LX59DDF	MG
292	LX59CZK	NX	312	LX59CZY	BX	332	LX59DDJ	SW
293	LX59CZL	NX	313	LX59CZZ	MG	333	LX59DDK	MG

The second-generation of the Wright Eclipse Gemini body can be found in considerable number within the Go-Ahead London fleet, this time on the later Volvo B9TL chassis. WVL331 is seen in Bexleyheath on route 89 heading to Slade Green

334*	LX59DDL	C	362	LX60DWN	A	399	LX11CWA	NX
335*	LX59DDN	C	363	LX60DWO	A	407	LX11CWM	NX
336*	LX59DDO	C	364	LX60DWP	A	408	LX11CWN	NX
337*	LX59DDU	C	365	LX60DWU	A	409	LX11CWO	NX
338*	LX59DDV	C	366	LX60DWV	C	410	LX11CWP	NX
339*	LX59DDY	C	367	LX60DWW	NP	411	LX11CWR	NX
340*	LX59DDZ	C	368	LX60DWY	w	412	LX11CWT	NX
341*	LX59DEU	C	375	LX60DXF	w	413	LX11CWU	RR
342*	LX59DFA	C	376	LX60DXG	w	414	LX11CWV	RR
343*	LX59DFC	C	378	LX60DXJ	w	415	LX11CWW	RR
344*	LX59DFD	C	379	LX60DXK	w	416	LX11CWY	RR
345	LX59DFE	RR	380	LX60DXM	SW	417	LX11CWZ	RR
346	LX59DFF	RR	381	LX60DXO	SW	418	LX11CXA	RR
347	LX59DFG	RR	382	LX60DXP	SW	419	LX11CXB	RR
348	LX59DFJ	RR	383	LX60DXR	SW	420	LX11CXC	RR
349	LX59DFK	RR	384	LX60DXS	SW	421	LX11CXD	RR
350	LX60DVY	MG	385	LX60DXT	SW	422	LX11FHV	SI
351	LX60DVZ	MG	386	LX11CVL	NX	423	LX11FHW	SI
352	LX60DWA	MG	387	LX11CVM	NX	424	LX11FHY	SI
353	LX60DWC	MG	388	LX11CVN	NX	425	LX11FHZ	SI
354	LX60DWD	MG	390	LX11CVP	NX	426	LX11FJA	SI
355	LX60DWE	MG	391	LX11CVR	NX	427	LX11FJC	SI
356	LX60DWF	NX	392	LX11CVS	NX	428	LX11FJD	SI
357	LX60DWG	MG	393	LX11CVT	NX	429	LX11FJE	SI
358	LX60DWJ	NP	395	LX11CVV	NX	430	LX11FJF	SI
359	LX60DWK	NP	396	LX11CVW	NX	431	LX11FJJ	SI
360	LX60DWL	A	397	LX11CVY	NX	432	LX11FJK	SI
361	LX60DWM	A	398	LX11CVZ	NX	433	LX11FJN	SI

434	LX11FJO	SI	442	LJ61GXB	A	450	LJ61GWL	NP
435	LJ61GWU	AF	443	LJ61GXC	A	451	LJ61GWM	RR
436	LJ61GWV	SW	444	LJ61GXD	A	452	LJ61GWN	RR
437	LJ61GWW	SW	445	LJ61GWD	A	453	LJ61GWO	RR
438	LJ61GWX	SW	446	LJ61GWE	AL	454	LJ61GWP	RR
439	LJ61GWY	SW	447	LJ61GWF	A	455	LJ61GVP	BX
440	LJ61GWZ	A	448	LJ61GWG	NP	456	LJ61GVT	BX
441	LJ61GXA	A	449	LJ61GWK	NP			

WVL457-495		Volvo B9TL		Wright Eclipse Gemini 2 10.5m			H39/23D	
457	LJ61NUM	NP	470	LJ61NWZ	RR	483	LJ12CHF	AL
458	LJ61NUO	NP	471	LJ61NXA	RR	484	LJ12CHG	RR
459	LJ61NUP	NP	472	LJ61NXB	RR	485	LJ61NWU	RR
460	LJ61NUU	NP	473	LJ61NXC	RR	486	LJ61NWV	RR
461	LJ61NUV	NP	474	LJ61NXD	RR	487	LJ61NVZ	RR
462	LJ61NUW	NP	475	LJ61NXE	RR	488	LJ61NWA	RR
463	LJ61NUX	NP	476	LJ61NXF	RR	489	LJ61NWB	RR
464	LJ61NUY	NP	477	LJ61NWL	RR	490	LJ61NWC	RR
465	LJ61NVA	NP	478	LJ61NWM	RR	491	LJ61NWD	RR
466	LJ61NVB	NP	479	LJ61NWN	RR	492	LJ61NWE	RR
467	LJ61NWW	NP	480	LJ61NWO	RR	493	LJ61NWF	RR
468	LJ61NWX	RR	481	LJ12CHD	AL	494	LJ61NWG	RR
469	LJ12CHC	RR	482	LJ61NWR	AL	495	LJ61NWH	RR

During 2012, Go-Ahead London purchased the Northumberland Park Garage, including vehicles and routes, from First London. WVN5, one of a number of vehicles included in that acquisition, is seen in Tottenham while on route 259 heading to King's Cross

WVL509	BF63HDE	Volvo B5TL	Wright Eclipse Gemini 3 10.5m	H41/22D	C
WVL510	BF63HDG	Volvo B5TL	Wright Eclipse Gemini 3 10.5m	H41/21D	C

	WVN1-45		Volvo B9TL		Wright Eclipse Gemini 2 10.4m		H39/23D	
1	LK59FEP	NP	16	LK59FDF	NP	31	BV10WVD	AL
2	LK59FET	NP	17	LK59FDJ	NP	32	BV10WVE	AL
3	LK59FEU	NP	18	LK59FDL	NP	33	BV10WVF	AL
4	LK59FDV	NP	19	LK59FDM	NP	34	BV10WVG	AL
5	LK59FDX	NP	20	LK59FDN	NP	35	BV10WVH	AL
6	LK59FDY	NP	21	LK59FDO	NP	36	BV10WVJ	AL
7	LK59FDZ	NP	22	LK59FDP	NP	37	BV10WVK	AL
8	LK59FEF	NP	23	LK59FDU	NP	38	BV10WVL	AL
9	LK59FEG	NP	24	BG59FXA	NP	39	BV10WWA	AL
10	LK59FEH	NP	25	BG59FXB	NP	40	BV10WWC	AL
11	LK59FEO	NP	26	BG59FXC	AL	41	BV10WWD	AL
12	LK59FDG	NP	27	BG59FXD	AL	42	BV10WWF	AL
13	LK59FEJ	NP	28	BG59FXE	AL	43	BV10WWO	AL
14	LK59FEM	NP	29	BG59FXF	AL	44	BV10WWP	AL
15	LK59FDE	NP	30	BG59FXH	AL	45	BV10WWR	AL

	WVN46-53		Volvo B9TL		Wright Eclipse Gemini 2 10.5m		H39/23D	
46	BL61ACY	NP	49	BL61ACZ	NP	52	BL61ADX	NP
47	BL61ACX	NP	50	BL61ADV	NP	53	BL61ADZ	NP
48	BL61ADU	NP	51	BL61ADO	NP			

Previous registrations

LUT1	WX55HWF		VC2	LK53KWE, NX52AAA
LUT2	WX55HWG		VC4	LSK845
LUT3	WX55HWH		VC6	YN55WSV, Y50HMC, YN55WSV,
LUT4	YJ07LVX			L700SGB
RML2516	CUV283C		WHV111	141-D-21502
VC1	LK53KVY, NX51AAA			

Liveries

Unless stated below, all vehicles in this fleet carry standard fleet livery;

Cream-based Go-Ahead London Commercial: 256, MEC11, MEC15-19, MEC22-26, MEC28, MEC29, MEC31, MEC33, MEC35, MEC36, MEC38-41, PHD271, VC1-4
HereEast: LDP186, WS35, WS36, WS38
1920-style General: LT50
1930-style General: LT60, WVL83, WVL93
East London Transit: LT903-910, LT914-953, WVL468-480
Allover purple: LUT1-5
London by Night: PVL224
London Transport: RM9
Allover white: VC5, VC6

Metrobus

Garage
CY   Crawley – Wheatstone Close, Crawley, RH10 9UA

6001-6018		Volvo B7RLE		Wright Eclipse 2 12.0m			B40D	
6001	BN14CUC	CY	6007	BN14CUU	CY	6013	BN14CVB	CY
6002	BN14CUG	CY	6008	BN14CUV	CY	6014	BN14CVC	CY
6003	BN14CUH	CY	6009	BN14CUW	CY	6015	BU14EFS	CY
6004	BN14CUJ	CY	6010	BN14CUX	CY	6016	BU14EFT	CY
6005	BN14CUK	CY	6011	BN14CUY	CY	6017	BU14EHK	CY
6006	BN14CUO	CY	6012	BN14CVA	CY	6018	BU14EHL	CY

Part of the Metrobus network in Crawley is Route 10, branded as the Fastway, linking Crawley with Gatwick Airport and using some guided busway. 6008 is seen turning into Crawley Bus Station while on route 10 heading to Gatwick Airport

6019-6022		Volvo B8RLE		Wright Eclipse 2 12.0m			B40D	
6019	BJ15TWU	CY	6021	BV17CKF	CY			
6020	BJ15TWV	CY	6022	BV17CKG	CY			

6101	LK13AEJ	Wright Streetlite Max		Wright Streetlite 11.5m			B45F	CY

6102-6117		Wright Streetlite DF		Wright Streetlite 10.8m			B41F	
6102	SK66HSV	CY	6108	SK66HTE	CY	6114	SK66HTO	CY
6103	SK66HSX	CY	6109	SK66HTF	CY	6115	SK66HTP	CY
6104	SK66HSY	CY	6110	SK66HTG	CY	6116	SK66HTT	CY
6105	SK66HTA	CY	6111	SK66HTJ	CY	6117	SK66HTU	CY
6106	SK66HTC	CY	6112	SK66HTL	CY			
6107	SK66HTD	CY	6113	SK66HTN	CY			

New in 2017 as part of a fleet upgrade were 16 Wright Streetlites. 6113 is seen here in Crawley Town Centre while on route 5 heading to Pound Hill

6287	SN03YCL	Dennis Dart SLF SFD6BA	Alexander Pointer 2 8.8m	B29F	CY
6288	SN03YCM	Dennis Dart SLF SFD6BA	Alexander Pointer 2 8.8m	B29F	CY
6289	SN03YCT	Dennis Dart SLF SFD6BA	Alexander Pointer 2 8.8m	B29F	CY
6320	LX03OJP	Dennis Dart SLF SFD3CA	Alexander Pointer 2 10.7m	B37F	CY
6321	LX03OJN	Dennis Dart SLF SFD3CA	Alexander Pointer 2 10.7m	B37F	CY

6476-6497		Scania N94UD		East Lancs OmniDekka 10.6m		H45/29D	
6476	YN53RYF	CY	6490	YN53RZC	CY	6493	YN53RZF	CY
6478	YN53RYK	CY	6492	YN53RZE	CY	6496	YN54AJX	CY

6513-6558		Scania CN94UB		Scania OmniCity 12.0m		B34D	
				* - B42F, $ - B37D, % - B41F			
6513*	YP52CTO	CY	6552	YN55PWJ	CY	6556	YN55PWU	CY
6531$	YN03UWU	CY	6553	YN55PWK	CY	6557	YN55PWW	CY
6550%	YN05HCF	CY	6554	YN55PWL	CY	6558	YN55PWX	CY
6551%	YN05HCG	CY	6555	YN55PWO	CY			

| 6559 | YN07LKF | Scania CN230UB | Scania OmniCity 12.0m | B40F | CY |
| 6560 | YN07LKG | Scania CN230UB | Scania OmniCity 12.0m | B40F | CY |

6615-6623		Scania N94UB		East Lancs Esteem 10.6m		B36F	
6615	YN06JXU	CY	6618	YN06JXX	CY	6621	YM55SXR	CY
6616	YN06JXV	u	6619	YM55SXO	CY	6622	YN06JXY	CY
6617	YN06JXW	CY	6620	YM55SXP	CY	6623	YN06JXZ	CY

Showing the original version of the Metrobus livery for the Crawley operation is 6555, seen in Horsham while on route 23 heading to Worthing

6624-6633		Scania CN230UB		Scania OmniCity 10.9m			B33F	
6624	YN08DFJ	CY	6628	YN08DFP	CY	6632	YN08DFY	CY
6625	YN08DFK	CY	6629	YN08DFU	CY	6633	YN08DFZ	CY
6626	YN08DFL	CY	6630	YN08DFV	CY			
6627	YN08DFO	CY	6631	YN08DFX	CY			

6725-6730		Dennis E200Dart SFD511		Alexander Enviro 200 10.2m			B36F	
6725	GN07AVR	CY	6727	GN07AVU	CY	6729	GN07AVW	CY
6726	GN07AVT	CY	6728	GN07AVV	CY	6730	GN07AUY	CY

6734-6772		ADL E20D SFD7E1		ADL Enviro 200 10.8m			B38F	
6734	SN12AAE	CY	6763	YX63ZWW	CY	6769	YX63ZXD	CY
6735	SN12AAF	CY	6764	YX63ZWY	CY	6770	YX63ZXE	CY
6736	SN12AAJ	CY	6765	YX63ZWZ	CY	6771	YX63ZXF	CY
6737	SN12AAK	CY	6766	YX63ZXA	CY	6772	YX63ZXG	CY
6738	SN12AAO	CY	6767	YX63ZXB	CY			
6739	SN12AAU	CY	6768	YX63ZXC	CY			

6773-6782		ADL E20D SFD7LB		ADL Enviro 200 10.8m			B38F	
6773	YY15GBZ	CY	6777	YY15GCU	CY	6781	YY15GDA	CY
6774	YY15GCF	CY	6778	YY15GCV	CY	6782	YY15GDE	CY
6775	YY15GCK	CY	6779	YY15GCX	CY			
6776	YY15GCO	CY	6780	YY15GCZ	CY			

6938	YN56FDO	Scania N94UD	East Lancs Omnidekka 10.6m	H45/31F	CY
6939	YN56FDP	Scania N94UD	East Lancs Omnidekka 10.6m	H45/31F	CY
6953	YN08OBP	Scania CN230UD	Scania OmniCity 10.8m	H45/31F	CY

6954	YN08OBR	Scania CN230UD	Scania OmniCity 10.8m	H45/31F	CY
6955-6985		Scania CN270UD	Scania OmniCity 10.8m	H45/31F	

6955	YP09HWB	CY	6966	YP58UGG	CY	6977	YP09HWJ	CY
6956	YP09HWA	CY	6967	YP58UGH	CY	6978	YP09HWK	CY
6957	YP09HWC	CY	6968	YP58UGJ	CY	6979	YP09HWL	CY
6958	YP09HWD	CY	6969	YP58UGK	CY	6980	YP09HWM	CY
6959	YP09HWS	CY	6970	YP58UGL	CY	6981	YP09HWN	CY
6960	YP58UGA	CY	6971	YP58UGM	CY	6982	YP09HWO	CY
6961	YP58UGB	CY	6972	YP58UGN	CY	6983	YP09HWR	CY
6962	YP58UGC	CY	6973	YP09HWE	CY	6984	YP09HWT	CY
6963	YP58UGD	CY	6974	YP09HWF	CY	6985	YP09HWU	CY
6964	YP58UGE	CY	6975	YP09HWG	CY			
6965	YP58UGF	CY	6976	YP09HWH	CY			

The Metrobus fleet is undergoing a fleet upgrade, with Scania OmniCity double-deckers cascaded from Brighton & Hove replacing older East Lancs Omnidekka-bodied Scanias. 6955 is seen in Brighton Town centre, a location it would be more than familiar with.

7209	SN03WLU	Dennis Dart SLF SFD3CA	Alexander Pointer 2 10.7m	B36D	CYt
7546	YN05HCA	Scania CN94UB	Scania OmniCity	B24D	CYt
7547	YN05HCC	Scania CN94UB	Scania OmniCity	B24D	CYt

Liveries

Unless stated below, all vehicles carry standard Metrobus Crawley livery (two-tone blue with yellow crescent);

Fastway: 6001-6022, 6102-6104, 6624-6633
Older Metrobus Crawley livery: 6287-6289, 6320, 6321, 6490, 6492, 6496, 6550-6552, 6554, 6555, 6557, 6559, 6615-6623, 6725-6730, 6734-6739, 6763-6773, 6939
Red and blue training: 7209
White training: 7546, 7547

Oxford

Garage
OX   Oxford - Cowley House, Watlington Road, Oxford, OX4 6GA

1-9		Scania K360EB			Plaxton Panther 2			C44FT	
1	AF61OXF	OX	4	DF61OXF	OX	7		GF61OXF	OX
2	BF61OXF	OX	5	EF61OXF	OX	9		JF61OXF	OX
3	CF61OXF	OX	6	FF61OXF	OX				

19	BV66GVJ	Mercedes-Benz Tourismo M	Mercedes-Benz 13.0m	C57FT	OX

21-25		Volvo B11R			Plaxton Panther			C44FT	
21	AF14OXF	u	23	CF14OXF	u	25		EF14OXF	u
22	BF14OXF	u	24	DF14OXF	u				

41-46		Scania K360EB			Plaxton Panther 2			C44FT	
41	MF61OXF	OX	43	PF61OXF	OX	45		SF61OXF	OX
42	OF61OXF	OX	44	LF61OXF	OX	46		TF61OXF	OX

51	FJ60KVP	Volvo B9R	Caetano Levante 12.6m	C48FTL	OX
52	FJ60KVR	Volvo B9R	Caetano Levante 12.6m	C48FTL	OX
53	BX65WAO	Volvo B8R	Caetano Levante 12.6m	C48FTL	OX
54	BX65WAU	Volvo B8R	Caetano Levante 12.6m	C48FTL	OX
55	BX65WCK	Volvo B8R	Caetano Levante 12.6m	C48FTL	OX
56	BV67JYR	Volvo B11RT	Caetano Levante 14.2m	C56FTL	OX
57	BV67JYS	Volvo B11RT	Caetano Levante 14.2m	C56FTL	OX

Oxford Bus Company's route X90, linking London with Oxford, has been in direct competition with Stagecoach's Oxford Tube for many years. Part of the fleet which operate this service are two Scania coaches with Plaxton Panther 2 bodywork, as seen here on 81, pictured at Hyde Park Corner while heading for Oxford

61-78   Volvo B11RT   Plaxton Elite i   CH62/3FT
* - CH60/3FT

61	GB63OXF	OX	69*	X90PLS	OX	75	X90OXD	OX
62	GO63OXF	OX	70*	X90WAY	OX	76	X90SVC	OX
63	TO63OXF	OX	71	X90LON	OX	77	OX15BUS	OX
65	XS63OXF	OX	72	X90LDN	OX	78	OX15LON	OX
67*	X90APP	OX	73	X90OBC	OX			
68*	X90YES	OX	74	X90OFD	OX			

81	KF61OXF	Scania K360EB	Plaxton Panther 2	C44FT	OX
82	RF61OXF	Scania K360EB	Plaxton Panther 2	C44FT	OX

201-227   Scania N230UD   Alexander Enviro 400 10.9m   H51/29F

201	AF09OXF	OX	205	EF09OXF	OX	225	PF10OXF	OX
202	BF09OXF	OX	206	FF09OXF	OX	226	RF10OXF	OX
203	CF09OXF	OX	223	MF10OXF	OX	227	SF10OXF	OX
204	DF09OXF	OX	224	OF10OXF	OX			

During 2009 and 2010, Oxford Bus Company received two batches of Scania double-deckers with Alexander Enviro 400 bodywork. 227, which has recently received this livery for Route 2, is seen in St Giles, Oxford while on route 2B, heading for Kidington

300-317   ADL E40H SFD4BR   ADL Enviro 400 10.8m   H47/30F
* - H45/31F

300*	R12OXF	OX	306	HF11OXF	OX	312	HM11OXF	OX
301	HY11BRD	OX	307	HG11OXF	OX	313	HN11OXF	OX
302	HB11OXF	OX	308	HH11OXF	OX	314	HP11OXF	OX
303	HC11OXF	OX	309	HJ11OXF	OX	315	HR11OXF	OX
304	HD11OXF	OX	310	HK11OXF	OX	317	HY11OXF	OX
305	HE11OXF	OX	311	HL11OXF	OX			

351-369 — Volvo B5LH — Wright Eclipse Gemini 2 10.5m — H45/27F

351	R1OXF	OX	358	R8OXF	OX	365	V15OXF	OX
352	R2OXF	OX	359	R9OXF	OX	366	V16OXF	OX
353	R3OXF	OX	360	J1OXF	OX	367	V17OXF	OX
354	R4OXF	OX	361	R11OXF	OX	368	N1OXF	OX
355	R5OXF	OX	362	K1OXF	OX	369	Y25OXF	OX
356	R6OXF	OX	363	M1OXF	OX			
357	R7OXF	OX	364	V14OXF	OX			

601-614 — ADL E40H SFD911 — ADL Enviro 400MMC 10.9m — H47/32F

601	GB14OXF	OX	606	SC64OXF	OX	611	LM64OXF	OX
602	UK14OXF	OX	607	SB64OXF	OX	612	GA64OXF	OX
603	GX14OXF	OX	608	RW64OXF	OX	613	JG64OXF	OX
604	SU14OXF	OX	609	PS64OXF	OX	614	GH64OXF	OX
605	SM64OXF	OX	610	PK64OXF	OX			

Oxford Bus Company were awarded the BrookesBus contract in 2009, for which new vehicles were ordered, and later replaced in 2015 by a batch of hybrid ADL Enviro 400MMCs. 605 is seen near Oxford Station while on route U1 heading for the Wheatley Campus

651-691 — Wright Streetdeck — Wright Streetdeck 10.6m — H45/29F
* - H36/29F

651	SL15ZGC	OX	659	SL15ZGM	OX	667*	SK66HUA	OX
652	SL15ZGD	OX	660	SL15ZGN	OX	668*	SK66HUH	OX
653	SL15ZGE	OX	661	SL15ZGO	OX	669*	SK66HUJ	OX
654	SL15ZGF	OX	662*	SK66HVG	OX	670*	SK66HUO	OX
655	SL15ZGG	OX	663*	SK66HTV	OX	671*	SK66HUP	OX
656	SL15ZGH	OX	664*	SK66HTX	OX	672*	SK66HUU	OX
657	SL15ZGJ	OX	665*	SK66HTY	OX	673*	SK66HUV	OX
658	SL15ZGK	OX	666*	SK66HTZ	OX	674*	SK66HUY	OX

675*	SK66HUZ	OX	681*	SK66HVF	OX	688	SK17HHT	OX
676*	SK66HVA	OX	683	SK17HHN	OX	689	SK17HHU	OX
677*	SK66HVB	OX	684	SK17HHO	OX	690	SK17HHV	OX
678*	SK66HVC	OX	685	SK17HHP	OX	691	SK17HHW	OX
679*	SK66HVD	OX	686	SK17HHR	OX			
680*	SK66HVE	OX	687	SK17HHS	OX			

Most of the routes in Oxford have their own dedicated livery, with route 3 having Yellow as its dedicated colour. 682 is in Oxford High Street while heading for Rose Hill

807	YJ56WVT	Optare Tempo X1260			Optare Tempo 12.6m		B49F	OXt

837-883		Mercedes-Benz O530			Mercedes-Benz Citaro 12.0m * - B40F, % - B42F		B37D	
837%	GX53WYV	u	843	EF55OXF	OX	869*	KF57OXF	OX
838%	GX53WDA	u	844	FF55OXF	OX	870*	LF57OXF	OX
839	AF55OXF	OX	845	GF55OXF	OX	882*	BT09GPE	OX
840	BF55OXF	OX	846	HF55OXF	OX	883*	BT09GPF	OX
841	CF55OXF	OX	847	JF55OXF	OX			
842	DF55OXF	OX	848	KF55OXF	OX			

962	YJ06FXW	Optare Tempo X1260	Optare Tempo 12.6m	B46F	OXt
7284	V284SBW	Volvo B10M-62	Plaxton Excalibur 12.0m	C16FT	OXt
	SN59AWW	Dennis Trident SFD16M	Alexander Enviro 400 10.2m		u

Previous registrations

44	RF61OXF		838	X8OXF
82	LF61OXF		962	YJ06FXW, C1WYC
300	SN60BXW		7284	V16OXF
837	X7OXF			

Liveries
Unless stated below, all vehicles in this fleet carry standard fleet livery;

Airline: 1-9, 41-46
Allover white: 19
Oxford Express (route X90): 21-25, 61-63, 65, 67-78, 81, 82
National Express: 51-57
BrookesBus: 201-206, 601-614
City 2 (blue): 223-227
Oxford Park & Ride: 301-314, 316, 317, 369, 671
City 5 (fuchsia): 651-661
City 3 (yellow): 682-685
City 8 and 9 (orange): 686-691
Oxford Bus Company Training: 7284

After replacement with fully electric single-deckers in London on the Red Arrow routes, a number of Mercedes-Benz Citaros were cascaded from London to Oxford Bus Company. 883 is seen here in Oxford High Street while on route 3A, heading for Oxford Science Park

Plymouth Citybus

16-25		Dennis Dart SLF SFD322		Plaxton Pointer 2 10.7m			B39F	
16	R116OFJ	w	23	R123OFJ	w			
17	R117OFJ	PH	25	R125OFJ	w			

29-48		Dennis Dart SPD SFD476		Plaxton Pointer 2 11.3m			B41F	
				* - B43F				
29*	T129EFJ	PH	46	Y646NYD	r			
39*	T139EFJ	PH	48	Y648NYD	w			

53	GU52HKA	Dennis Dart SLF SFD3CA	Alexander Pointer 2 10.7m	B38F	PH
54	GU52HKB	Dennis Dart SLF SFD3CA	Alexander Pointer 2 10.7m	B38F	PH

60-66		Dennis Dart SPD SFD4D6		Alexander Pointer 2 11.3m			B41F	
60	WJ52GNY	u	63	WJ52GOC	PH	66	WJ52GOK	PH
61	WJ52GNZ	PH	64	WJ52GOE	PH			
62	WJ52GOA	PH	65	WJ52GOH	PH			

Plymouth Citybus operate a batch of Dennis Dart SPDs. One of these, 63, is seen here at the eastern end of Royal Parade, pictured while on route 61 heading for Transit Way. This vehicle has since been repainted into current standard livery

67-71		Dennis Dart SPD SFD4DB		Alexander Pointer 2 11.3m			B41F	
67	WA03BHW	r	69	WA03BHY	PH	71	WA03BJE	r
68	WA03BHX	PH	70	WA03BHZ	r			

72-79		Dennis Dart SLF SFD3CA		Alexander Pointer 2 10.7m			B37F	
72	WA54JVV	PH	75	WA54JVY	PH	78	WA54JWD	PH
73	WA54JVW	PH	76	WA54JVZ	PH	79	WA54JWE	PH
74	WA54JVX	PH	77	WA54JWC	PH			

80-94		Mercedes-Benz O530		Mercedes-Benz Citaro 12.0m * - B39F			B42F	
80	WJ55HLG	PH	85	WJ55HLO	PH	90*	WA56OZP	PH
81	WJ55HLH	PH	86	WJ55HLP	PH	91*	WA56OZR	PH
82	WJ55HLK	PH	87	WJ55HLR	PH	92*	WA56OZS	PH
83	WJ55HLM	PH	88*	WA56OZM	PH	93*	WA56OZT	PH
84	WJ55HLN	PH	89*	WA56OZO	PH	94*	WA56OZU	PH

Amongst the wide variety of vehicle types in the Plymouth Citybus fleet is the Mercedes-Benz Citaro. 90 is seen here in Western Approach while on route 62 heading to Transit Way

100-109		Volvo B7RLE		Wright Eclipse 2 12.0m			B41F	
100	WA12ACJ	PH	104	WA12ACX	PH	108	WA12ADU	PH
101	WA12ACO	PH	105	WA12ACY	PH	109	WA12ADV	PH
102	WA12ACU	PH	106	WA12ACZ	w			
103	WA12ACV	PH	107	WA12ADO	PH			

133	WA56HHO	Dennis E200Dart SFD321	Alexander Enviro 200 10.8m	B37F	PH
134	WA56HHP	Dennis E200Dart SFD321	Alexander Enviro 200 10.8m	B37F	PH
135	WA56HHN	Dennis E200Dart SFD321	Alexander Enviro 200 10.8m	B37F	PH
137	VJY137V	Leyland Atlantean	East Lancs	H43/28D	p

136-146		Dennis E200Dart SFD373		Alexander Enviro 200 10.8m			B38F	
136	WA08LDF	PH	138	WA08LDK	PH	140	WA08LDN	PH
137	WA08LDJ	PH	139	WA08LDL	PH	141	WA08LDU	PH

| 142 | WA08LDV | PH | 144 | WA08LDZ | PH | 146 | WA08LEJ | PH |
| 143 | WA08LDX | PH | 145 | WA08LEF | PH | | | |

Plymouth Citybus also operate a number of Alexander Enviro 200s. 136 is seen loading in Royal Parade while on route 9 heading to Efford and Laira

147-159				ADL E20D SFD7E1		ADL Enviro 200 10.8m		B37F
147	WJ65HMA	PH	152	WJ65HMG	PH	157	WJ65HMV	PH
148	WJ65HMC	PH	153	WJ65HMH	PH	158	WJ65HMW	PH
149	WJ65HMD	PH	154	WJ65HMK	PH	159	WJ65HMY	PH
150	WJ65HME	PH	155	WJ65HMO	PH			
151	WJ65HMF	PH	156	WJ65HMU	PH			

201	DDR201C	Leyland Titan PDR1/1	Metro-Cammell	H43/34F	p

250-256			Dennis Dart SLF SFD6BA	Alexander Pointer 2 8.8m		B23F	
250	LX05EYP	PH	253	LX05EYS	PH	256	LX05EXZ	PH
251	LX05EYV	PH	254	LX05EYU	PH			
252	LX05EYY	PH	255	LX05EYW	PH			

311	JSK264	Volvo B10M-62	Plaxton Premiere 350 12.0m	C53F	PH
313	JSK261	Volvo B10M-62	Plaxton Paragon 12.0m	C49FT	PH
314	JSK262	Volvo B10M-62	Plaxton Paragon 12.0m	C49FT	PH
315	JSK263	Volvo B12M	Plaxton Paragon 12.0m	C49FT	PH
316	JSK265	Volvo B12M	Plaxton Paragon 12.0m	C49FT	PH
317	BX11GVP	Volvo B9R	Plaxton Panther 12.3m	C49FT	PH
318	BX61DKV	Volvo B12B	Plaxton Panther 12.3m	C49FT	PH
319	WA64FZY	Volvo B11R	Plaxton Panther	C53FT	PH
320	YX14SFE	Volvo B11R	Plaxton Panther 2	C49FT	PH
321	YX14SFN	Volvo B11R	Plaxton Panther 2	C49FT	PH
322	UF61OXF	Scania K360EB	Plaxton Panther 2	C44FTL	PH

Plymouth Citybus also have a small coach operation, under the name Plymouth Citycoach. 318 is seen here in London while on a private hire duty

| 358 | MCO658 | Leyland Titan PD2/12 | | Leyland | | | O30/26R | p |

| 370-373 | | Scania N94UB | | East Lancs Esteem | | | B31F | |

| 370 | PF06ENL | w | 372 | PF06ENN | w | | | |
| 371 | PF06ENM | w | 373 | PF06ENO | w | | | |

| 401-418 | | Volvo B7TL | | East Lancs Myllennium Vyking 11.0m | | | H45/24F | |
| | | | | * - H45/20D | | | | |

| 401 | PN02XBX | PH | 404 | PN02XCG | PH | 417* | PL51LGU | PHt |
| 403 | PN02XCE | w | 405 | PN02XCH | PH | 418* | PL51LGW | PHt |

| 433-442 | | Volvo B7TL | | Plaxton President 10.0m | | | H41/23F | |

433	X501EGK	PH	436	X571EGK	PH	442	Y814TGH	PH
434	X546EGK	PH	437	X702EGK	PH			
435	X568EGK	PH	440	X504EGK	PH			

| 480-487 | | Dennis Trident SFD34D | | Plaxton President 10.5m | | | H47/31F | |

480	PK02RFF	PH	483	PK02RDV	PH	486	PK02RFJ	PH
481	PK02RFL	PH	484	PK02RDZ	PH	487	PK02RFE	PH
482	PK02RDU	PH	485	PK02RDY	PH			

| 501-538 | | ADL E40D SFD4DS | | ADL Enviro 400 10.8m | | | H45/30F | |
| | | | | * - H45/29F | | | | |

501	WF63LYA	PH	505	WF63LYO	PH	509	WF63LYT	PH
502	WF63LYB	PH	506	WF63LYP	PH	510	WF63LYU	PH
503	WF63LYC	PH	507	WF63LYR	PH	511	WF63LYV	PH
504	WF63LYD	PH	508	WF63LYS	PH	512	WF63LYW	PH

513	WF63LYX	PH	522*	WJ65BYN	PH	531*	WJ65BYX	PH
514	WF63LYY	PH	523*	WJ65BYO	PH	532	WJ65BYY	PH
515	WF63LYZ	PH	524*	WJ65BYP	PH	533	WJ65BYZ	PH
516	WF63LZE	PH	525*	WJ65BYR	PH	534	WJ65BZA	PH
517	WG63HHV	PH	526*	WJ65BYS	PH	535	WJ65BZB	PH
518	WG63HHW	PH	527*	WJ65BYT	PH	536	WJ65BZC	PH
519	WG63HHX	PH	528*	WJ65BYU	PH	537	WJ65BZD	PH
520	WG63HHY	PH	529*	WJ65BYV	PH	538	WJ65BZE	PH
521*	WJ65BYM	PH	530*	WJ65BYW	PH			

There has been a fair-sized investment in new double-deck vehicles for the Plymouth fleet, including two batches totalling 38 ADL Enviro 400s delivered between 2013 and 2016. 537 is seen here at Derrys Cross roundabout while on route 50A, heading for Holly Park

550-565				ADL E40D SFDB38		ADL Enviro 400City 10.5m			H45/29F	
550	WA17FSU	PH	556	WA17FTD	PH	562	WA17FTV	PH		
551	WA17FSV	PH	557	WA17FTE	PH	563	WA17FTX	PH		
552	WA17FSX	PH	558	WA17FTF	PH	564	WA17FTY	PH		
553	WA17FSY	PH	559	WA17FTP	PH	565	WA17FTZ	PH		
554	WA17FSZ	PH	560	WA17FTT	PH					
555	WA17FTC	PH	561	WA17FTU	PH					

701-713				MAN EcoCity		Caetano			B43F	
701	AU62DWC	PH	706	WX62HGU	PH	711	AU13FBK	PH		
702	AU62DWG	PH	707	WX62HHE	PH	712	AU13FBL	PH		
703	AU62DWL	PH	708	WX62HHF	PH	713	WX62HGG	PH		
704	AU62DWN	PH	709	WX62HHP	PH					
705	WX62HFU	PH	710	AU13FBJ	PH					

1557	FDV787V	Bristol LHS	ECW	B35F	p
	OCO502	Leyland Titan PD2/40	Metro-Cammell	H30/26R	PH

Previous registrations

311	W311SDV	315	WA03MGE
313	Y313NYD	316	WA03MGJ
314	Y314NYD		

Liveries

Unless stated below, all vehicles in this fleet carry standard fleet livery;

Old Plymouth Citybus: 48, 71, 137 (Atlantean)
Blue Flash: 100-105, 109
Green Flash: 134, 135, 154-159
London red: 252
Plymouth Citycoach: 311, 313-322
Plymouth Citybus Training: 417, 418
Red Flash: 501, 503, 505-507, 509, 510, 512-516
Yellow Flash: 521-530, 537, 538
Spark: 550-564
Orange Flash: 701-705
Anglian Bus: 713
Blue Bus: 1557
Plymouth Corporation: 201, 358, OCO502

Towards the end of 2016, a batch of gas-powered MAN EcoCity buses were transferred from Anglian Bus to Plymouth Citybus. 711 is seen here at St Andrew's Cross in Plymouth while on route 28 heading to Crownhill

South Coast

1-4		Volvo B11R		Plaxton Elite		C51FT
1	HF17AZA	PI	3	HF17AZC	SA	
2	HF17AZB	PI	4	HF17AZD	SA	

Tourist Coaches is one of the fleet names carried by coaches in the Go South Coast fleet. 4 is seen here in Winchester while on a private hire duty

5	HF18CKJ	Volvo B11RT	Volvo 9700	C51FT	BO
6	HF18CKK	Volvo B11RT	Volvo 9700	C51FT	BO
103	NK04UTJ	Dennis Dart SLF SFD6BA	Alexander Pointer 2 8.8m	B29F	w
104	NK04UTL	Dennis Dart SLF SFD6BA	Alexander Pointer 2 8.8m	B29F	w

105-109		ADL E20D SFD1D1		ADL Enviro 200 8.9m			B29F	
105	MX13AZV	TD	107	MX13BBZ	TD	109	YY16YJF	TD
106	MX13BBV	TD	108	YY16YJE	TD			

145	JAM145E	Daimler CVG6/30		Northern Counties			H40/30F	p

198-210		Dennis Dart SPD SFD4D8		Alexander Pointer 2 11.3m			B41F	
201	WU52YWE	w	204	WU52YWH	w	209	WX03YFD	w
202	WU52YWF	w	207	WU52YWL	w	210	WX03YFE	w
203	WU52YWG	w	208	WU52YWM	w			

211	WX03ZNS	Dennis Dart SPD SFD4D6	Alexander Pointer 2 11.3m	B41F	w
212	WX04CZH	Dennis Dart SPD SFD4D8	Alexander Pointer 2 11.3m	B41F	w
213	WX04CZJ	Dennis Dart SPD SFD4D8	Alexander Pointer 2 11.3m	B41F	w
214	WX04CZK	Dennis Dart SPD SFD4D8	Alexander Pointer 2 11.3m	B41F	w

216-219		ADL E20D SFD6F3		ADL Enviro 200 11.3m		B38F
216	OY16JVK	TD	218	OY16JWA	TD	
217	OY16JVL	TD	219	OY16JVZ	TD	

In 2017, Go-Ahead acquired Thamesdown and integrated the operation into their South Coast operation. With this acquisition brought this new bright livery to the streets of Swindon. 217 is seen in Fleming Way while on route 13 heading for Eldene

220-260		ADL E20D SFDDPC		ADL Enviro 200MMC			B38F	
220	HF67EUA	PO	225	HF67EUH	PO	230	HF67EUN	PO
221	HF67EUB	PO	226	HF67EUJ	PO	231	HF18CGV	PO
222	HF67EUC	PO	227	HF67EUK	PO	232	HF18CGX	PO
223	HF67EUD	PO	228	HF67EUL	PO	233	HF18CGY	PO
224	HF67EUE	PO	229	HF67EUM	PO	234	HF18CGZ	PO

235	HF18CHC	PO	244	HF18CHV	PO	253	HF18CJX	PO
236	HF18CHD	PO	245	HF18CHX	PO	254	HF18CJY	PO
237	HF18CHG	PO	246	HF18CHY	PO	255	HF18CJZ	PO
238	HF18CHH	PO	247	HF18CHZ	PO	256	HF18CKA	PO
239	HF18CHJ	PO	248	HF18CJE	PO	257	HF18CKC	PO
240	HF18CHK	PO	249	HF18CJJ	PO	258	HF18CKD	PO
241	HF18CHL	PO	250	HF18CJO	PO	259	HF18CKE	PO
242	HF18CHN	PO	251	HF18CJU	PO	260	HF18CKG	PO
243	HF18CHO	PO	252	HF18CJV	PO			

363	SN51AXW	Dennis Trident SFD344	Plaxton President 10.5m	H47/25F	PO
365	SN51AYO	Dennis Trident SFD344	Plaxton President 10.5m	H47/25F	TD
366	SN51AYP	Dennis Trident SFD344	Plaxton President 10.5m	H47/25F	PO

Prior to acquisition by Go-Ahead, Thamesdown purchased a handful of Plaxton President-bodied Dennis Tridents from Lothian. 365 is seen here, in the original Thamesdown livery, close to the outlet centre while on route 19 heading to Swindon Town Centre

371-379		Scania N94UD		East Lancs Omnidekka 10.6m			H45/30F	
371	YN55NHD	TD	374	YN55NHH	TD	377	YN55NHL	TD
372	YN55NHE	TD	375	YN55NHJ	TD	378	YN55NHM	TD
373	YN55NHG	TD	376	YN55NHK	TD	379	YN55NHO	TD

383	R189NFE	Dennis Dart SLF SFD322	Plaxton Pointer 2 10.7m	B43F	TDt

401-408		Optare Versa V1110		Optare Versa 11.1m			B37F	
401	WX60EEB	TD	404	WX60EDU	TD	407	WX60EDO	TD
402	WX60EEA	TD	405	WX60EDR	TD	408	WX60EDL	TD
403	WX60EDV	TD	406	WX60EDP	TD			

A batch of Optare Versa joined the Thamesdown fleet in 2011. 406 is seen in Farringdon Road while on route 22 heading to Barnfield. This vehicle was on diversion due to road works in Bristol Street

411-417		Wright Streetlite DF		Wright Streetlite 10.8m			B41F	
				* - B40F				
411	WX12GEJ	TD	414	WX12GDV	TD	417*	SK63GAA	TD
412	WX12GDZ	TD	415	WX12GDU	TD			
413	WX12GDY	TD	416	WX12GDO	TD			

501-510		Scania L94IB		Wright Solar			B40F	
501	WX55ZZR	r	504	WX06JXS	TD	507	WX06JYC	TD
502	WX06JYD	TD	505	WX06JXT	TD	508	WX06JYB	TD
503	WX06JXR	TD	506	WX06JYE	TD	509	WX06JYA	TD

511-528		Scania K230UB		Wright Solar			B40F	
511	WX57TLY	TD	517	WX08SXD	TD	523	WX59GJF	TD
512	WX57TLU	TD	518	WX08SXE	TD	524	WX59GJG	TD
513	WX57TLV	TD	519	WX08SXF	TD	525	WX59GJJ	TD
514	WX57TLZ	TD	520	XMW120	TD	526	WX59GJK	TD
515	WX57TLN	TD	521	WX08SXG	TD	527	WX59GJO	TD
516	WX57TLO	TD	522	WX08SXH	TD	528	WX59GJU	TD

598	R435MEH	Volvo B10M-62		Plaxton Excalibur 12.0m			C49FT	u
702	CDL889	Bristol K5G		ECW			O30/26R	p
1001	YN54AFK	Scania N94UD		East Lancs OmniDekka			H51/39F	SA
1002	YN54AFX	Scania N94UD		East Lancs OmniDekka			H51/39F	SA

1011-1022		Scania N94UD		East Lancs OmniDekka 10.6m			H47/33F	
1011	YN06JWD	PI	1013	YN06JWG	PI	1015	YN06JWM	PI
1012	YN06JWE	PI	1014	YN06JWJ	LY	1016	YN06JWO	LY

1017	YN06JWU	LY	1019	YN06JWW	SA	1021	YN06JWY	PI
1018	YN06JWV	PI	1020	YN06JWX	SA	1022	YN06JWZ	PI

1091	YN55NFP	Scania N94UD	East Lancs OmniDekka	H51/25D	EH

The Southern Vectis part of the Go South Coast operation is the main operator on the Isle of Wight. Within that is the Island Breezer, a group of three open-top routes serving the island. 1111 is seen in Yarmouth while on the Needles Breezer, heading for the Needles lighthouse

1101-1199		Scania CN230UD		Scania OmniCity 10.8m	H45/31F			
				* - PO45/28F, $ - H45/29F, % - H45/27F				
1101	HW08AOP	PO	1122$	HF58GZB	PO	1143	HW09BBV	PI
1102	HW08AOR	PO	1123$	HF58GZC	PO	1144	HW09BBX	PI
1103	HW08AOS	PO	1124$	HF58GZD	PO	1145	HW09BBZ	SA
1104	HW08AOT	PO	1125	HF58GZP	EH	1146	HW09BCE	SV
1105	HW58ARU	PO	1126$	HF58KCA	EH	1147	HW09BCF	SV
1106	HW58ARX	PO	1127	HF58KCC	EH	1148	HW09BCK	SV
1107	HW58ARZ	EH	1128	HF58KCE	EH	1149	HW09BCO	SV
1108	HW58ASO	PI	1129	HF58KCG	EH	1150	HW09BCU	SV
1109	HW58ASU	PO	1130	HF58KCJ	EH	1151	HW09BCV	SV
1110	HW58ASV	PI	1131	HF58KCK	EH	1152	HW09BAA	SV
1111*	VDL744	SV	1132	HF09BJE	SA	1191%	HF58GZE	PO
1112	HW58ASZ	EH	1133	HF09BJJ	SA	1192%	HF58GZG	PO
1113	HW58ATF	EH	1134	HF09BJK	SA	1193%	HF58GZH	PO
1114	HW58ATK	EH	1135	HF09BJO	SA	1194%	HF58GZJ	PO
1115	HW58ATN	EH	1136	HF09BJU	SA	1195%	HF58GZK	PO
1116	HW58ATO	EH	1137	HF09BJV	SA	1196%	HF58GZL	PO
1117	HW58ATP	PO	1138	HF09BJX	SA	1197%	HF58GZM	PO
1118$	HF58GYW	RI	1139	HF09BJY	SA	1198%	HF58GZN	PO
1119$	HF58GYY	RI	1140	HF09BJZ	SA	1199%	HF58GZO	PO
1120$	HF58GYZ	RI	1141	HF09BKA	SA			
1121$	HF58GZA	RI	1142	HW09BBU	PO			

During 2009, a batch of over 60 Scania Omnicity double-deckers were delivered to what is now the Go South Coast operation. 1198 is seen here in Poole Bus Station in More livery, pictured while on route 14 heading to Broadstone

1401-1409		Scania N230UD		East Lancs Visionaire * - PO51/29F			CO51/29F	
1401*	HF09BVU	SV	1404	HF09FVX	PO	1407	HF59DMU	PO
1402*	HF09BVV	SV	1405	HF09FVY	PO	1408	HF59DMV	PO
1403*	HF09FVW	SV	1406	HF59DMO	PO	1409	HF59DMX	PO

1410	HF09FVR	Scania N230UD	East Lancs Olympus	H51/29F	PO
1411	HF09FVS	Scania N230UD	East Lancs Olympus	H51/29F	PO
1412	HF09FVT	Scania N230UD	East Lancs Olympus	H51/29F	PO

1501-1506		Scania N230UD		Alexander Enviro 400 10.9m			H47/29F	
1501	HF59FAA	SA	1503	HF59FAK	SA	1505	HF59FAO	SA
1502	HF59FAJ	SA	1504	HF59FAM	SA	1506	HF59FAU	SA

1507-1547		ADL E40D SFD4DS		ADL Enviro 400 10.8m * - H47/29F			H47/32F	
1507*	HW62CVF	PI	1517*	HW62CZY	SV	1527	HJ63JHV	TN
1508*	HW62CVL	SV	1518*	HW62CAO	SV	1528	HJ63JHX	TN
1509*	HW62CVM	EH	1519*	HW62CCD	SV	1529	HJ63JHY	TN
1510*	HW62CVO	SV	1520*	HW62CEJ	SV	1530	HJ63JHZ	TN
1511*	HW62CVZ	SV	1521*	HW62CMZ	SV	1531	HJ63JJE	TN
1512*	HW62CWN	SV	1522*	HW62CNA	SV	1532	HJ63JJF	TN
1513*	HW62CXK	SV	1523*	HW62CNE	SV	1533	HJ63JJK	TN
1514*	HW62CXR	SV	1524*	HW62CNU	SV	1534	HJ63JJL	LY
1515*	HW62CYJ	SV	1525*	HW62CLV	SV	1535	HJ63JJO	LY
1516*	HW62CZO	SV	1526*	HW62CMU	SV	1536	HJ63JJU	LY

Above: *Vectis Blue is another of the fleet names seen across the Go South Coast operation, as seen here on 1524. This is just backing off the stands at Ryde Bus Station while on the Island Coaster heading for Yarmouth*

Below: *Bluestar's route 1 links Southampton with Winchester, using a batch of ADL Enviro 400s. 1533 is seen here loading in Southampton while heading to Winchester*

1537	HJ63JJV	LY	1541	HJ63JKE	RI	1545	HJ63JKO	SA
1538	HJ63JJX	LY	1542	HJ63JKF	SA	1546	HJ63JKU	SA
1539	HJ63JJY	LY	1543	HJ63JKK	SA	1547	HJ63JKV	PO
1540	HJ63JJZ	RI	1544	HJ63JKN	SA			

1548-1570		ADL E40D SFD1DS		ADL Enviro 400 10.2m		H41/24D	
1548	HJ63JKX	EH	1556	HJ63JMU	EH	1564	HJ63JNU	EH
1549	HJ63JKY	EH	1557	HJ63JMV	EH	1565	HJ63JNV	EH
1550	HJ63JKZ	EH	1558	HJ63JMX	EH	1566	HJ63JNX	EH
1551	HJ63JLO	EH	1559	HJ63JNF	EH	1567	HJ63JNZ	EH
1552	HJ63JLU	EH	1560	HJ63JNK	EH	1568	HJ63JOA	EH
1553	HJ63JLV	EH	1561	HJ63JNL	EH	1569	HJ63JOH	EH
1554	HJ63JLX	EH	1562	HJ63JNN	EH	1570	HJ63JOU	EH
1555	HJ63JMO	EH	1563	HJ63JNO	EH			

A number of buses in Salisbury carry the Salisbury Reds fleet name, with this red-based livery. 1598 is in Fleming Way Swindon starting its journey on route X5, heading for Pewsey and Salisbury

1571-1622		ADL E40D SFD4DS		ADL Enviro 400 10.8m		H47/32F	
1571	HW63FGM	SA	1587	HW63FHJ	SV	1599	HF64BTE	SA
1572	HW63FGN	SA	1588	HW63FHK	SV	1600	HF64BTO	SA
1573	HW63FGO	SA	1589	HW63FHL	SV	1601	HF64BOV	EH
1574	HW63FGP	SA	1590	HW63FHM	SV	1602	HF64BPE	EH
1575	HW63FGU	SA	1591	HW63FHN	SV	1603	HF64BPK	EH
1576	HW63FGV	SA	1592	HW63FHO	SV	1604	HF64BPO	EH
1577	HW63FGX	SA	1593	HW63FHP	SV	1605	HF65AXY	EH
1578	HW63FGZ	SA	1594	HW63FHR	SV	1606	HF65AXZ	EH
1579	HW63FHA	SV	1595	HF64BSV	SV	1607	HF65AYA	EH
1580	HW63FHB	SV	1596	HF64BSX	SV	1608	HF65AYB	PO
1585	HW63FHG	SV	1597	HF64BSY	SA	1609	HF65AYN	RI
1586	HW63FHH	SV	1598	HF64BSZ	SA	1610	HF65AYO	RI

1611	HF65AYP	PI	1615	HJ16HSE	SV	1619	HJ16HSL	SV
1612	HF65AYS	PI	1616	HJ16HSF	SV	1620	HJ16HSN	SV
1613	HJ16HSC	SV	1617	HJ16HSG	SV	1621	HJ16HSO	SV
1614	HJ16HSD	SV	1618	HJ16HSK	SV	1622	HJ16HSU	SV

Go South Coast also operate special university services for Bournemouth University, with buses carrying this striking livery pattern. Colours used include Purple, Pink & Green. 1628 is seen approaching its terminus in Bournemouth while on route 16

1623-1654		ADL E40D SFD911		ADL Enviro 400MMC 10.9m			DPH39/32F	
				* - H47/32F				
1623*	HF66CDY	PO	1634*	HF66CFA	PO	1645	HF66CFU	EH
1624*	HF66CDZ	PO	1635*	HF66CFD	SA	1646	HF66CFV	EH
1625*	HF66CEA	PO	1636*	HF66CFE	SA	1647	HF66CFX	EH
1626*	HF66CEJ	PO	1637*	HF66CFG	SA	1648	HF66CFY	RI
1627*	HF66CEK	PO	1638	HF66CFJ	EH	1649	HF66CFZ	RI
1628*	HF66CEN	PO	1639	HF66CFK	EH	1650	HF66CGE	RI
1629*	HF66CEO	PO	1640	HF66CFL	EH	1651	HF66CGG	RI
1630*	HF66CEU	PO	1641	HF66CFM	EH	1652	HF66CGK	RI
1631*	HF66CEV	PO	1642	HF66CFN	EH	1653	HF66CHD	RI
1632*	HF66CEX	PO	1643	HF66CFO	EH	1654	HF66CHG	RI
1633*	HF66CEY	PO	1644	HF66CFP	EH			

1655-1671		ADL E40D SFD917		ADL Enviro 400MMC 10.9m			H47/32F	
1655	HW67AHO	PO	1661	HW67AHZ	SV	1667	HW67AKG	SV
1656	HW67AHP	SV	1662	HW67AJO	SV	1668	HW67AKJ	SV
1657	HW67AHU	SV	1663	HW67AJU	SV	1669	HW67AKK	SV
1658	HW67AHV	SV	1664	HW67AJV	SV	1670	HW67AKN	SV
1659	HW67AHX	SV	1665	HW67AJY	SV	1671	HW67AKO	SV
1660	HW67AHY	SV	1666	HW67AKF	SV			

Above: *Another fleet name used is More, with this red and two-tone blue livery. 1650 is seen approaching Bournemouth Town Centre while on route X3*

Below: *Route 50 is Bournemouth is branded as the Purbeck Breezer, linking Bournemouth with Swanage and Sandbanks. 1704 is seen approaching Bournemouth Town Centre while heading for Swanage*

1701-1712		Volvo B5TL		MCV EvoSeti 10.5m			CO45/29F	
				* - H45/30F, $ - PO43/30F				
1701*	HJ16HSV	SW	1705$	HJ16HTA	SW	1709	HF66DSU	SW
1702*	HJ16HSX	SW	1706$	HJ16HTC	SW	1710	HF66DSV	SW
1703*	HJ16HSY	SW	1707	HF66DSE	SW	1711	HF66DSX	SW
1704$	HJ16HSZ	SW	1708	HF66DSO	SW	1712	HF66DSY	SW

1801-1833		Volvo B7TL		East Lancs Myllennium Vyking 11.0m CO49/29F				
				* - H46/27F				
1801*	HX51ZRA	PI	1824	HF54KXW	LY	1829	HF05GGP	LY
1802*	HX51ZRC	PI	1825	HF05GGE	PO	1830	HF05GGU	LY
1821	HF54KXT	LY	1826	HF05GGJ	LY	1831	HF05GGV	LY
1822	HF54KXU	SV	1827	HF05GGK	LY	1832	HF05GGX	LY
1823	HF54KXV	LY	1828	HF05GGO	LY	1833	HF05GGY	LY

1851	SN56AWX	Volvo B7TL		Alexander Enviro 400			H45/32F	EH

1901-1973		Volvo B7TL		Plaxton President 10.0m			H41/20D	
				* - H41/19D, $ - O--/--D, % - H41/16D				
1901*	W501WGH	u	1940	Y704TGH	SV	1947%	Y747TGH	SV
1904*	W504WGH	SV	1941	Y741TGH	SA	1972	X572EGK	EH
1910*	VJI3968	EHt	1942	Y742TGH	EH	1973	X573EGK	PO
1928*	W498WGH	PO	1943	Y743TGH	PO			
1939	Y739TGH	SAt	1946$	Y746TGH	Pla			

The London PVL-class Plaxton Presidents have found themselves scattered far and wide following their replacement with newer vehicles in London. 1910 now earns its keep as a trainer in the South Coast fleet, and is seen here entering Salisbury depot

1991-1997   Volvo B7TL   Plaxton President 10.6m   H51/28F
                                                       * - PO47/28F

1991*	WDL691	SV	1994	HW52EPO	SA	1997	HW52EPV	SA
1992*	GSK962	SV	1995	HW52EPP	SA			
1993	HW52EPN	SA	1996	HW52EPU	SA			

2001   YN06CGO   Scania N94UB   Scania OmniCity 12.0m   B39F   r

2002-2012   Scania CN230UB   Scania OmniCity 12.0m   B39F
                                                      * - B35D

2002	HF58HTG	EH	2006	HF58HTN	PO	2010	HF58HTU	PO
2003	HF58HTJ	EH	2007	HF58HTO	r	2011*	HF61FWL	EH
2004	HF58HTK	EH	2008	HF58HTP	r	2012*	HF61FWM	EH
2005	HF58HTL	EH	2009	HF58HTT	PO			

2101   YT59SFJ   Scania K230UB   Wright Solar   B44F   PO

2203-2238   Volvo B7RLE   Wright Eclipse Urban 12.0m   DP35F
                                                      * - B40F

2203	HF54HFR	PO	2213	HF54HGD	PO	2229	HF54HHD	r
2204	HF54HFT	PO	2217	HF54HGK	r	2232	HF54HHK	r
2205	HF54HFU	PO	2219	HF54HGM	r	2233	HF54HHL	r
2206	HF54HFV	PO	2222	HF54HGP	r	2234*	HF54HHM	r
2207	HF54HFW	PO	2223	HF54HGU	r	2236	HF05HXE	PO
2208	HF54HFX	PO	2225	HF54HGY	r	2237	HF05HXG	r
2209	HF54HFY	PO	2228	HF54HHC	PO	2238	HF05HXH	PO

2273 is part of a considerable batch of Wright Eclipse 2s in the Go South Coast fleet, and is approaching Bournemouth Town Centre while on route m2 heading to Southbourne

2251-2292		Volvo B7RLE		Wright Eclipse 2 12.0m * - B40D			B41F	
2251	HF12GVP	PO	2265	HF12GWJ	PO	2279	HF12GXB	PO
2252	HF12GVR	PO	2266	HF12GWK	PO	2280	HF12GXC	PO
2253	HF12GVT	PO	2267	HF12GWL	PO	2281	HF12GXD	PO
2254	HF12GVU	PO	2268	HF12GWM	PO	2282	HF12GXE	PO
2255	HF12GVV	PO	2269	HF12GWN	PO	2283	HF12GXG	PO
2256	HF12GVW	PO	2270	HF12GWO	PO	2284	HF12GXH	PO
2257	HF12GVX	PO	2271	HF12GWP	PO	2285	HF12GXJ	PO
2258	HF12GVY	PO	2272	HF12GWU	PO	2286	HF12GXK	PO
2259	HF12GVZ	PO	2273	HF12GWV	PO	2287*	HJ63JOV	EH
2260	HF12GWA	PO	2274	HF12GWW	PO	2288*	HJ63JPF	EH
2261	HF12GWC	PO	2275	HF12GWX	PO	2289*	BN64CNO	EH
2262	HF12GWD	PO	2276	HF12GWY	PO	2290*	BN64CNU	EH
2263	HF12GWE	PO	2277	HF12GWZ	PO	2291*	BN64CSV	EH
2264	HF12GWG	PO	2278	HF12GXA	PO	2292*	HF64BSU	EH

2401-2457		Mercedes-Benz O530		Mercedes-Benz Citaro 12.0m			B39F	
2401	HF55JYX	EH	2417	HF55JZT	r	2436	HX06EZE	TN
2402	HF55JYY	EH	2421	HF06FTO	TN	2438	HX06EZG	TN
2403	HF55JYZ	EH	2422	HF06FTP	TN	2439	HX06EZH	TN
2404	HF55JZA	EH	2423	HF06FTT	TN	2451	HW07CXR	TN
2405	HF55JZC	EH	2424	HF06FTU	TN	2452	HW07CXS	TN
2406	HF55JZD	EH	2425	HF06FTV	TN	2453	HW07CXT	TN
2407	HF55JZE	EH	2427	HF06FTY	TN	2454	HW07CXU	TN
2408	HF55JZG	EH	2428	HF06FTZ	TN	2455	HW07CXV	TN
2409	HF55JZJ	u	2433	HX06EZB	TN	2456	HW07CXX	TN
2410	HF55JZK	EH	2434	HX06EZC	TN	2457	HW07CXY	TN
2411	HF55JZL	u	2435	HX06EZD	TN			

2610	HJ02WDE	Optare Excel L1180		Optare Excel 11.8m			B42F	TDt
2611	HJ02WDF	Optare Excel L1180		Optare Excel 11.8m			B42F	POt
2612	HJ02WDG	Optare Excel L1180		Optare Excel 11.8m			B42F	r
2700	YY17GRX	ADL E20D SFDDWC		ADL Enviro 200MMC 11.8m			B40F	PO

2701-2708		ADL E20D SFD7EB		ADL Enviro 200 10.8m			B39F	
2701	YX64VOB	SA	2704	YX64VOF	SA	2707	YX64VOJ	SA
2702	YX64VOC	SA	2705	YX64VOG	SA	2708	YX64VOK	SA
2703	YX64VOD	SA	2706	YX64VOH	SA			

2709-2717		ADL E20D SFD1DA		ADL Enviro 200 8.9m			B29F	
2709	HW64AWZ	SV	2712	HW64AXC	SV	2715	HW64AXG	SV
2710	HW64AXA	SV	2713	HW64AXD	SV	2716	HW64AXH	SV
2711	HW64AXB	SV	2714	HW64AXF	SV	2717	HW64AXJ	SV

The ADL Enviro 200 features in varying lengths in the Go South Coast fleet. 2717 has just left Newport Bus Station while on route 1 to Cowes Red Jet Park & Ride site

2718-2732		ADL E20D SFD7EB		ADL Enviro 200 10.8m			B39F	
2718	HF64BPU	SA	2723	HF64BRV	SA	2728	HF65AYH	SA
2719	HF64BPV	SA	2724	HF65AYC	SA	2729	HF65AYJ	SA
2720	HF64BPX	SA	2725	HF65AYD	SA	2730	HF65AYK	DO
2721	HF64BPY	SA	2726	HF65AYE	SA	2731	HF65AYL	PI
2722	HF64BPZ	SA	2727	HF65AYG	SA	2732	HF65AYM	PI

2733-2750		ADL E20D SFDDLA		ADL Enviro 200MMC 11.5m			B43F	
2733	HF65CXE	EH	2739	HF65CXM	EH	2745	HF65CXV	EH
2734	HF65CXG	EH	2740	HF65CXN	EH	2746	HF65CXW	EH
2735	HF65CXH	EH	2741	HF65CXO	EH	2747	HF65CXX	EH
2736	HF65CXJ	EH	2742	HF65CXP	EH	2748	HF65CXY	EH
2737	HF65CXK	EH	2743	HF65CXT	EH	2749	HF65CXZ	EH
2738	HF65CXL	EH	2744	HF65CXU	EH	2750	HF65CYA	EH

As part of a vehicle upgrade on route 18 in Southampton, a batch of ADL Enviro 200MMCs were delivered in 2016. 2734 is seen here passing through Southampton while heading for Thornthill

2751	HF66CHH		ADL E20D SFD1RA		ADL Enviro 200 8.9m		B29F	SV

2752-2763		ADL E20D SFDDLA		ADL Enviro 200MMC 11.5m			B43F	
2752	HF66DPU	TN	2756	HF66DPZ	TN	2760	HF66DPE	TN
2753	HF66DPV	TN	2757	HF66DRO	TN	2761	HF66DPK	TN
2754	HF66DPX	TN	2758	HF66DRV	TN	2762	HF66DPN	TN
2755	HF66DPY	TN	2759	HF66DOU	TN	2763	HF66DPO	TN

2764-2771		ADL E20D SFD7S1		ADL Enviro 200 10.8m			B37F	
2764	YX17NHP	TD	2767	YX17NHV	TD	2770	YX17NJE	TD
2765	YX17NHT	TD	2768	YX17NHY	TD	2771	YX17NJF	TD
2766	YX17NHU	TD	2769	YX17NHZ	TD			

2772-2784		ADL E20D SFDDPC		ADL Enviro 200MMC			B36F	
2772	HF67ATN	TD	2777	HF67ATY	TD	2782	HF67AUH	TD
2773	HF67ATO	TD	2778	HF67ATZ	TD	2783	HF67AUJ	TD
2774	HF67ATU	TD	2779	HF67AUA	TD	2784	HF67AUK	TD
2775	HF67ATV	TD	2780	HF67AUC	TD			
2776	HF67ATX	TD	2781	HF67AUE	TD			

2785-2790		ADL E20D SFDBL1		ADL Enviro 200MMC 10.4m			B38F	
2785	HF67AUL	SA	2787	HF67AUN	SA	2789	HF67AUP	SA
2786	HF67AUM	SA	2788	HF67AUO	SA	2790	HF67AUR	SA

Soon after acquisition by Go-Ahead, the Thamesdown operation took delivery of a batch of long-wheelbase ADL Enviro 200MMCs. 2775 is seen on its way into Swindon Town centre on route 5 heading to Park North

3301-3329		Dennis Dart SLF SFD6BA		Alexander Pointer 2 8.8m			B29F	
				* - B27F, $ - B26F				
3301	HW52EPX	SA	3313	SN03LDU	SA	3321*	HW54BUF	u
3304	SN03EBV	r	3314*	HW54BTU	u	3325*	HW54BUP	r
3310	SN03LDJ	r	3317*	HW54BTY	u	3326*	HW54BUU	r
3311	SN03LDK	SA	3319*	HW54BUA	r	3328$	HW54DBZ	DO
3312	SN03LDL	SA	3320*	HW54BUE	r	3329$	HW54DCE	DO

3344	381VHX	Dennis Dart SLF SFD3C2	Caetano Nimbus 10.7m	B26D	TN
3351	PE55WPP	Dennis Dart SLF SFD2BA	East Lancs Myllenium	B29D	TN
3352	PE55WSU	Dennis Dart SLF SFD2BA	East Lancs Myllenium	B34F	DO
3361	HW54DCF	Dennis Dart SLF SFD3CA	Alexander Pointer 2 10.7m	B36F	PI
3362	HW54DCO	Dennis Dart SLF SFD3CA	Alexander Pointer 2 10.7m	B36F	PI
3363	HW54DCU	Dennis Dart SLF SFD3CA	Alexander Pointer 2 10.7m	B36F	PI
3412	YG52CMF	DAF DE12BSSB120	Wright Cadet 10.8m	B39F	TN

3413-3416		VDL DE12BSSB120		Wright Cadet 10.8m		B39F
3413	NK04FOV	EH	3415	YJ07JTX	EH	
3414	NK04FPA	TN	3416	YJ07JTY	EH	

3634-3688		Optare Solo M850		Optare Solo 8.5m			B30F	
3634	T634AJT	SA	3656	V656DFX	u	3663	V663DFX	r
3636	T636AJT	SA	3660	V660DFX	r	3669	V669DFX	r

| 3671 | V671FEL | r | 3687 | X687XJT | SA |
| 3672 | V672FEL | r | 3688 | X688XJT | SA |

| 3701 | NK54DEU | Optare Solo M880 | Optare Solo 8.5m | B25F | LY |

3688 used to carry full advertising livery for Tesco, and was used on a special few service to a Tesco store. It is seen in the entrance to Salisbury depot having had the branding removed from the livery

3703	NK54DFC	Optare Solo M880	Optare Solo 8.5m	B25F	LY
3704	NK54DFD	Optare Solo M880	Optare Solo 8.5m	B25F	SW
3707	MV07DWM	Optare Solo M880SL	Optare Solo Slimline 8.8m	B28F	r
3708	MX07NSV	Optare Solo M880SL	Optare Solo Slimline 8.8m	B29F	HE

3709-3712   Optare Solo M880   Optare Solo 8.8m   B29F
           * - B28F

| 3709 | MX57CAO | PO | 3711 | MX57CAV | r |
| 3710 | MX57CAU | PO | 3712* | MX08MYP | r |

| 3716 | MX53FEF | Optare Solo M850 | Optare Solo 8.5m | B29F | PO |
| 3722 | YJ05XMR | Optare Solo M780 | Optare Solo 7.8m | B21F | LY |

3751-3758   Optare Solo M920   Optare Solo 9.2m   B31F
           * - B32F, $ - B33F

3751*	GP02DPV	SA	3754$	MX03YDD	SA	3757	YJ06FYD	SA
3752$	VU02TTK	SA	3755	YJ06FYB	SA	3758	YJ06FYE	SA
3753$	VU52UES	SA	3756	YJ06FYC	SA			

3759-3777   Optare Solo M950   Optare Solo 9.5m   B33F
           * - B29F

| 3759 | MX07JNV | PO | 3761 | MX07NTD | r | 3763 | MX57CCU | r |
| 3760 | MX07NTC | r | 3762 | MX57CAA | r | 3764 | MX08MZF | LY |

3765	MX08MZJ	LY	3776*	MX57UPC	RI	3777*	MX57UPY	DO
3778	CE52UXC	Optare Solo M920		Optare Solo 9.2m			B33F	PI
3779	CE52UXD	Optare Solo M920		Optare Solo 9.2m			B33F	PI
3801	BP09ONE	Optare Solo SR M960		Optare Solo SR 9.6m			B29F	PO
3802	PB09ONE	Optare Solo SR M960		Optare Solo SR 9.6m			B29F	PO

Part of the fleet upgrade in 2015 saw a batch of Optare Solo SRs delivered to Salisbury where they were applied with the Damory fleet name. 3827 is entering Yeovil Bus Station while on route 74 heading to Sherborne

3803-3819		Optare Solo SR M890		Optare Solo SR 8.9m * - B30F			B25F	
3803	HW62CGF	SV	3809	HW62CJJ	SV	3815*	HW62CNJ	SV
3804	HW62CGO	SV	3810	HW62CKV	SV	3816*	HW62CNK	SV
3805	HW62CGY	SV	3811	HW62CKY	SV	3817*	HW62CNO	SV
3806	HW62CHC	SV	3812	HW62CMK	SV	3818*	HW62CNV	SV
3807	HW62CHZ	SV	3813*	HW62CMV	SV	3819*	HW62CPK	SA
3808	HW62CJE	SV	3814*	HW62CMY	SV			

3822-3832		Optare Solo SR M900SL		Optare Solo SR Slimline 9.0m			B30F	
3822	HF64BNN	SA	3826	HF64BNX	SA	3830	HF64BOJ	PI
3823	HF64BNO	SA	3827	HF64BNY	SA	3831	HF64BOU	RI
3824	HF64BNU	SA	3828	HF64BNZ	SA	3832	HF64BRZ	RI
3825	HF64BNV	SA	3829	HF64BOH	DO			

3833	HF15BMV	Optare Solo SR M925SL		Optare Solo SR Slimline 9.25m			B30F	SA
3834	HF15BMY	Optare Solo SR M925SL		Optare Solo SR Slimline 9.25m			B30F	SA
3835	HF15BMZ	Optare Solo SR M925SL		Optare Solo SR Slimline 9.25m			B30F	SA
4413	BFX666T	Bristol VRT		ECW			H43/31F	p
4637	R737XRV	Volvo Olympian		NC Palatine 1			PO44/29F	SV

Preserved by Go South Coast is 4413, a Bristol VRT which has spent all of its life in the Wilts & Dorset fleet or that of its predecessor, Hants & Dorset. It is seen on display at a Winchester running day

4706	F706RDL	Leyland Olympian		Leyland			DPH39/29F	u
5129	BJ03FHZ	LDV Convoy		LDV			M16	u
5130	WA03CRV	LDV Convoy		LDV			M16	u
5601	R601NFX	Optare Solo M850		Optare Solo 8.5m			B30F	u
7017	M376MRU	Volvo B10M-62		Plaxton Premiere 350 12.0m			C53F	w

7031-7044		Volvo B12M		Van Hool Alizee T9			C53F	
7031	MV02ULK	SV	7036	MV02UML	SV	7042	MV02UMU	SV
7032	MV02ULL	SV	7038	MV02UMO	SV	7043	MV02UMW	SV
7033	MV02ULM	SV	7039	MV02UMR	SV	7044	MV02UMX	SV
7034	MV02UMJ	SV	7040	MV02UMS	SV			
7035	MV02UMK	SV	7041	MV02UMT	SV			

7051	FJ61EVX	Volvo B9R	Caetano Levante 12.6m	C48FTL	SA
7052	BF63ZSO	Volvo B9R	Caetano Levante 12.6m	C49FTL	SA
7053	BF63ZSP	Volvo B9R	Caetano Levante 12.6m	C49FTL	SA
7061	DIG5295	Volvo B7R	Jonckheere Modulo	C57F	SA
7062	NXI5358	Volvo B7R	Jonckheere Modulo	C57F	SA
7071	SF05KWM	Volvo B7R	Plaxton Profile 12.0m	C70F	SA
7081	HJI7615	Volvo B10M-62	Plaxton Paragon 12.0m	C49FT	SA
7084	UJI2507	Volvo B10M-62	Plaxton Paragon 12.0m	C49FT	SA

7091-7099		Volvo B12M		Plaxton Paragon 12.0m			C57F	
				* - C53F, $ - C49FT				
7091*	OJI1875	SA	7096	PX03KCN	r	7099	TIL6719	PI
7092*	NBZ2184	SA	7097	TIL6717	DO			
7093$	WV52HTT	SV	7098	VU03VVX	r			

7101-7105		Scania K340EB4		Irizar PB			C49FT	
7101	HF08UHS	PI	7104	HF08UHV	SA			
7103	HF08UHU	PI	7105	HF08UHW	SA			
7131	YN07EWS	Scania K340EB		Caetano Levante 12.6m			C49FTL	r
7132	SIL7914	Scania K340EB		Caetano Levante 12.6m			C49FTL	SA

Coaches working under the Tourist Coaches fleet name can often be found on school duties. 7132 is seen in Salisbury while heading out of service to start work on a school duty

7174-7180		Scania K114IB4		Irizar Century			C53F	
7174	YSU875	SV	7177	XAA299	SA	7180	YN04GHV	SV
7175	YN04GHF	SV	7178	USV115	SV			
7176	LSV749	SA	7179	YMW843	SA			

7311	KP51UEO	Dennis R SFD122	Plaxton Paragon 12.0m	C70F	DO
7312	KP51UES	Dennis R SFD112	Plaxton Paragon 12.0m	C70F	DO
7314	KT51BXH	Dennis R SFD112	Plaxton Panther 12.0m	C34FT	DO
7315	YR02ZKV	Dennis R SFD112	Plaxton Panther 12.0m	C34FT	DO
7316	YR02ZKW	Dennis R SFD112	Plaxton Panther 12.0m	C34FT	PI
7318	YR02ZKY	Dennis R SFD112	Plaxton Panther 12.0m	C70F	r
7400	FJ17PVY	Mercedes-Benz 1223L	Plaxton Cheetah 3	C36F	SA

7801-7813		Volvo B9R		Caetano Levante 12.6m * - C48FTL, $ - C53FL			C70FL	
7801*	FJ60EHB	SA	7806$	FJ11GNP	DO	7811	FJ11GNZ	PI
7802*	FJ60EHC	SA	7807$	FJ11GNU	DO	7812	FJ61EWX	PI
7803*	FJ60EHD	SA	7808	FJ11GNV	DO	7813	FJ61EWY	DO
7804*	FJ60EHE	PI	7809	FJ11GNX	DO			
7805*	FJ60EHF	PI	7810	FJ11GNY	PI			

Go South Coast also operate National Express services towards the southwest of England. 7814 is seen in Winchester while on National Express route 032, heading for Southampton

7814-7831		Volvo B11RT			Caetano Levante 14.2m			C56FTL	
7814	BX16CLV	EH	7820	BW16LCO	EH	7826	BV66WOA		PO
7815	BX16CLY	EH	7821	BW16LCP	PO	7827	BV66WOB		PO
7816	BX16CLZ	EH	7822	BW16LCT	PO	7828	BV66WOC		PO
7817	BW16LCL	EH	7823	BV66WNX	PO	7829	BV66WOD		PO
7818	BW16LCM	EH	7824	BV66WNY	PO	7830	BV66WOH		PO
7819	BW16LCN	EH	7825	BV66WNZ	PO	7831	BV66WOJ		PO

7832	XEL24	Volvo B12M		Plaxton Paragon 12.8m	C57F	PI
7833	XEL31	Volvo B12M		Plaxton Paragon 12.8m	C57F	PI
7834	XEL158	Volvo B12M		Plaxton Paragon 12.8m	C51FT	BO

7835-7843		Volvo B11R			Jonckheere SHV			C53FT	
7835	A12XEL	BO	7838	A15XEL	BO	7841	A18XEL		BO
7836	A13XEL	BO	7839	A16XEL	BO	7842	A19XEL		BO
7837	A14XEL	BO	7840	A17XEL	BO	7843	A20XEL		BO

7844	A3XEL	Volvo B12M		Jonckheere SHV	C53F	BO
7845	A4XEL	Volvo B12M		Jonckheere SHV	C53F	BO
7846	FJ55BXZ	Volvo B12B		Caetano Enigma	C53F	PI
7847	FJ55BXV	Volvo B12B		Caetano Enigma	C53F	PI
7849	FJ55BXY	Volvo B12B		Caetano Enigma	C53F	DO
7850	XEL254	Volvo B12B		Caetano Enigma	C53F	DO

7943-7966		Ford Transit			Ford			M8	
					* - M16				
7943*	NG56HGO	DO	7964	EY67ZDD	DO	7966	EX67CWA		DOa
7952	EX06AYD	u	7965	EJ67KNM	Pla				

During 2017, Go-Ahead acquired Bournemouth-based coach company, Excelsior, and integrated them into the South Coast fleet. 7845 is seen in Swindon soon after the acquisition and prior to renumbering, pictured while on a private hire duty

7982	XEL4	Mercedes-Benz City 45	Mercedes-Benz	M16	BO
7983	EN67OBW	Ford Transit	Ford	M16	DO
7984	EN67WLD	Ford Transit	Ford	M16	PI
8101	700GOO	Scania N270UD	East Lancs Olympus	CH51/35F	PI
8102	HF08TKY	Scania N270UD	East Lancs Olympus	CH51/35F	SA
8201	YJ05PXM	VDL DE02PSDB250	East Lancs Myllennium Lowlander	H51/30F	PI
8202	YJ05PXN	VDL DE02PSDB250	East Lancs Myllennium Lowlander	CH51/30F	PI

Previous registrations

520	WX08VDC	3707	T10BHN
598	A5FTG, R435MEH, VUV246	3751	A15GPS
1014	YN06JWJ, MRD1	4637	R737XRV, XDL872
1111	HW58ASX	7017	XEL24, M376MRU, OJI1875
1910	W474WGH	7061	AT02CJT
1991	HW52EPK	7062	BT02CJT
1992	HW52EPL	7081	Y781MFT, LIL2665, Y871MFT
2289	HF64BRX	7084	Y784MFT, WKZ8689, Y784MFT
2290	HF64BRZ	7091	WV52AKY, MIL9575, WV52AKY
2291	HF64BSO	7092	WV52FAO
2451	HW07CXS	7093	WV52HTT, XXI8502
2452	HW07CXR	7096	PX03KCN, HSV342, PX03KCN, TIL6716
3344	HX51LPN	7097	PX03KCU, TIL6717, PX03KCU
3634	T634AJT, LIL9974	7098	VU03VVX, TIL6718
3660	V660DFX, TIL6727	7099	VU03VVY
3663	V663DFX, ONZ1208	7131	YN07EWS, SIB5373
3669	V669DFX, WIL2574	7132	YN07EWT

7174	YN04GHD		7839	BF65WHV
7175	YN04GHF, WDL691		7840	BF65WKK
7176	YN04GHG		7841	BF65WKL
7177	YN04GHH		7842	BF65WLA
7178	YN04GHJ		7843	BF65WLB
7179	YN04GHK		7844	LSK821, CT10OUG
7180	YN04GHV, XDL872		7845	LSK824, CT10OUH
7314	Y5HMC		7846	FJ55BXZ, A17XEL
7832	YN08NKK		7847	FJ55BXV, A18XEL
7833	YN08NKL		7849	FJ55BXY, A20XEL
7834	YN08NKM		7850	HF05AXS
7835	BG15RPO		7982	BV14UAA
7836	BG15RPU		8101	HF08TKX
7837	BG15RPV			
7838	BP15OLJ			

Liveries

Unless stated below, all vehicles in this fleet carry standard fleet livery;

Excelsior: 5, 6, 7832-7847, 7849, 7850
Swindon Bus Company (new Thamesdown): 105-109, 216-219, 405, 406, 411, 412, 415, 417, 504, 505, 510, 524, 526, 2764-2784
Old Thamesdown: 103, 104, 145, 198, 200-205, 207-214, 363, 365, 366, 371-379, 401-404, 407, 408, 413, 414, 416, 501-503, 506-509, 511-523, 525, 527, 528
More: 220-260, 1014, 1016, 1017, 1021, 1022, 1104, 1119-1122, 1124, 1191, 1535, 1538, 1547, 1609-1612, 1648-1654, 1822, 1824, 2203-2208, 2210-2215, 2217-2226, 2228-2230, 2417, 2419, 3765, 3832
Blue and white: 383
Vintage Southern Vectis: 702
Stonehenge: 1001, 1002, 1635-1637, 2785-2790, 3672
Bluestar: 1011-1013, 1125-1131, 1527-1534, 1638-1647, 1801, 1802, 1851, 2404-2410, 2422, 2423, 2432-2436, 2438, 2439, 2451, 2454, 2457, 2733-2750, 2752-2763, 3304, 3412, 3413, 3415, 3416, 3634, 3660
Forest Bus: 1015, 1018, 1827, 1829, 3764
Vintage Wilts & Dorset: 1019, 1020, 4413
Unilink: 1091, 1192-1195, 1197-1199, 1548-1570, 1910, 2001-2012, 2287-2292, 3344, 3352
Southern Vectis: 1101-1103, 1105-1110, 1112-1117, 1142-1152, 1579, 1580, 1585-1594, 1613-1622, 1656-1671, 1991-1997, 2452, 2453, 2455, 2456, 2711-2717, 2751, 3301, 3310, 3312, 3314, 3317, 3319-3321, 3325
Island Breezer: 1111, 1401-1403, 4637
Wilts & Dorset: 1118, 1132-1138, 1140, 1536, 1537, 1539-1544, 1546, 1821, 1823, 1825, 1826, 1828, 1830-1833, 2209, 2251-2286, 2401-2403, 2411, 2412, 2421, 2424, 2425, 2427, 2428, 2610-2612, 3656, 3663, 3669, 3671, 3687, 3701, 3703, 3754
Bournemouth Universitybus: 1123, 1196, 1501, 1502, 1504, 1519, 1623-1633, 1655, 2101
Salisbury Reds: 1139, 1141, 1503, 1505, 1506, 1571-1578, 2701-2708, 2718-2723, 3313, 3751, 3753, 3755-3758, 3822-3826
Purbeck Breezer: 1404-1402, 1701-1712
Vectis Blue: 1507-1518, 1520-1526, 3803-3819, 7031-7036, 7038-7044, 7093, 7175, 7180
Activ8: 1545
London red: 1901, 1904, 1942
Allover blue: 1940, 1941, 1943, 1972, 1973, 3704
Allover yellow: 1946
Island Coaster: 1947
Salisbury Park & Ride: 2231-2238
Allover white: 2700, 3707-3711, 3752, 3759-3763, 3777-3779, 7071, 7131, 7176, 7311, 7312, 7314-7316, 7318, 7806-7813, 7965, 7966
Damory: 2730-2732, 3326, 3328, 3329, 3362, 3363, 3716, 3776, 3827-3831, 7103, 7174, 7178, 7943, 8102
Red Rocket: 3311
Tourist Coaches: 7017, 8101
National Express: 7051-7053, 7096-7099, 7814-7831
Allover silver: 8201, 8202, 7983, 7984

Tappins

Garage

OX   Oxford - Osney Mead, Oxford, OX2 0ES

55	PO55NXU	Volvo B7TL	East Lancs Myllennium Vyking 11.0m	PO49/35F	OX
56	PO56JEJ	Volvo B7TL	East Lancs Myllennium Vyking 11.0m	PO49/35F	OX
58	T110DBW	Dennis Trident SFD323	Alexander ALX400 10.5m	PO51/27F	OX
59	T115DBW	Dennis Trident SFD323	Alexander ALX400 10.5m	PO51/27F	OX
902	V902FEC	Dennis Trident SFD113	East Lancs Lolyne 10.0m	O45/23F	OX
903	PJ53NKC	Volvo B7TL	Plaxton President 10.6m	O45/24F	OX
904	V904FEC	Dennis Trident SFD113	East Lancs Lolyne 10.0m	O45/23F	OX
905	V905FEC	Dennis Trident SFD113	East Lancs Lolyne 10.0m	O45/23F	OX
906	LY02OAE	Dennis Trident SFD134	Alexander ALX400 9.9m	O47/23F	OX
907	LY02OBK	Dennis Trident SFD134	Alexander ALX400 9.9m	O47/23F	OX
908	V908FEC	Dennis Trident SFD113	East Lancs Lolyne 10.0m	O45/23F	OX

Starting life with Oxford Bus Company before being acquired by Tappins is 59, seen approaching the town centre in St Giles while on the Oxford Tour

Liveries

Unless stated below, all vehicles in this fleet carry City Sightseeing livery;

The Oxford Tour: 58, 59, 906, 907

Thames Travel

Garage

WL   Wallingford - Lester Way, Wallingford, OX10 9TA

| 114 | T114DBW | Dennis Trident SFD323 | Alexander ALX400 10.5m | | | H47/24D | | u |

207-231		Scania N230UD	Alexander Enviro 400 10.9m			H51/29F	
207	GF09OXF	WL	212	AF10OXF	WL	230	VF10OXF	WL
208	HF09OXF	WL	213	BF10OXF	WL	231	WF10OXF	WL
209	JF09OXF	WL	228	TF10OXF	WL			
210	KF09OXF	WL	229	UF10OXF	WL			

During 2016, a batch of Alexander Enviro 400-bodied Scania double-deckers were cascaded from Oxford Bus Company to sister company Thames Travel. 207 is seen here arriving in Oxford while on route X2, showing the Connector livery carried by this vehicle

251-254		ADL E40D SFD4DS	ADL Enviro 400 10.8m		H47/32F
251	HW63FHC	WL	253	HW63FHE	WL
252	HW63FHD	WL	254	HW63FHF	WL

441	SK66HRN	Wright Streetlite DF	Wright Streetlite 10.8m	B41F	WL
442	SK66HRO	Wright Streetlite DF	Wright Streetlite 10.8m	B41F	WL

| 849-881 | | Mercedes-Benz O530 | Mercedes-Benz Citaro 12.0m | B40F | |
			* - B42F		
849*	LF56OXF	WL	854*	SF56OXF	WL	859*	YF56OXF	WL
850*	MF56OXF	WL	855*	TF56OXF	WL	860	AF57OXF	WL
851*	OF56OXF	WL	856*	UF56OXF	WL	861	BF57OXF	WL
852*	PF56OXF	WL	857*	VF56OXF	WL	862	CF57OXF	WL
853*	RF56OXF	WL	858*	WF56OXF	WL	863	DF57OXF	WL

864	EF57OXF	u	867	HF57OXF	u	880	BT09GOP	WL
865	FF57OXF	u	868	JF57OXF	u	881	BT09GOX	WL
866	GF57OXF	u	879	BT09GOK	WL			

Also new to Oxford Bus Company, but cascaded in 2012 were a batch of Mercedes-Benz Citaros. 849 is seen here on route X39 at Reading, while making its way to Oxford City Centre

912	OU08HGM	Scania CN230UD		Scania OmniCity 10.8m		H45/30F	WL
913	OU08HGN	Scania CN230UD		Scania OmniCity 10.8m		H45/30F	WL
933-937		Volvo B7TL		Wright Eclipse Gemini 10.1m		H41/21D	
933	LX06EAC	WL	935	LX06EAF	WL	937	LX05FBY	WL
934	LX06EAE	WL	936	LX06EAG	WL			

Liveries
Unless stated below, all vehicles in this fleet carry standard fleet livery;

Connector: 207, 231, 862-868
Two-tone red: 208, 230
Blue River Rapids: 228, 229, 251-254
Red River Rapids: 879-881
London red: 936

Southeastern (including Javelin services)

Depots
Ashford
Gillingham
Ramsgate
Slade Green

Class 375   Bombardier Electrostar 3-car sets

375 301	375 303	375 305	375 307	375 309
375 302	375 304	375 306	375 308	375 310

Class 375   Bombardier Electrostar 4-car sets

375 601	375 618	375 705	375 807	375 824	375 911
375 602	375 619	375 706	375 808	375 825	375 912
375 603	375 620	375 707	375 809	375 826	375 913
375 604	375 621	375 708	375 810	375 827	375 914
375 605	375 622	375 709	375 811	375 828	375 915
375 606	375 623	375 710	375 812	375 829	375 916
375 607	375 624	375 711	375 813	375 830	375 917
375 608	375 625	375 712	375 814	375 901	375 918
375 609	375 626	375 713	375 815	375 902	375 919
375 610	375 627	375 714	375 816	375 903	375 920
375 611	375 628	375 715	375 817	375 904	375 921
375 612	375 629	375 801	375 818	375 905	375 922
375 613	375 630	375 802	375 819	375 906	375 923
375 614	375 701	375 803	375 820	375 907	375 924
375 615	375 702	375 804	375 821	375 908	375 925
375 616	375 703	375 805	375 822	375 909	375 926
375 617	375 704	375 806	375 823	375 910	375 927

Class 375 sets feature quite prominently in the Southeastern fleet. 375 927 is seen here at Faversham while heading for London Victoria (photo courtesy of Kevin Cooper)

Class 376   Bombardier Electrostar 5-car sets

376 001	376 007	376 013	376 019	376 025	376 031
376 002	376 008	376 014	376 020	376 026	376 032
376 003	376 009	376 015	376 021	376 027	376 033
376 004	376 010	376 016	376 022	376 028	376 034
376 005	376 011	376 017	376 023	376 029	376 035
376 006	376 012	376 018	376 024	376 030	376 036

Class 377   Bombardier Electrostar 4-car sets

377 163	377 504	377 509	377 514	377 519
377 164	377 505	377 510	377 515	377 520
377 501	377 506	377 511	377 516	377 521
377 502	377 507	377 512	377 517	377 522
377 503	377 508	377 513	377 518	377 523

Class 395   Hitachi A Train "Javelin" 6-car sets

395 001	395 006	395 011	395 016	395 021	395 026
395 002	395 007	395 012	395 017	395 022	395 027
395 003	395 008	395 013	395 018	395 023	395 028
395 004	395 009	395 014	395 019	395 024	395 029
395 005	395 010	395 015	395 020	395 025	

The Javelin service was introduced by Southeastern, using the high-speed rail link to London St Pancras. 395 025 is seen here at Margate while heading for London St Pancras

Class 465   BREL Networker 4-car sets

465 001	465 004	465 007	465 010	465 013	465 016
465 002	465 005	465 008	465 011	465 014	465 017
465 003	465 006	465 009	465 012	465 015	465 018

465 019	465 025	465 031	465 037	465 043	465 049
465 020	465 026	465 032	465 038	465 044	465 050
465 021	465 027	465 033	465 039	465 045	
465 022	465 028	465 034	465 040	465 046	
465 023	465 029	465 035	465 041	465 047	
465 024	465 030	465 036	465 042	465 048	

Southeastern operate both London suburban and mainline services in Kent and Sussex. 465 035 is seen here on a suburban working while leaving London Bridge (photo courtesy of Kevin Cooper)

Class 465		ABB Networker 4-car sets			
465 151	465 159	465 167	465 175	465 183	465 191
465 152	465 160	465 168	465 176	465 184	465 192
465 153	465 161	465 169	465 177	465 185	465 193
465 154	465 162	465 170	465 178	465 186	465 194
465 155	465 163	465 171	465 179	465 187	465 195
465 156	465 164	465 172	465 180	465 188	465 196
465 157	465 165	465 173	465 181	465 189	465 197
465 158	465 166	465 174	465 182	465 190	

Class 465		GEC Alsthom Networker 4-car sets			
465 235	465 244	465 903	465 912	465 921	465 930
465 236	465 245	465 904	465 913	465 922	465 931
465 237	465 246	465 905	465 914	465 923	465 932
465 238	465 247	465 906	465 915	465 924	465 933
465 239	465 248	465 907	465 916	465 925	465 934
465 240	465 249	465 908	465 917	465 926	
465 241	465 250	465 909	465 918	465 927	
465 242	465 901	465 910	465 919	465 928	
465 243	465 902	465 911	465 920	465 929	

Class 466

GEC Alsthom Networker 2-car sets

466 001	466 009	466 017	466 025	466 033	466 041
466 002	466 010	466 018	466 026	466 034	466 042
466 003	466 011	466 019	466 027	466 035	466 043
466 004	466 012	466 020	466 028	466 036	
466 005	466 013	466 021	466 029	466 037	
466 006	466 014	466 022	466 030	466 038	
466 007	466 015	466 023	466 031	466 039	
466 008	466 016	466 024	466 032	466 040	

Class 466 sets also operate the London suburban services. 466 007 is seen here at London Charing Cross awaiting its departure to Orpington (photo courtesy of Kevin Cooper)

Named sets

There are no named sets in this fleet.

Common workings

Class 375   London Charing Cross to Dover Priory, Ramsgate, Hastings and Tunbridge Wells
London Victoria to Ramsgate, Dover Priory, Canterbury West and Ashford International
Strood to Maidstone West and Tonbridge
Sittingbourne to Sheerness-on-Sea

Class 376   London Cannon Street loop service via Bexleyheath and Slade Green, loop service via Sidcup and Slade Green, loop service via Woolwich Arsenal and Slade Green, Orpington
London Charing Cross to Dartford, Hayes, Sevenoaks, Gravesend, Gillingham
London Victoria to Dartford, Orpington
Bromley North to Grove Park

Class 377	London Charing Cross to Dover Priory, Ramsgate, Hastings, Tunbridge Wells
	London Victoria to Ramsgate, Dover Priory, Canterbury West, Ashford International
	Strood to Maidstone West and Tonbridge
	Sittingbourne to Sheerness-on-Sea
Class 395	High speed services from London St Pancras International to Faversham, Margate and Dover Priory, and loop service via Chatham, Ramsgate, Dover and Ashford
Class 465	London Cannon Street loop service via Bexleyheath and Slade Green, loop service via Sidcup and Slade Green, loop service via Woolwich Arsenal and Slade Green, Orpington
	London Charing Cross to Dartford, Hayes, Sevenoaks, Gravesend, Gillingham
	London Victoria to Dartford, Orpington
	Bromley North to Grove Park
Class 466	London Cannon Street loop service via Bexleyheath and Slade Green, loop service via Sidcup and Slade Green, loop service via Woolwich Arsenal and Slade Green, Orpington
	London Charing Cross to Dartford, Hayes, Sevenoaks, Gravesend, Gillingham
	London Victoria to Dartford, Orpington
	Bromley North to Grove Park

Southern Railway (including Gatwick Express)

Depots

Brighton (Lovers Walk)		Selhurst		Stewarts Lane	

73 202		Electro-diesel locomotive			
171 201		Bombardier Turbostar 2-car set			
171 202		Bombardier Turbostar 2-car set			
171 401		Bombardier Turbostar 4-car set			
171 402		Bombardier Turbostar 4-car set			

Class 171 — Bombardier Turbostar 2-car sets

| 171 721 | 171 723 | 171 725 | 171 727 | 171 729 | |
| 171 722 | 171 724 | 171 726 | 171 728 | 171 730 | |

Class 171 — Bombardier Turbostar 4-car sets

| 171 801 | 171 802 | 171 803 | 171 804 | 171 805 | 171 806 |

Class 313 — BREL 3-car sets

313 201	313 205	313 209	313 213	313 217	
313 202	313 206	313 210	313 214	313 219	
313 203	313 207	313 211	313 215	313 220	
313 204	313 208	313 212	313 216		

Class 313 units can be found operating numerous stopping services along the south coast within the Southern fleet. Restored to original British Rail livery is 313 201, seen here awaiting its departure from Bognor Regis (photo courtesy of Kevin Cooper)

Class 377 — Bombardier Electrostar 4-car sets

| 377 101 | 377 103 | 377 105 | 377 107 | 377 109 | 377 111 |
| 377 102 | 377 104 | 377 106 | 377 108 | 377 110 | 377 112 |

377 113	377 124	377 135	377 146	377 157	377 206
377 114	377 125	377 136	377 147	377 158	377 207
377 115	377 126	377 137	377 148	377 159	377 208
377 116	377 127	377 138	377 149	377 160	377 209
377 117	377 128	377 139	377 150	377 161	377 210
377 118	377 129	377 140	377 151	377 162	377 211
377 119	377 130	377 141	377 152	377 201	377 212
377 120	377 131	377 142	377 153	377 202	377 213
377 121	377 132	377 143	377 154	377 203	377 214
377 122	377 133	377 144	377 155	377 204	377 215
377 123	377 134	377 145	377 156	377 205	

Class 377   Bombardier Electrostar 3-car sets

377 301	377 306	377 311	377 316	377 321	377 326
377 302	377 307	377 312	377 317	377 322	377 327
377 303	377 308	377 313	377 318	377 323	377 328
377 304	377 309	377 314	377 319	377 324	377 342
377 305	377 310	377 315	377 320	377 325	

Class 377 Electrostars, in varying lengths form the backbone of the Southern rail fleet. 377 448, a four-car example, is seen leaving Chichester while heading for Brighton

Class 377   Bombardier Electrostar 4-car sets

377 401	377 410	377 419	377 428	377 437	377 447
377 402	377 411	377 420	377 429	377 438	377 448
377 403	377 412	377 421	377 430	377 439	377 449
377 404	377 413	377 422	377 431	377 440	377 450
377 405	377 414	377 423	377 432	377 441	377 451
377 406	377 415	377 424	377 433	377 443	377 452
377 407	377 416	377 425	377 434	377 444	377 453
377 408	377 417	377 426	377 435	377 445	377 454
377 409	377 418	377 427	377 436	377 446	377 455

377 456	377 460	377 464	377 468	377 472	
377 457	377 461	377 465	377 469	377 473	
377 458	377 462	377 466	377 470	377 474	
377 459	377 463	377 467	377 471	377 475	

Class 377		Bombardier Electrostar 5-car sets			
377 601	377 607	377 613	377 619	377 625	377 705
377 602	377 608	377 614	377 620	377 626	377 706
377 603	377 609	377 615	377 621	377 701	377 707
377 604	377 610	377 616	377 622	377 702	377 708
377 605	377 611	377 617	377 623	377 703	
377 606	377 612	377 618	377 624	377 704	

Class 387		Bombardier Electrostar 4-car sets			
387 201	387 206	387 211	387 216	387 221	387 226
387 202	387 207	387 212	387 217	387 222	387 227
387 203	387 208	387 213	387 218	387 223	
387 204	387 209	387 214	387 219	387 224	
387 205	387 210	387 215	387 220	387 225	

Previous page: *Class 455 sets are the mainstay on the London suburban part of the Southern rail network. 455 824 is seen here at Victoria heading for West Croydon (photo courtesy of Kevin Cooper)*

Class 455		BREL 4-car sets			
455 801	455 808	455 815	455 822	455 829	455 836
455 802	455 809	455 816	455 823	455 830	455 837
455 803	455 810	455 817	455 824	455 831	455 838
455 804	455 811	455 818	455 825	455 832	455 839
455 805	455 812	455 819	455 826	455 833	455 840
455 806	455 813	455 820	455 827	455 834	455 841
455 807	455 814	455 821	455 828	455 835	455 842

455 843   455 844   455 845   455 846

Named sets

There are no named sets in this fleet

Common workings

Class 171   Brighton to Ashford International
               London Bridge to Uckfield

Class 313   Brighton to Lewes, Eastbourne, Hastings, Ore, Seaford, Ashford International, Littlehampton,
               Bognor Regis and Southampton (stopping services)

Class 377   Throughout Southern network with the exception of Oxted to Uckfield, and Ore to Ashford
               International

Class 387   London Victoria to Brighton and Gatwick Airport (latter non-stop)

Class 455   Brighton and Three Bridges to Bedford
               Brighton to London Bridge
               London Victoria to Epsom, Horsham, Dorking, Caterham, Sutton (both via
               Norbury and via Gipsy Hill), London Bridge (via Gipsy Hill)
               London Bridge to Caterham, Tattenham Corner, West Croydon, Beckenham
               Junction

Thameslink and Great Northern

Depots
Bedford
Cambridge
Cauldwell Walk, Bedford

Cricklewood
Hornsey (Great Northern)
Peterborough

Three Bridges

Class 313 — BREL 3-car sets

313 018	313 031	313 040	313 048	313 056	313 064
313 024	313 032	313 041	313 049	313 057	313 122
313 025	313 033	313 042	313 050	313 058	313 123
313 026	313 035	313 043	313 051	313 059	313 134
313 027	313 036	313 044	313 052	313 060	
313 028	313 037	313 045	313 053	313 061	
313 029	313 038	313 046	313 054	313 062	
313 030	313 039	313 047	313 055	313 063	

Class 365 — BREL 4-car sets

365 502	365 508	365 515	365 522	365 532	365 539
365 503	365 510	365 516	365 524	365 534	365 540
365 504	365 511	365 518	365 528	365 536	365 541
365 506	365 512	365 520	365 530	365 537	
365 507	365 514	365 521	365 531	365 538	

Class 387 — Bombardier Electrostar 4-car sets

387 101	387 106	387 111	387 116	387 121	387 126
387 102	387 107	387 112	387 117	387 122	387 127
387 103	387 108	387 113	387 118	387 123	387 128
387 104	387 109	387 114	387 119	387 124	387 129
387 105	387 110	387 115	387 120	387 125	

Class 700 — Siemens Desiro City 8-car sets

700 001	700 011	700 021	700 031	700 041	700 051
700 002	700 012	700 022	700 032	700 042	700 052
700 003	700 013	700 023	700 033	700 043	700 053
700 004	700 014	700 024	700 034	700 044	700 054
700 005	700 015	700 025	700 035	700 045	700 055
700 006	700 016	700 026	700 036	700 046	700 056
700 007	700 017	700 027	700 037	700 047	700 057
700 008	700 018	700 028	700 038	700 048	700 058
700 009	700 019	700 029	700 039	700 049	700 059
700 010	700 020	700 030	700 040	700 050	700 060

Class 700 — Siemens Desiro City 12-car sets

700 101	700 111	700 121	700 131	700 141	700 151
700 102	700 112	700 122	700 132	700 142	700 152
700 103	700 113	700 123	700 133	700 143	700 153
700 104	700 114	700 124	700 134	700 144	700 154
700 105	700 115	700 125	700 135	700 145	700 155
700 106	700 116	700 126	700 136	700 146	
700 107	700 117	700 127	700 137	700 147	
700 108	700 118	700 128	700 138	700 148	
700 109	700 119	700 129	700 139	700 149	
700 110	700 120	700 130	700 140	700 150	

Class 717 — Siemens Desiro City 6-car sets (on order)

717 001	717 003	717 005	717 007	717 009	717 011
717 002	717 004	717 006	717 008	717 010	717 012

717 013	717 016	717 019	717 022	717 025
717 014	717 017	717 020	717 023	
717 015	717 018	717 021	717 024	

Class 700s now form the backbone of the Thameslink fleet. 700 039 is seen here at Brighton awaiting its departure towards London (photo courtesy of Kevin Cooper)

Named sets

313 054	Captain William Leefe Robinson VC
313 122	Eric Roberts 1946-2012 "The Flying Nottsman"
365 506	The Royston Express
365 514	Captain George Vancouver
365 518	The Fenman
365 530	The Interlink Partnership
365 536	Rufus Barnes – Chief Executive of London Travelwatch for 25 years
365 537	Daniel Edwards – Cambridge Driver 1974-2010

Common workings

Class 313   London Moorgate/King's Cross to Welwyn Garden City, Hertford North, Stevenage and Letchworth Garden City

Class 365   London King's Cross to Peterborough, Cambridge and Ely

Class 387   London King's Cross to Peterborough, Cambridge and King's Lynn

Class 700   Bedford to Brighton, Gatwick Airport, Cambridge, East Grinstead and Littlehampton
Peterborough to Horsham
Cambridge to Maidstone East
Luton to Rainham and Orpington
Sutton to St Albans and Luton
Welwyn Garden City to Sevenoaks
London King's Cross to Peterborough and Cambridge

Bus Registration Index

This section consists of an index of all of the buses with the UK operation of Go-Ahead, along with the operating company. All registrations are in age order, from old to new. The list of division codes is as follows:

BH	Brighton & Hove	KO	Konnectbus	OX	Oxford	TT	Thames Travel
CA	Carousel	LN	London	PL	Plymouth Citybus		
CH	Chambers	MB	Metrobus	SC	South Coast		
HD	Hedingham & District	NE	North East	TA	Tappins		

Reg	No	Div
574CPT	3965	NE
700GOO	8101	SC
340GUP	6144	NE
381VHX	3344	SC
CU6860	6147	NE
CU7661	6148	NE
CDL889	702	SC
DIG5295	7061	SC
FCU190	3943	NE
GSK962	1992	SC
HJI7615	7081	SC
JCN822	3962	NE
JSK261	313	PL
JSK262	314	PL
JSK263	315	PL
JSK264	311	PL
JSK265	316	PL
LSV749	7176	SC
LTZ1041	LT41	LN
LTZ1042	LT42	LN
LTZ1043	LT43	LN
LTZ1044	LT44	LN
LTZ1045	LT45	LN
LTZ1046	LT46	LN
LTZ1047	LT47	LN
LTZ1048	LT48	LN
LTZ1049	LT49	LN
LTZ1050	LT50	LN
LTZ1051	LT51	LN
LTZ1052	LT52	LN
LTZ1053	LT53	LN
LTZ1054	LT54	LN
LTZ1055	LT55	LN
LTZ1056	LT56	LN
LTZ1057	LT57	LN
LTZ1058	LT58	LN
LTZ1059	LT59	LN
LTZ1060	LT60	LN
LTZ1061	LT61	LN
LTZ1062	LT62	LN
LTZ1063	LT63	LN
LTZ1064	LT64	LN
LTZ1065	LT65	LN
LTZ1066	LT66	LN
LTZ1067	LT67	LN
LTZ1068	LT68	LN
LTZ1118	LT118	LN
LTZ1119	LT119	LN
LTZ1189	LT189	LN
LTZ1273	LT273	LN
LTZ1274	LT274	LN
LTZ1275	LT275	LN
LTZ1276	LT276	LN
LTZ1277	LT277	LN
LTZ1278	LT278	LN
LTZ1279	LT279	LN
LTZ1280	LT280	LN
LTZ1281	LT281	LN
LTZ1282	LT282	LN
LTZ1283	LT283	LN
LTZ1284	LT284	LN
LTZ1285	LT285	LN
LTZ1286	LT286	LN
LTZ1287	LT287	LN
LTZ1288	LT288	LN
LTZ1289	LT289	LN
LTZ1290	LT290	LN
LTZ1291	LT291	LN
LTZ1292	LT292	LN
LTZ1293	LT293	LN
LTZ1294	LT294	LN
LTZ1295	LT295	LN
LTZ1296	LT296	LN
LTZ1297	LT297	LN
LTZ1298	LT298	LN
LTZ1299	LT299	LN
LTZ1300	LT300	LN
LTZ1301	LT301	LN
LTZ1302	LT302	LN
LTZ1303	LT303	LN
LTZ1304	LT304	LN
LTZ1305	LT305	LN
LTZ1306	LT306	LN
LTZ1307	LT307	LN
LTZ1308	LT308	LN
LTZ1309	LT309	LN
LTZ1310	LT310	LN
LTZ1311	LT311	LN
LTZ1391	LT391	LN
LTZ1392	LT392	LN
LTZ1393	LT393	LN
LTZ1394	LT394	LN
LTZ1395	LT395	LN
LTZ1396	LT396	LN
LTZ1397	LT397	LN
LTZ1398	LT398	LN
LTZ1399	LT399	LN
LTZ1400	LT400	LN
LTZ1401	LT401	LN
LTZ1402	LT402	LN
LTZ1403	LT403	LN
LTZ1404	LT404	LN
LTZ1405	LT405	LN
LTZ1406	LT406	LN
LTZ1407	LT407	LN
LTZ1408	LT408	LN
LTZ1409	LT409	LN
LTZ1410	LT410	LN
LTZ1411	LT411	LN
LTZ1412	LT412	LN
LTZ1413	LT413	LN
LTZ1414	LT414	LN
LTZ1415	LT415	LN
LTZ1416	LT416	LN
LTZ1417	LT417	LN
LTZ1418	LT418	LN
LTZ1419	LT419	LN
LTZ1420	LT420	LN
LTZ1421	LT421	LN
LTZ1422	LT422	LN
LTZ1423	LT423	LN
LTZ1424	LT424	LN
LTZ1425	LT425	LN
LTZ1426	LT426	LN
LTZ1427	LT427	LN
LTZ1428	LT428	LN
LTZ1429	LT429	LN
LTZ1430	LT430	LN
LTZ1431	LT431	LN
LTZ1432	LT432	LN
LTZ1433	LT433	LN
LTZ1434	LT434	LN
LTZ1435	LT435	LN
LTZ1436	LT436	LN
LTZ1437	LT437	LN
LTZ1438	LT438	LN
LTZ1439	LT439	LN
LTZ1440	LT440	LN
LTZ1441	LT441	LN
LTZ1442	LT442	LN
LTZ1443	LT443	LN
LTZ1444	LT444	LN
LTZ1445	LT445	LN
LTZ1446	LT446	LN
LTZ1447	LT447	LN
LTZ1448	LT448	LN
LTZ1449	LT449	LN
LTZ1450	LT450	LN
LTZ1451	LT451	LN
LTZ1452	LT452	LN
LTZ1453	LT453	LN
LTZ1454	LT454	LN
LTZ1455	LT455	LN
LTZ1456	LT456	LN
LTZ1457	LT457	LN
LTZ1458	LT458	LN
LTZ1459	LT459	LN
LTZ1478	LT478	LN
LTZ1479	LT479	LN
LTZ1480	LT480	LN
LTZ1481	LT481	LN
LTZ1482	LT482	LN
LTZ1483	LT483	LN
LTZ1484	LT484	LN
LTZ1485	LT485	LN
LTZ1486	LT486	LN
LTZ1487	LT487	LN
LTZ1501	LT501	LN
LTZ1502	LT502	LN
LTZ1503	LT503	LN
LTZ1504	LT504	LN
LTZ1505	LT505	LN
LTZ1506	LT506	LN
LTZ1507	LT507	LN
LTZ1508	LT508	LN
LTZ1509	LT509	LN
LTZ1510	LT510	LN
LTZ1511	LT511	LN
LTZ1512	LT512	LN
LTZ1664	LT664	LN
LTZ1665	LT665	LN
LTZ1666	LT666	LN
LTZ1667	LT667	LN
LTZ1668	LT668	LN
LTZ1669	LT669	LN
LTZ1670	LT670	LN
LTZ1671	LT671	LN
LTZ1672	LT672	LN
LTZ1673	LT673	LN
LTZ1674	LT674	LN
LTZ1675	LT675	LN
LTZ1676	LT676	LN
LTZ1677	LT677	LN
LTZ1678	LT678	LN
LTZ1679	LT679	LN
LTZ1680	LT680	LN
LTZ1681	LT681	LN
LTZ1682	LT682	LN
LTZ1683	LT683	LN
LTZ1684	LT684	LN
LTZ1685	LT685	LN
LTZ1686	LT686	LN
LTZ1688	LT688	LN
LTZ1689	LT689	LN
LTZ1690	LT690	LN
LTZ1845	LT845	LN
LTZ1846	LT846	LN
LTZ1847	LT847	LN
LTZ1848	LT848	LN
LTZ1849	LT849	LN
LTZ1850	LT850	LN
LTZ1851	LT851	LN
LTZ1852	LT852	LN
LTZ1853	LT853	LN
LTZ1854	LT854	LN
LTZ1855	LT855	LN
LTZ1856	LT856	LN
LTZ1857	LT857	LN
LTZ1858	LT858	LN
LTZ1859	LT859	LN
LTZ1860	LT860	LN
LTZ1861	LT861	LN
LTZ1862	LT862	LN
LTZ1863	LT863	LN
LTZ1864	LT864	LN
LTZ1865	LT865	LN
LTZ1866	LT866	LN
LTZ1867	LT867	LN
LTZ1868	LT868	LN
LTZ1869	LT869	LN
LTZ1870	LT870	LN
LTZ1871	LT871	LN
LTZ1872	LT872	LN
LTZ1873	LT873	LN
LTZ1874	LT874	LN
LTZ1875	LT875	LN
LTZ1876	LT876	LN
LTZ1877	LT877	LN
LTZ1878	LT878	LN
LTZ1879	LT879	LN
LTZ1880	LT880	LN
LTZ1881	LT881	LN
LTZ1882	LT882	LN
LTZ1883	LT883	LN
LTZ1884	LT884	LN
LTZ1885	LT885	LN
LTZ1886	LT886	LN
LTZ1887	LT887	LN
LTZ1888	LT888	LN
LTZ1889	LT889	LN
LTZ1890	LT890	LN
LTZ1891	LT891	LN
LTZ1892	LT892	LN
LTZ1893	LT893	LN
LTZ1894	LT894	LN
LTZ1895	LT895	LN
LTZ1896	LT896	LN
LTZ1897	LT897	LN
LTZ1898	LT898	LN
LTZ1899	LT899	LN
LTZ1900	LT900	LN
LTZ2101	LT901	LN
LTZ2102	LT902	LN
LTZ2103	LT903	LN
LTZ2104	LT904	LN
LTZ2105	LT905	LN
LTZ2106	LT906	LN
LTZ2107	LT907	LN
LTZ2108	LT908	LN
LTZ2109	LT909	LN
LTZ2110	LT910	LN
LTZ2111	LT911	LN
LTZ2112	LT912	LN
LTZ2113	LT913	LN
LTZ2114	LT914	LN
LTZ2115	LT915	LN
LTZ2116	LT916	LN
LTZ2117	LT917	LN
LTZ2118	LT918	LN
LTZ2119	LT919	LN
LTZ2120	LT920	LN
LTZ2121	LT921	LN
LTZ2122	LT922	LN
LTZ2123	LT923	LN
LTZ2124	LT924	LN
LTZ2125	LT925	LN
LTZ2126	LT926	LN
LTZ2127	LT927	LN
LTZ2128	LT928	LN
LTZ2129	LT929	LN
LTZ2130	LT930	LN
LTZ2131	LT931	LN
LTZ2132	LT932	LN
LTZ2133	LT933	LN
LTZ2134	LT934	LN
LTZ2135	LT935	LN
LTZ2136	LT936	LN
LTZ2137	LT937	LN
LTZ2138	LT938	LN
LTZ2139	LT939	LN
LTZ2140	LT940	LN
LTZ2141	LT941	LN
LTZ2142	LT942	LN
LTZ2143	LT943	LN
LTZ2144	LT944	LN
LTZ2145	LT945	LN
LTZ2146	LT946	LN
LTZ2147	LT947	LN
LTZ2148	LT948	LN
LTZ2149	LT949	LN
LTZ2150	LT950	LN
LTZ2151	LT951	LN
LTZ2152	LT952	LN
LTZ2153	LT953	LN
MCO658	358	PL
NBZ2184	7092	SC
NXI5358	7062	SC
OCO502		PL
OJI1875	7091	SC
SIL7914	7132	SC
TIL6717	7097	SC
TIL6719	7099	SC
UJI2507	7084	SC
USV115	7178	SC
VDL744	1111	SC

Code	No.	Rgn
VJI3968	1910	SC
VLT9	RM9	LN
WDL691	1991	SC
WLT516	RML2516	LN
XAA299	7177	SC
XEL4	7982	SC
XEL24	7832	SC
XEL31	7833	SC
XEL158	7834	SC
XEL254	7850	SC
XMW120	520	SC
YMW843	7179	SC
YSU875	7174	SC
CUV305C	RML2305	LN
CUV317C	RML2317	BH
CUV318C	RML2318	LN
DDR201C	201	PL
JAM145E	145	SC
NML604E	RML2604	LN
BFX666T	4413	SC
FDV787V	1557	PL
VJY137V	137a	PL
A3XEL	7844	SC
A4XEL	7845	SC
A12XEL	7835	SC
A13XEL	7836	SC
A14XEL	7837	SC
A15XEL	7838	SC
A16XEL	7839	SC
A17XEL	7840	SC
A18XEL	7841	SC
A19XEL	7842	SC
A20XEL	7843	SC
C1WYC	551	CA
C2WYC	552	CA
C3WYC	553	CA
F706RDL	4706	SC
J1OXF	360	OX
K1OXF	362	OX
K3VOY	7093	NE
M655KVU	3	CH
M376MRU	7017	SC
M1OXF	363	OX
M571XKY	4	HD
N21GNE	5321	NE
N427JBV	90	HD
N1OXF	368	OX
N664THO	5	HD
N667THO	6	HD
P530CLJ	7	HD
P735RYL	LDP35	LN
R453FWT	8	HD
R221HCD	7221	BH
R236HCD	7236	BH
R273LGH	93	HD
R279LGH	95	HD
R435MEH	598	SC
R189NFE	383	SC
R601NFX	5601	SC
R116OFJ	16	PL
R117OFJ	17	PL
R123OFJ	23	PL
R125OFJ	25	PL
R1OXF	351	OX
R2OXF	352	OX
R3OXF	353	OX
R4OXF	354	OX
R5OXF	355	OX
R6OXF	356	OX
R7OXF	357	OX
R8OXF	358	OX
R9OXF	359	OX
R11OXF	361	OX
R12OXF	300	OX
R737XRV	4637	SC
S977ABR	7077	NE
S818OFT	3818	NE
S819OFT	3819	NE
S832OFT	3832	NE
S290TVW	9	HD
S291TVW	10	CH
S300XHK	75	HD
T636AJT	3636	SC
T107DBW	737	HD
T108DBW	738	HD
T110DBW	58	LN
T114DBW	114	TT
T115DBW	59	TA
T129EFJ	29	PL
T139EFJ	39	PL
T3FCC	LUT1	LN
T4FCC	LUT2	LN
T5FCC	LUT3	LN
T6FCC	LUT4	LN
T801RFG	701	HD
T802RFG	702	HD
T812RFG	712	HD
T817RFG	717	HD
V656DFX	3656	SC
V989ETN	4899	NE
V902FEC	902	TA
V904FEC	904	TA
V905FEC	905	TA
V908FEC	908	TA
V816KGF	6016	NE
V923KGF	6023	NE
V209LGC	6009	NE
V218LGC	6018	NE
V220LGC	6020	NE
V233LGC	6033	NE
V301LGC	561	HD
V302LGC	6039	NE
V307LGC	563	HD
V310LGC	6010	NE
V315LGC	6015	NE
V317LGC	6017	NE
V319LGC	6019	NE
V325LGC	6025	NE
V330LGC	6030	NE
V331LGC	6031	NE
V161MEV	740	KO
V14OXF	364	OX
V15OXF	365	OX
V16OXF	366	OX
V17OXF	367	OX
V284SBW	7284	OX
W821NNJ	721	HD
W822NNJ	722	HD
W823NNJ	723	HD
W824NNJ	724	CH
W826NNJ	726	HD
W827NNJ	727	HD
W829NNJ	729	HD
W834NNJ	734	HD
W404WGH	PVL140	LN
W408WGH	PVL80	LN
W409WGH	564	CH
W425WGH	565	CH
W428WGH	566	CH
W435WGH	PVL135	LN
W457WGH	567	CH
W458WGH	568	CH
W484WGH	569	HD
W487WGH	570	CH
W488WGH	571	HD
W489WGH	572	CH
W491WGH	573	HD
W498WGH	1928	SC
W501WGH	1901	SC
W504WGH	1904	SC
W506WGH	574	HD
W516WGH	575	HD
W517WGH	576	HD
W518WGH	577	HD
W519WGH	578	HD
W526WGH	579	HD
W527WGH	580	HD
W534WGH	PVL134	LN
W536WGH	PVL136	LN
W537WGH	PVL137	LN
W538WGH	PVL138	LN
W539WGH	PVL139	LN
W541WGH	PVL141	LN
W542WGH	PVL142	LN
W543WGH	PVL143	LN
W956WGH	581	HD
X90APP	67	OX
X501EGK	433	PL
X504EGK	440	PL
X546EGK	434	PL
X548EGK	PVL148	LN
X568EGK	435	PL
X571EGK	436	PL
X572EGK	1972	SC
X573EGK	1973	SC
X702EGK	437	PL
X171FBB	VP18	LN
X21GNE	6146	NE
X90LDN	72	OX
X90LON	71	OX
X386NNO	743	HD
X90OBC	73	OX
X90OFD	74	OX
X90OXD	75	OX
X90PLS	69	OX
X90SVC	76	OX
X90WAY	70	OX
X687XJT	3687	SC
X688XJT	3688	SC
X90YES	68	OX
Y926ERG	4926	NE
Y929ERG	4929	NE
Y932ERG	4932	NE
Y933ERG	4933	NE
Y934ERG	4934	NE
Y493ETN	4930	NE
Y186HNH	LUT5	LN
Y648NYD	48	PL
Y25OXF	369	OX
Y704TGH	1940	SC
Y729TGH	PVL229	LN
Y739TGH	1939	SC
Y741TGH	1941	SC
Y742TGH	1942	SC
Y743TGH	1943	SC
Y746TGH	1946	SC
Y747TGH	1947	SC
Y748TGH	PVL248	LN
Y814TGH	442	PL
Y818TGH	PVL218	LN
Y819TGH	PVL219	LN
Y821TGH	PVL221	LN
Y822TGH	PVL222	LN
Y823TGH	PVL223	LN
Y824TGH	PVL224	LN
Y986TGH	LDP186	LN
HX51ZRA	1801	SC
HX51ZRC	1802	SC
KP51UEO	7311	SC
KP51UES	7312	SC
KT51BXH	7314	SC
LN51DWO	DMN4	LN
NK51OKW	4937	NE
NK51OKX	4938	NE
NK51OLB	4940	NE
NK51OLH	4944	NE
NK51OLJ	4945	NE
NK51OLN	4947	NE
NK51OLO	4948	NE
NK51OLP	4949	NE
PL51LDK	7951	BH
PL51LDN	7952	BH
PL51LGO	9000	HD
PL51LGV	417	PL
PL51LGW	418	PL
SN51AXW	363	SC
SN51AYO	365	SC
SN51AYP	366	SC
SN51UAD	LDP191	LN
SN51UAG	LDP194	LN
SN51UAL	LDP198	LN
SN51UAO	LDP200	LN
SN51UAT	LDP204	LN
SN51UAV	LDP206	LN
VX51RHZ	900	KO
VX51RJZ	901	KO
YN51MKV	4989	NE
YN51MKX	4990	NE
YT51EBF	907	KO
EJ02KYY	289	HD
EX02RYR	290	HD
GP02DPV	3751	SC
HJ02WDE	2610	SC
HJ02WDF	2611	SC
LB02YWX	510	HD
LB02YWY	511	HD
LB02YXA	512	HD
LB02YXE	513	HD
LB02YXF	514	HD
LG02KHT	WVL18	LN
LG02KHX	WVL22	LN
LG02KJA	WVL25	LN
LG02KJF	WVL27	LN
LT02NUK	DMN1	LN
LT02NUM	DMN7	LN
LT02NUO	DMN8	LN
LT02NUP	DMN9	LN
LT02NUV	DMN11	LN
LT02NVE	DMN12	LN
LT02NVH	DMN15	LN
LT02NVU	DMN16	LN
LT02ZDR	142	LN
LY02OAE	906	TA
LY02OBK	907	TA
MV02ULK	7031	SC
MV02ULL	7032	SC
MV02ULM	7033	SC
MV02UMJ	7034	SC
MV02UMK	7035	SC
MV02UML	7036	SC
MV02UMO	7038	SC
MV02UMR	7039	SC
MV02UMS	7040	SC
MV02UMT	7041	SC
MV02UMU	7042	SC
MV02UMW	7043	SC
MV02UMX	7044	SC
PJ02PYU	3968	NE
PJ02PYW	3970	NE
PJ02PYX	3971	NE
PJ02PYZ	3973	NE
PJ02PZA	3974	NE
PJ02PZB	3975	NE
PJ02PZC	3976	NE
PJ02PZD	3977	NE
PJ02PZL	3983	NE
PJ02RCF	PVL282	LN
PJ02RCU	PVL284	LN
PJ02REU		HD
PJ02RFE	PVL296	LN
PK02RDU	482	PL
PK02RDY	483	PL
PK02RDY	485	PL
PK02RDZ	484	PL
PK02RFE	487	PL
PK02RFF	480	PL
PK02RFJ	486	PL
PK02RFL	481	PL
PN02XBL	PVL263	LN
PN02XBO	PVL265	LN
PN02XBX	401	PL
PN02XCE	403	PL
PN02XCG	404	PL
PN02XCH	405	PL
PN02XCL	3967	NE
VU02TTK	3752	SC
YR02ZKV	7315	SC
YR02ZKW	7316	SC
YR02ZYK	4991	NE
YR02ZYM	4992	NE
YU02GHA	9016	HD
YU02GHD	9017	HD
YU02GHN	9018	KO
CE52UXC	3778	SC
CE52UXD	3779	SC
GU52HKA	53	PL
GU52HKB	54	PL
HW52EPN	1993	SC
HW52EPO	1994	SC
HW52EPP	1995	SC
HW52EPU	1996	SC
HW52EPV	1997	SC
LF52ZLZ	WVL102	LN
LF52ZMU	WVL104	LN
LF52ZNE	WVL93	LN
LF52ZNG	WVL94	LN
LF52ZNH	WVL95	LN
LF52ZNJ	WVL96	LN
LF52ZNR	WVL83	LN
LF52ZNY	WVL90	LN
LF52ZPE	WVL75	LN
LF52ZPK	WVL79	LN
LT52WUM	DMN17	LN
LT52WUP	DMN13	LN
LT52WUR	DMN18	LN
NL52WVM	4956	NE
NL52WVN	4957	NE
NL52WVO	4958	NE
NL52WVP	4959	NE
NL52WVR	4960	NE
NL52WVS	4961	NE
NL52WVT	4962	NE
NL52WVU	4963	NE
NL52WVV	4964	NE
NL52WVW	4965	NE
VU52UES	3753	SC
WJ52GNY	60	PL
WJ52GNZ	61	PL
WJ52GOA	62	PL
WJ52GOC	63	PL
WJ52GOE	64	PL
WJ52GOH	65	PL
WJ52GOK	66	PL
WU52YWE	201	SC
WU52YWF	202	SC
WU52YWG	203	SC
WU52YWH	204	SC
WU52YWL	207	SC
WU52YWM	208	SC
WV52HTT	7093	SC
YG52CMF	3412	SC
YP52CTO	6513	MB
YR52VFK	9019	KO
BJ03FHZ	5129	SC
EU03BZK	252	CH
GX03SSU	6122	NE
GX03SSV	616	BH
GX03SSZ	3995	NE
GX03STZ	3996	NE
GX03SUA	6136	NE

Callsign	No.	Reg
GX03SUH	6123	NE
GX03SUU	6124	NE
GX03SUV	6125	NE
GX03SUY	6126	NE
GX03SVA	6127	NE
GX03SVC	6128	NE
GX03SVD	6129	NE
GX03SVE	6130	NE
GX03SVF	6137	NE
GX03SVG	6138	NE
GX03SVJ	6139	NE
LX03ECV	WVL119	LN
LX03ECW	WVL120	LN
LX03ECY	WVL121	LN
LX03EDV	WVL111	LN
LX03EEF	WVL114	LN
LX03EEG	WVL115	LN
LX03EEJ	WVL117	LN
LX03EEM	WVL118	LN
LX03OJN	6321	MB
LX03OJP	6320	MB
MX03YDD	3754	SC
SN03LDK	3311	SC
SN03LDL	3312	SC
SN03LDU	3313	SC
SN03WLU	7209	MB
SN03WMG	214	LN
SN03WMK	215	LN
SN03YBA	PHD271	LN
SN03YCK	286	LN
SN03YCL	6287	MB
SN03YCM	6288	MB
SN03YCT	6289	MB
WA03BHW	67	PL
WA03BHX	68	PL
WA03BHY	69	PL
WA03CRV	5130	SC
WX03YFD	209	SC
WX03YFE	210	SC
YN03UWU	6531	MB
YN03WRJ	462	KO
EU53PYJ	DP201	LN
GX53WDA	838	OX
GX53WYV	837	OX
LK53KVY	VC1	LN
LK53KVZ	VC5	LN
LK53KWE	VC2	LN
LX53AZN	WVL137	LN
LX53BAO	WVL159	LN
LX53BGE	WVL153	LN
MX53FDM	904	KO
MX53FDO	905	KO
MX53FDP	903	KO
MX53FEF	3716	SC
NK53TKY	559	NE
NK53UNT	4967	NE
NK53UNV	4969	NE
NK53UNX	4971	NE
NK53UNZ	4973	NE
NK53UOA	4974	NE
NK53UOB	4975	NE
NK53UOC	4976	NE
PJ53NKC	903	TA
PJ53NKO	9015	KO
PJ53SOE	PVL362	LN
PJ53SOH	PVL363	LN
PJ53SOU	PVL364	LN
PJ53SRU	PVL370	LN
YN53RYC	6474	MB
YN53RYF	6476	MB
YN53RYK	6478	MB
YN53RYP	1500	CH
YN53RZC	6490	MB
YN53RZE	6492	MB
YN53RZZ	6493	MB
AU04JKN	906	KO
EU04BVF	253	HD
NK04FPA	3414	SC
NK04UTJ	103	SC
NK04UTL	104	SC
WX04CZH	212	SC
WX04CZJ	213	SC
WX04CZK	214	SC
YN04AOM	637	BH
YN04AOO	638	BH
YN04AOP	639	BH
YN04AOR	640	BH
YN04AOT	641	BH
YN04AOU	642	BH
YN04AOV	643	BH
YN04AOW	644	BH
YN04AOX	645	BH
YN04AOY	646	BH
YN04GHF	7175	SC
YN04GHV	7180	SC
YN04GJE	6131	NE
YN04GJF	6132	NE
YN04GJG	6133	NE
YN04GJJ	6140	NE
YN04GJK	623	BH
YN04GJU	6134	NE
YN04GJV	6135	NE
YN04GJX	631	BH
YN04GJY	6141	NE
YN04GJZ	6142	NE
YN04GKA	6143	NE
YN04GKC	629	BH
YN04GKD	630	BH
YN04GKE	632	BH
YN04GKF	633	BH
YN04GKG	634	BH
YN04GKJ	635	BH
YN04GKK	636	BH
YN04LWP	902	KO
HF54HFR	2203	SC
HF54HFT	2204	SC
HF54HFU	2205	SC
HF54HFV	2206	SC
HF54HFW	2207	SC
HF54HFX	2208	SC
HF54HFY	2209	SC
HF54HGD	2213	SC
HF54HHC	2228	SC
HF54KXT	1821	SC
HF54KXU	1822	SC
HF54KXV	1823	SC
HF54KXW	1824	SC
HW54BTU	3314	SC
HW54BTY	3317	SC
HW54BUF	3321	SC
HW54DBZ	3328	SC
HW54DCE	3329	SC
HW54DCF	3361	SC
HW54DCO	3362	SC
HW54DCU	3363	SC
LX54GYV	PVL406	LN
LX54GYW	PVL407	LN
LX54GYY	PVL408	LN
LX54GYZ	PVL409	LN
LX54GZB	PVL410	LN
LX54GZC	PVL411	LN
LX54GZD	PVL412	LN
LX54GZE	PVL413	LN
LX54GZF	PVL414	LN
LX54GZG	PVL396	LN
LX54GZH	PVL397	LN
LX54GZK	PVL398	LN
LX54GZL	PVL399	LN
LX54GZM	PVL400	LN
LX54GZN	PVL401	LN
LX54GZO	PVL402	LN
LX54GZP	PVL403	LN
LX54GZR	PVL404	LN
LX54GZT	PVL405	LN
LX54GZU	PVL415	LN
LX54GZV	PVL416	LN
LX54GZW	PVL417	LN
LX54GZY	PVL418	LN
LX54GZZ	PVL419	LN
LX54HAA	PVL390	LN
LX54HAE	PVL391	LN
LX54HAO	PVL392	LN
LX54HAU	PVL393	LN
LX54HBA	PVL394	LN
LX54HBB	PVL395	LN
NK54DEU	3701	SC
NK54DFC	3703	SC
NK54DFD	3704	SC
NK54NUH	4978	NE
NK54NUJ	4979	NE
NK54NUM	4980	NE
NK54NUO	4981	NE
NK54NUP	4982	NE
NK54NUU	5201	NE
NK54NUV	5202	NE
NK54NUW	5203	NE
NK54NUX	5204	NE
NK54NUY	5205	NE
NK54NVA	5206	NE
NK54NVB	5207	NE
NK54NVC	5208	NE
NK54NVD	5209	NE
NK54NVE	5210	NE
NK54NVF	5211	NE
NK54NVG	5212	NE
NK54NVH	5213	NE
NK54NVJ	5214	NE
NK54NVL	5215	NE
NK54NVM	5216	NE
NK54NVN	5217	NE
NK54NVO	5218	NE
NK54NVP	5219	NE
NK54NVT	5220	NE
NK54NVU	5221	NE
NK54NVV	5222	NE
NK54NVW	5223	NE
NK54NVX	5224	NE
NK54NVY	5225	NE
NK54NVZ	5226	NE
NK54NWA	5227	NE
NK54NWB	5228	NE
SN54GRK	256	LN
WA54JVV	72	PL
WA54JVW	73	PL
WA54JVX	74	PL
WA54JVY	75	PL
WA54JVZ	76	PL
WA54JWC	77	PL
WA54JWD	78	PL
WA54JWE	79	PL
YN54AFK	1001	SC
YN54AFX	1002	SC
YN54AJX	6496	MB
EU05AUR	254	HD
EU05AUT	255	HD
EU05CLJ	470	HD
HF05GGE	1825	SC
HF05GGJ	1826	SC
HF05GGK	1827	SC
HF05GGO	1828	SC
HF05GGP	1829	SC
HF05GGU	1830	SC
HF05GGV	1831	SC
HF05GGX	1832	SC
HF05GGY	1833	SC
HF05HXE	2236	SC
HF05HXH	2238	SC
LX05EXZ	256	PL
LX05EYP	250	PL
LX05EYR	LDP264	LN
LX05EYS	253	PL
LX05EYU	254	PL
LX05EYV	251	PL
LX05EYW	255	PL
LX05EYY	252	PL
LX05EYZ	WVL203	LN
LX05EZA	WVL204	LN
LX05EZB	WVL205	LN
LX05EZC	WVL206	LN
LX05EZD	WVL207	LN
LX05EZE	WVL208	LN
LX05EZF	WVL209	LN
LX05EZG	WVL210	LN
LX05EZH	WVL211	LN
LX05EZK	515	KO
LX05EZL	516	KO
LX05EZM	WVL195	LN
LX05EZN	WVL196	LN
LX05EZO	WVL197	LN
LX05EZP	WVL198	LN
LX05EZR	517	HD
LX05EZS	WVL200	LN
LX05EZT	WVL201	LN
LX05EZU	WVL202	LN
LX05EZV	WVL190	LN
LX05EZW	518	KO
LX05EZZ	519	KO
LX05FBC	WVL189	LN
LX05FBY	937	TT
MX05ELH	404	KO
NK05GZO	3941	NE
NK05GZP	3942	NE
SF05KWM	7071	SC
SF05XEC	VC4	LN
UK05BCL	VC3	LN
YJ05PXM	8201	SC
YJ05PXN	8202	SC
YJ05XMR	3722	SC
YN05GZH	649	BH
YN05GZJ	650	BH
YN05GZK	647	BH
YN05GZM	648	BH
YN05GZO	652	BH
YN05HCA	7546	MB
YN05HCC	7547	MB
YN05HCD	7548	BH
YN05HCE	7549	BH
YN05HCF	6550	MB
YN05HCG	6551	MB
YN05HFF	460	KO
YN05HFG	461	KO
YN05HFH	458	KO
YN05HFJ	459	KO
AF55OXF	839	OX
BF55OXF	840	OX
BX55FYH	1	CH
BX55FYJ	2	CH
CF55OXF	841	OX
DF55OXF	842	OX
EF55OXF	843	OX
EU55BWC	256	HD
FF55OXF	844	OX
FJ55BXV	7847	SC
FJ55BXY	7849	SC
FJ55BXZ	7846	SC
GF55OXF	845	OX
HF55JYY	2401	SC
HF55JYZ	2402	SC
HF55JYZ	2403	SC
HF55JZA	2404	SC
HF55JZC	2405	SC
HF55JZD	2406	SC
HF55JZE	2407	SC
HF55JZG	2408	SC
HF55JZJ	2409	SC
HF55JZK	2410	SC
HF55JZL	2411	SC
HF55OXF	846	OX
JF55OXF	847	OX
KF55OXF	848	OX
LA55WWN	7092	NE
LX55EAC	WHY2	LN
LX55EAE	WHY3	LN
LX55EAF	WHY4	LN
LX55EAG	WHY5	LN
LX55EAJ	WHY6	LN
NK55OLG	5229	NE
NK55OLH	5230	NE
NK55OLJ	5231	NE
NK55OLM	5232	NE
NK55RUV	618	NE
NK55RUW	619	NE
PE55WPP	3351	SC
PE55WSU	3352	SC
PO55NXU	55	TA
WJ55HLG	80	PL
WJ55HLH	81	PL
WJ55HLK	82	PL
WJ55HLM	83	PL
WJ55HLN	84	PL
WJ55HLO	85	PL
WJ55HLP	86	PL
WJ55HLR	87	PL
YJ55BLX	414	KO
YM55SXO	6619	MB
YM55SXP	6620	MB
YM55SXR	6621	MB
YN55NFA	663	BH
YN55NFC	6145	NE
YN55NFD	665	BH
YN55NFF	655	BH
YN55NFG	666	BH
YN55NFH	657	BH
YN55NFJ	662	BH
YN55NFK	658	BH
YN55NFL	659	BH
YN55NFM	660	BH
YN55NFO	656	BH
YN55NFP	1091	SC
YN55NHD	371	SC
YN55NHE	372	SC
YN55NHG	373	SC
YN55NHH	374	SC
YN55NHJ	375	SC
YN55NHK	376	SC
YN55NHL	377	SC
YN55NHM	378	SC
YN55NHO	379	SC
YN55PWJ	6552	MB
YN55PWK	6553	MB
YN55PWL	6554	MB
YN55PWO	6555	MB
YN55PWU	6556	MB
YN55PWW	6557	MB
YN55PWX	6558	MB
YN55PZC	801	CH
YN55PZD	802	CH
YN55PZE	803	CH
YN55PZF	804	CH
YN55PZG	805	CH
YN55PZH	806	CH
YN55PZJ	807	CH
YN55PZL	808	CH
YN55PZM	809	CH
YN55PZO	810	CH
YN55PZP	811	CH
YN55PZR	812	HD
YN55PZU	813	HD
YN55PZV	814	HD
YN55PZW	815	HD
YN55PZX	816	HD
YN55WSV	VC6	LN
EU06KCX	291	HD
EX06AYD	7952	SC
HF06FTO	2421	SC

Call	Code	Reg	Call	Code	Reg	Call	Code	Reg	Call	Code	Reg	Call	Code	Reg
HF06FTP	2422	SC	LX06EZK	LDP294	LN	YN06SZY	669	BH	VF56OXF	857	TT	LX07BYH	E57	LN
HF06FTT	2423	SC	LX06EZL	E16	LN	YN06SZZ	670	BH	WA56HHN	135	PL	LX07BYP	ED24	LN
HF06FTU	2424	SC	LX06EZN	E18	LN	AE56OUO	ED15	LN	WA56HHO	133	PL	LX07BYU	ED28	LN
HF06FTV	2425	SC	LX06EZO	E19	LN	EU56FLM	257	HD	WA56HHP	134	PL	MX07NSV	3708	SC
HF06FTY	2427	SC	LX06EZP	E20	LN	EU56FLN	258	HD	WA56OZM	88	PL	NK07KPG	5275	NE
HF06FTZ	2428	SC	LX06EZR	E21	LN	EU56FLP	259	HD	WA56OZO	89	PL	NK07KPJ	5276	NE
HF06FUA	5337	NE	LX06EZS	E22	LN	LF56OXF	849	TT	WA56OZP	90	PL	NK07KPL	5277	NE
HF06FUB	5338	NE	LX06EZT	E23	LN	LX56ETD	E40	LN	WA56OZR	91	PL	NK07KPN	5278	NE
HX06EZB	2433	SC	LX06EZZ	LDP292	LN	LX56ETE	E41	LN	WA56OZS	92	PL	NK07KPO	5279	NE
HX06EZC	2434	SC	LX06FBF	WVL256	LN	LX56ETF	E42	LN	WA56OZT	93	PL	NK07KPP	5280	NE
HX06EZD	2435	SC	LX06FKL	E36	LN	LX56ETJ	E43	LN	WA56OZU	94	PL	NK07KPR	5281	NE
HX06EZE	2436	SC	LX06FKM	E37	LN	LX56ETK	E44	LN	WF56OXF	858	TT	NK07KPT	5282	NE
HX06EZG	2438	SC	LX06FKN	E38	LN	LX56ETL	E45	LN	YF56OXF	859	TT	NK07KPU	5283	NE
HX06EZH	2439	SC	LX06FKO	E39	LN	LX56ETO	E46	LN	YJ56WUE	805	CA	SK07DZM	SE18	LN
LX06DYS	WVL212	LN	MX06YXU	406	KO	LX56ETR	E47	LN	YJ56WVA	407	KO	SK07DZN	SE19	LN
LX06DYT	WVL213	LN	NK06JXC	3964	NE	LX56ETT	E48	LN	YJ56WVB	408	KO	SK07DZO	SE20	LN
LX06DYW	WVL216	LN	NK06JXD	3963	NE	LX56ETU	E49	LN	YJ56WVT	807	OX	SK07HLO	SEN38	LN
LX06DYY	WVL217	LN	PF06ENL	370	PL	LX56ETV	E50	LN	YN56FDK	935	LN	YJ07JTX	3415	SC
LX06DZB	WVL219	LN	PF06ENM	371	PL	LX56ETY	E51	LN	YN56FDO	6938	MB	YJ07JTY	3416	SC
LX06DZE	WVL222	LN	PF06ENN	372	PL	LX56ETZ	E52	LN	YN56FDP	6939	MB	YN07EXF	947	LN
LX06DZG	WVL224	LN	PF06ENO	373	PL	LX56EUA	E53	LN	YN56FEF	945	LN	YN07EXG	948	LN
LX06DZH	WVL225	LN	SN06BNA	E1	LN	LX56EUB	E54	LN	YN56FEG	946	LN	YN07EXH	949	LN
LX06DZJ	WVL226	LN	SN06BNB	E2	LN	LX56EUC	E55	LN	YN56FFA	901	BH	YN07EXK	950	LN
LX06DZL	WVL228	LN	SN06BND	E3	LN	LX56EUD	E56	LN	YN56FFB	902	BH	YN07EXM	951	LN
LX06DZN	WVL230	LN	SN06BNE	E4	LN	MF56OXF	850	TT	YN56FFC	903	BH	YN07EXO	952	LN
LX06DZO	WVL231	LN	SN06BNF	E5	LN	NG56HGO	7943	SC	YN56FFD	904	BH	YN07EZB	451	KO
LX06DZP	WVL232	LN	SN06BNJ	E6	LN	NK56KHB	5234	NE	YN56FFE	905	BH	YN07LFU	450	KO
LX06DZR	WVL233	LN	SN06BNK	E7	LN	NK56KHC	5235	NE	YN56FFG	906	BH	YN07LKF	6559	MB
LX06DZS	WVL234	LN	SN06BNL	E8	LN	NK56KHD	5236	NE	YN56FFH	907	BH	YN07LKG	6560	MB
LX06DZT	WVL235	LN	SN06BNO	E9	LN	NK56KHE	5237	NE	YN56FFJ	908	BH	YN07UOF	673	BH
LX06DZV	WVL237	LN	SN06BNU	E10	LN	NK56KHF	5238	NE	YN56FFK	909	BH	YN07UOG	674	BH
LX06DZW	WVL238	LN	SN06BNV	E11	LN	NK56KHG	5239	NE	YN56FFL	910	BH	YN07UOT	671	BH
LX06DZY	WVL239	LN	SN06BNX	E12	LN	NK56KHH	5240	NE	YN56FFM	911	BH	YN07UOU	672	BH
LX06DZZ	WVL240	LN	SN06BNY	E13	LN	NK56KHL	5241	NE	YN56FFO	912	BH	AF57OXF	860	TT
LX06EAA	WVL241	LN	SN06BNZ	E14	LN	NK56KHL	5242	NE	YN56FFP	913	BH	AO57BDY	952	KO
LX06EAC	933	TT	SN06BOF	E15	LN	NK56KHM	5243	NE	YN56FFR	914	BH	AO57EZL	551	KO
LX06EAE	934	TT	WX06JXR	503	SC	NK56KHO	5244	NE	YN56FFS	915	BH	AO57EZM	550	KO
LX06EAF	935	TT	WX06JXS	504	SC	NK56KHP	5245	NE	YN56FFT	916	BH	AO57HCC	553	KO
LX06EAG	936	TT	WX06JXT	505	SC	NK56KHR	5246	NE	YN56FFU	917	BH	AO57HCD	852	HD
LX06EAJ	WVL246	LN	WX06JYA	509	SC	NK56KHT	5247	NE	YN56FFV	918	BH	BD57WCZ	802	KO
LX06EAK	WVL247	LN	WX06JYB	508	SC	NK56KHV	5249	NE	AU07KMK	951	KO	BD57WDA	800	KO
LX06EAM	WVL248	LN	WX06JYC	507	SC	NK56KHW	5250	NE	AU07KMM	950	KO	BD57WDC	105	BH
LX06EAO	WVL249	LN	WX06JYD	502	SC	NK56KHX	5251	NE	EU07GVY	615	HD	BD57WDE	106	BH
LX06EAP	WVL250	LN	WX06JYE	506	SC	NK56KHY	5252	NE	GN07AUY	6730	MB	BD57WDK	107	BH
LX06EAY	WVL252	LN	YJ06FXW	962	OX	NK56KHZ	5253	NE	GN07AVR	6725	MB	BD57WDL	108	BH
LX06EBA	WVL253	LN	YJ06FYB	3755	SC	NK56KJA	5254	NE	GN07AVT	6726	MB	BD57WDM	109	BH
LX06EBC	WVL254	LN	YJ06FYC	3756	SC	NK56KJE	5255	NE	GN07AVU	6727	MB	BD57WDN	110	BH
LX06EBD	WVL255	LN	YJ06FYD	3757	SC	NK56KJF	5256	NE	GN07AVV	6728	MB	BD57WDP	111	BH
LX06EBG	WVL257	LN	YJ06FYE	3758	SC	NK56KJJ	5257	NE	GN07AVW	6729	MB	BD57WDR	112	BH
LX06EBJ	WVL258	LN	YJ06FZK	415	KO	NK56KJN	5258	NE	HW07CXR	2451	SC	BD57WDS	113	BH
LX06EBK	WVL259	LN	YN06JWD	1011	SC	NK56KJO	5259	NE	HW07CXS	2452	SC	BD57WDT	114	BH
LX06EBL	WVL260	LN	YN06JWE	1012	SC	NK56KJU	5260	NE	HW07CXT	2453	SC	BF57OXF	861	TT
LX06EBM	WVL261	LN	YN06JWG	1013	SC	NK56KJV	5261	NE	HW07CXU	2454	SC	BL57OXJ	125	BH
LX06EBN	WVL262	LN	YN06JWJ	1014	SC	NK56KJX	5262	NE	HW07CXV	2455	SC	BL57OXK	119	BH
LX06EBO	WVL263	LN	YN06JWM	1015	SC	NK56KJY	5263	NE	HW07CXX	2456	SC	BL57OXM	130	BH
LX06EBP	WVL264	LN	YN06JWO	1016	SC	NK56KJZ	5264	NE	HW07CXY	2457	SC	BL57OXN	129	BH
LX06EBU	WVL265	LN	YN06JWU	1017	SC	NK56KKA	5265	NE	LX07BXH	SE1	LN	BL57OXP	126	BH
LX06EBV	WVL266	LN	YN06JWV	1018	SC	NK56KKB	5266	NE	LX07BXJ	SE2	LN	BP57UYE	120	BH
LX06EBZ	WVL267	LN	YN06JWW	1019	SC	NK56KKC	5267	NE	LX07BXK	SE3	LN	BP57UYF	121	BH
LX06ECA	WVL268	LN	YN06JWX	1020	SC	NK56KKD	5268	NE	LX07BXL	SE4	LN	BP57UYG	122	BH
LX06ECC	WVL269	LN	YN06JWY	1021	SC	NK56KKE	5269	NE	LX07BXM	SE5	LN	BP57UYH	123	BH
LX06ECD	WVL270	LN	YN06JWZ	1022	SC	NK56KKF	5270	NE	LX07BXN	SE6	LN	BP57UYJ	124	BH
LX06ECF	WVL272	LN	YN06JXT	613	LN	NK56KKG	5271	NE	LX07BXO	SE7	LN	BP57UYK	127	BH
LX06ECN	WHY1	LN	YN06JXU	6615	MB	NK56KKH	5272	NE	LX07BXP	SE8	LN	BP57UYL	128	BH
LX06ECT	E34	LN	YN06JXV	6616	MB	NK56KKJ	5273	NE	LX07BXR	SE9	LN	CF57OXF	862	TT
LX06ECV	E35	LN	YN06JXW	6617	MB	NK56KKL	5274	NE	LX07BXS	SE10	LN	DF57OXF	863	TT
LX06EYY	E24	LN	YN06JXX	6618	MB	OF56OXF	851	TT	LX07BXU	SE11	LN	EF57OXF	864	TT
LX06EYZ	E25	LN	YN06JXY	6623	MB	PF56OXF	852	TT	LX07BXV	SE12	LN	EY57FZE	261	CH
LX06EZA	E26	LN	YN06JXZ	6623	MB	PO56JEJ	56	TA	LX07BXW	SE13	LN	FF57OXF	865	TT
LX06EZB	E27	LN	YN06JYB	1517	HD	PO56JFE	230	LN	LX07BXY	SE14	LN	GF57OXF	866	TT
LX06EZC	E28	LN	YN06JYC	1518	HD	PO56JFF	231	LN	LX07BXZ	SE15	LN	HF57OXF	867	TT
LX06EZD	E29	LN	YN06JYD	819	HD	PO56JFG	232	LN	LX07BYB	SE16	LN	JF57OXF	868	TT
LX06EZE	E30	LN	YN06JYE	1520	HD	RF56OXF	853	TT	LX07BYB	SE17	LN	KF57OXF	869	OX
LX06EZF	E31	LN	YN06NYK	919	BH	SF56OXF	854	TT	LX07BYC	E58	LN	LF57OXF	870	OX
LX06EZG	E32	LN	YN06NYL	920	BH	SN56AWX	1851	SC	LX07BYD	E59	LN	LK57EJN	EN25	LN
LX06EZH	E33	LN	YN06SZW	667	BH	TF56OXF	855	TT	LX07BYF	E60	LN	LK57EJO	EN26	LN
LX06EZJ	LDP293	LN	YN06SZX	668	BH	UF56OXF	856	TT	LX07BYG	E61	LN	LX57CHV	E62	LN

LX57CHY	E63	LN	YN57HPU	954	KO	NK08MYG	5317	NE	HW58ARU	1105	SC	SN58CEU	EN8	LN			
LX57CHZ	E64	LN	YN57HPV	957	KO	NK08MZV	5318	NE	HW58ARX	1106	SC	SN58CEV	EN9	LN			
LX57CJE	E65	LN	YN57HPX	953	KO	NK08MZW	5319	NE	HW58ARZ	1107	SC	SN58CEX	EN10	LN			
LX57CJF	E66	LN	YN57HRA	956	KO	OU08HGM	912	TT	HW58ASO	1108	SC	SN58CEY	EN11	LN			
LX57CJJ	E67	LN	AU08DKL	302	KO	OU08HGN	913	TT	HW58ASU	1109	SC	SN58CFA	EN12	LN			
LX57CJO	E68	LN	AU08DKN	303	KO	OU08HGO	914	CA	HW58ASV	1110	SC	SN58CFD	EN13	LN			
LX57CJU	E69	LN	AU08GLY	959	KO	WA08LDF	136	PL	HW58ASZ	1112	SC	SN58CFE	EN14	LN			
LX57CJV	E70	LN	FJ08KLF	7094	NE	WA08LDJ	137	PL	HW58ATF	1113	SC	SN58CFF	EN15	LN			
LX57CJY	E71	LN	FJ08KLS	7095	NE	WA08LDK	138	PL	HW58ATK	1114	SC	SN58CFG	EN16	LN			
LX57CJZ	E72	LN	FJ08KLU	7096	NE	WA08LDL	139	PL	HW58ATN	1115	SC	SN58CFJ	EN17	LN			
LX57CKA	E73	LN	FJ08KLZ	7098	NE	WA08LDN	140	PL	HW58ATO	1116	SC	WK58EAE	706	NE			
LX57CKC	E74	LN	FJ08KMU	7099	NE	WA08LDU	141	PL	HW58ATP	1117	SC	WK58EAF	707	NE			
LX57CKD	E75	LN	FJ08KMV	7100	NE	WA08LDV	142	PL	LX58CWG	WDL1	LN	WK58EAG	708	NE			
LX57CKE	E76	LN	FJ08KNV	7101	NE	WA08LDX	143	PL	LX58CWK	VE1	LN	WK58EAJ	709	NE			
LX57CKF	E77	LN	FJ08KNW	7102	NE	WA08LDZ	144	PL	LX58CWL	VE2	LN	YN58BCE	51	BH			
LX57CKG	E78	LN	HF08TKY	8102	SC	WA08LEF	145	PL	LX58CWM	VE3	LN	YN58BCF	52	BH			
LX57CKJ	E79	LN	HF08UHS	7101	SC	WA08LEJ	146	PL	LX58CWN	DOE1	LN	YN58BCK	53	BH			
LX57CKK	E80	LN	HF08UHT	502	BH	WX08SXD	517	SC	LX58CWO	DOE2	LN	YN58BCO	54	BH			
LX57CKL	E81	LN	HF08UHU	7103	SC	WX08SXE	518	SC	LX58CWP	DOE3	LN	YN58BCU	55	BH			
LX57CKN	E82	LN	HF08UHV	7104	SC	WX08SXF	519	SC	LX58CWR	DOE4	LN	YN58BCV	56	BH			
LX57CKO	E83	LN	HF08UHW	7105	SC	WX08SXG	521	SC	LX58CWT	DOE5	LN	YN58BCY	57	BH			
LX57CKP	E84	LN	HW08AOP	1101	SC	WX08SXH	522	SC	LX58CWU	DOE6	LN	YN58BNA	562	LN			
LX57CKU	E85	LN	HW08AOR	1102	SC	YN08DFJ	6624	MB	LX58CWV	DOE7	LN	YP58UFV	957	LN			
LX57CKV	E86	LN	HW08AOS	1103	SC	YN08DFK	6625	MB	LX58CWW	DOE8	LN	YP58UGA	6960	MB			
LX57CKY	E87	LN	HW08AOT	1104	SC	YN08DFL	6626	MB	LX58CWY	DOE9	LN	YP58UGB	6961	MB			
LX57CLF	E88	LN	LK08FKX	EN27	LN	YN08DFO	6627	MB	LX58CWZ	DOE10	LN	YP58UGC	6962	MB			
LX57CLJ	E89	LN	LK08FLH	EN18	LN	YN08DFP	6628	MB	LX58CXA	DOE11	LN	YP58UGD	6963	MB			
LX57CLN	E90	LN	LK08FLJ	EN19	LN	YN08DFU	6629	MB	LX58CXB	DOE12	LN	YP58UGE	6964	MB			
LX57CLO	E91	LN	LK08FLL	EN20	LN	YN08DFV	6630	MB	LX58CXC	DOE13	LN	YP58UGF	6965	MB			
LX57CLV	E92	LN	LK08FLM	EN21	LN	YN08DFX	6631	MB	LX58CXD	DOE14	LN	YP58UGG	6966	MB			
LX57CLY	E93	LN	LK08FLN	EN22	LN	YN08DFY	6632	MB	LX58CXE	DOE15	LN	YP58UGH	6967	MB			
LX57CLZ	WHY7	LN	LK08FLR	EN23	LN	YN08DFZ	6633	MB	LX58CXF	DOE16	LN	YP58UGJ	6968	MB			
MX57CAO	3709	SC	LK08FLR	EN24	LN	YN08DMY	SE36	LN	LX58CXG	DOE17	LN	YP58UGK	6969	MB			
MX57CAU	3710	SC	LX08EBP	E94	LN	YN08OAS	561	LN	LX58CXH	DOE18	LN	YP58UGL	6970	MB			
MX57UPC	3776	SC	LX08EBU	E95	LN	YN08OAV	563	LN	LX58CXJ	DOE19	LN	YP58UGM	6971	MB			
MX57UPY	3777	SC	LX08EBV	E96	LN	YN08OAW	564	LN	LX58CXK	DOE20	LN	YP58UGN	6972	MB			
OU57FGV	502	CA	LX08EBZ	E97	LN	YN08OAX	565	LN	LX58CXL	DOE21	LN	YR58RUH	503	BH			
OU57FGX	503	CA	LX08ECA	E98	LN	YN08OAY	566	LN	LX58CXN	DOE22	LN	YR58RUU	504	BH			
OU57FGZ	294	KO	LX08ECC	E99	LN	YN08OAZ	567	LN	LX58CXO	DOE23	LN	YR58SNY	955	LN			
OU57FHA	298	KO	MX08MYV	709	CA	YN08OBP	6953	MB	LX58CXP	DOE24	LN	YR58SNZ	956	LN			
SN57DWG	SE21	LN	MX08MYY	710	CA	YN08OBR	6954	MB	LX58CXR	DOE25	LN	YX58DXC	707	LN			
SN57DWJ	SE22	LN	MX08MZF	3764	SC	AJ58WBG	717	LN	LX58CXS	DOE26	LN	AE09DHG	709	LN			
SN57DWK	SE23	LN	MX08MZJ	3765	SC	AJ58WBK	721	LN	LX58CXT	DOE27	LN	AE09DHJ	715	LN			
SN57DWL	SE24	LN	MX08UZT	300	KO	AU58AKK	960	KO	LX58CXU	DOE28	LN	AE09DHL	720	LN			
SN57DWM	SE25	LN	NK08CFP	5284	NE	AU58AKN	961	KO	LX58CXW	DOE29	LN	AE09DHP	713	LN			
SN57DWO	SE26	LN	NK08CFU	5285	NE	AU58AUV	452	KO	LX58CXW	DOE30	LN	AE09DHU	718	LN			
SN57DWP	SE27	LN	NK08CFV	5286	NE	EU58JCJ	262	HD	LX58CXY	DOE31	LN	AF09OXF	201	OX			
SN57DWU	SE28	LN	NK08CFX	5287	NE	HF58GYW	1118	SC	LX58CXZ	DOE32	LN	BD09ZPR	MEC11	LN			
SN57DWV	SE29	LN	NK08CFZ	5288	NE	HF58GYY	1119	SC	LX58CYA	DOE33	LN	BD09ZPS	MEC12	LN			
SN57DWW	SE30	LN	NK08CGE	5289	NE	HF58GYZ	1120	SC	LX58CYC	DOE34	LN	BD09ZPT	MEC13	LN			
SN57DWX	SE31	LN	NK08CGF	5290	NE	HF58GZA	1121	SC	LX58CYE	DOE35	LN	BD09ZPU	MEC14	LN			
SN57DWY	SE32	LN	NK08CGG	5291	NE	HF58GZB	1122	SC	LX58CYF	DOE36	LN	BD09ZPV	MEC15	LN			
SN57DWZ	SE33	LN	NK08CGO	5292	NE	HF58GZC	1123	SC	LX58CYG	DOE37	LN	BD09ZPW	MEC16	LN			
SN57DXA	SE34	LN	NK08CGU	5293	NE	HF58GZD	1124	SC	LX58DDJ	EH1	LN	BD09ZPX	MEC17	LN			
SN57DXB	SE35	LN	NK08CGV	5294	NE	HF58GZE	1191	SC	LX58DDK	EH2	LN	BD09ZPY	MEC18	LN			
WX57TLN	515	SC	NK08CGX	5295	NE	HF58GZG	1192	SC	LX58DDL	EH3	LN	BD09ZPZ	MEC19	LN			
WX57TLO	516	SC	NK08CGY	5296	NE	HF58GZH	1193	SC	LX58DDN	EH4	LN	BD09ZRA	MEC20	LN			
WX57TLU	512	SC	NK08CGZ	5297	NE	HF58GZJ	1194	SC	LX58DDO	EH5	LN	BD09ZRC	876	CA			
WX57TLV	513	SC	NK08CHC	5298	NE	HF58GZK	1195	SC	MX58AAF	711	CA	BD09ZRE	MEC22	LN			
WX57TLY	511	SC	NK08CHD	5299	NE	HF58GZL	1196	SC	MX58AAJ	712	CA	BD09ZRF	MEC23	LN			
WX57TLZ	514	SC	NK08CHF	5300	NE	HF58GZM	1197	SC	MX58AAN	713	CA	BD09ZRG	MEC24	LN			
YJ57EGX	410	KO	NK08CHG	5301	NE	HF58GZN	1198	SC	MX58ABV	411	KO	BD09ZRJ	MEC25	LN			
YJ57EGY	409	KO	NK08CHH	5302	NE	HF58GZO	1199	SC	MX58KYV	304	KO	BD09ZRK	MEC26	LN			
YN57FYA	677	BH	NK08CHJ	5303	NE	HF58GZP	1125	SC	NK58DVW	5320	NE	BD09ZVT	MEC28	LN			
YN57FYB	679	BH	NK08CHL	5304	NE	HF58HTG	2002	SC	NK58DVY	5322	NE	BD09ZVU	MEC29	LN			
YN57FYC	675	BH	NK08CHN	5305	NE	HF58HTJ	2003	SC	NK58DVZ	5323	NE	BD09ZVV	MEC30	LN			
YN57FYD	676	BH	NK08CHO	5306	NE	HF58HTK	2004	SC	NK58DWA	5324	NE	BD09ZVW	MEC31	LN			
YN57FYE	683	BH	NK08CHV	5307	NE	HF58HTL	2005	SC	NK58DWC	5325	NE	BD09ZVX	MEC32	LN			
YN57FYF	686	BH	NK08CHX	5308	NE	HF58HTN	2006	SC	NK58DWD	5326	NE	BD09ZVY	MEC33	LN			
YN57FYG	687	BH	NK08CHY	5309	NE	HF58HTT	2009	SC	NK58DWE	5327	NE	BD09ZVZ	MEC34	LN			
YN57FYH	688	BH	NK08MXY	5310	NE	HF58HTU	2010	SC	SN58CDY	EN1	LN	BD09ZWA	MEC35	LN			
YN57FYJ	678	BH	NK08MXZ	5311	NE	HF58KCA	1126	SC	SN58CDZ	EN2	LN	BD09ZWB	MEC36	LN			
YN57FYK	680	BH	NK08MYA	5312	NE	HF58KCC	1127	SC	SN58CEA	EN3	LN	BD09ZWC	MEC37	LN			
YN57FYL	681	BH	NK08MYB	5313	NE	HF58KCE	1128	SC	SN58CEF	EN4	LN	BD09ZWE	MEC38	LN			
YN57FYM	682	BH	NK08MYC	5314	NE	HF58KCG	1129	SC	SN58CEJ	EN5	LN	BD09ZWF	MEC39	LN			
YN57FYO	684	BH	NK08MYD	5315	NE	HF58KCJ	1130	SC	SN58CEK	EN6	LN	BD09ZWG	MEC40	LN			
YN57FYP	685	BH	NK08MYF	5316	NE	HF58KCK	1131	SC	SN58CEO	EN7	LN	BD09ZWH	MEC41	LN			

Code	No.	Area
BF09OXF	202	OX
BG09JJK	MEC1	LN
BG09JJL	MEC2	LN
BG09JJU	MEC3	LN
BG09JJV	MEC4	LN
BG09JJX	MEC5	LN
BG09JJY	MEC6	LN
BG09JJZ	MEC7	LN
BG09JKE	MEC8	LN
BG09JKF	MEC9	LN
BG09JKI	MEC10	LN
BP09ONE	3801	SC
BT09GOH	877	CA
BT09GOJ	878	CA
BT09GOK	879	TT
BT09GOP	880	TT
BT09GOU	MEC46	LN
BT09GOX	881	TT
BT09GPE	882	OX
BT09GPF	883	OX
BT09GPJ	MEC50	LN
CF09OXF	203	OX
DF09OXF	204	OX
EF09OXF	205	OX
FF09OXF	206	OX
GF09OXF	207	TT
HF09BJE	1132	SC
HF09BJJ	1133	SC
HF09BJK	1134	SC
HF09BJO	1135	SC
HF09BJU	1136	SC
HF09BJV	1137	SC
HF09BJX	1138	SC
HF09BJY	1139	SC
HF09BJZ	1140	SC
HF09BKA	1141	SC
HF09BVU	1401	SC
HF09BVV	1402	SC
HF09FVR	1410	SC
HF09FVS	1411	SC
HF09FVT	1412	SC
HF09FVW	1403	SC
HF09FVX	1404	SC
HF09FVY	1405	SC
HF09OXF	208	TT
HW09BAA	1152	SC
HW09BBU	1142	SC
HW09BBV	1143	SC
HW09BBX	1144	SC
HW09BBZ	1145	SC
HW09BCE	1146	SC
HW09BCF	1147	SC
HW09BCK	1148	SC
HW09BCO	1149	SC
HW09BCU	1150	SC
HW09BCV	1151	SC
JF09OXF	209	TT
KF09OXF	210	TT
LX09AXU	DOE45	LN
LX09AXV	DOE46	LN
LX09AXW	DOE47	LN
LX09AXY	DOE48	LN
LX09AXZ	DOE49	LN
LX09AYA	DOE50	LN
LX09AYB	DOE51	LN
LX09AYC	DOE52	LN
LX09AYD	DOE53	LN
LX09AYE	DOE54	LN
LX09AYF	SOE1	LN
LX09AYG	SOE2	LN
LX09AYH	SOE3	LN
LX09AYJ	SOE4	LN
LX09AYK	SOE5	LN
LX09AYL	SOE6	LN
LX09AYM	SOE7	LN
LX09AYN	SOE8	LN
LX09AYO	SOE9	LN
LX09AYP	SOE10	LN
LX09AYS	SOE11	LN
LX09AYT	SOE12	LN
LX09AYU	SOE13	LN
LX09AYV	SOE14	LN
LX09AYW	SOE15	LN
LX09AYY	SOE16	LN
LX09AYZ	SOE17	LN
LX09AZA	SOE18	LN
LX09AZB	SOE19	LN
LX09AZC	SOE20	LN
LX09AZD	SOE21	LN
LX09AZF	SOE22	LN
LX09AZG	SOE23	LN
LX09AZJ	SOE24	LN
LX09AZL	SOE25	LN
LX09AZN	SOE26	LN
LX09AZO	SOE27	LN
LX09AZP	SOE28	LN
LX09AZR	SOE29	LN
LX09AZT	SOE30	LN
LX09BXG	DOE38	LN
LX09BXH	DOE39	LN
LX09BXJ	DOE40	LN
LX09BXK	DOE41	LN
LX09BXL	DOE42	LN
LX09BXM	DOE43	LN
LX09BXO	DOE44	LN
LX09BXP	SOE31	LN
LX09BXR	SOE32	LN
LX09BXS	SOE33	LN
LX09EVB	SOE34	LN
LX09EVC	SOE35	LN
LX09EVD	SOE36	LN
LX09EVF	SOE37	LN
LX09EVG	SOE38	LN
LX09EVH	SOE39	LN
LX09EVJ	SOE40	LN
LX09EZU	E100	LN
LX09EZV	E101	LN
LX09EZW	E102	LN
LX09EZZ	E103	LN
LX09FAF	E104	LN
LX09FAJ	E105	LN
LX09FAK	E106	LN
LX09FAM	E107	LN
LX09FAO	E108	LN
LX09FAU	E109	LN
LX09FBA	E110	LN
LX09FBB	E111	LN
LX09FBC	E112	LN
LX09FBD	E113	LN
LX09FBE	E114	LN
LX09FBF	E115	LN
LX09FBG	E116	LN
LX09FBJ	E117	LN
LX09FBK	E118	LN
LX09FBN	E119	LN
LX09FBO	E120	LN
LX09FBU	E121	LN
LX09FBV	E122	LN
LX09FBY	E123	LN
LX09FBZ	E124	LN
LX09FCA	E125	LN
LX09FCC	E126	LN
LX09FCD	E127	LN
LX09FCE	E128	LN
NK09FUP	8294	NE
NK09FUT	8295	NE
NK09FUU	8296	NE
NK09FUV	8297	NE
NK09FUW	8298	NE
NK09FUY	8299	NE
NK09FVA	8300	NE
NK09FVB	8301	NE
NK09FVC	8302	NE
NK09FVE	8304	NE
NK09FVF	8305	NE
NK09FVG	8306	NE
NK09FVH	8307	NE
NK09FVJ	8308	NE
NK09FVL	8309	NE
PB09ONE	3802	SC
PN09EKR	870	LN
PN09EKT	871	LN
PN09EKU	872	LN
PN09EKV	873	LN
PN09EKW	874	LN
PN09EKX	875	LN
PN09EKY	876	LN
PN09ELO	877	LN
PN09ELU	878	LN
PN09ELV	879	LN
PN09ELW	880	LN
PN09ELX	881	LN
PN09EMF	882	LN
PN09EMK	883	LN
PN09EMV	884	LN
PN09EMX	885	LN
PN09ENC	886	LN
PN09ENE	887	LN
PN09ENF	888	LN
PN09ENH	889	LN
PN09ENK	890	LN
PN09ENL	891	LN
PN09ENM	892	LN
PN09ENO	893	LN
YJ09MHY	412	KO
YJ09MHZ	413	KO
YP09HWA	6956	MB
YP09HWB	6955	MB
YP09HWC	6957	MB
YP09HWD	6958	MB
YP09HWE	6973	MB
YP09HWF	6974	MB
YP09HWG	6975	MB
YP09HWH	6976	MB
YP09HWJ	6977	MB
YP09HWK	6978	MB
YP09HWL	6979	MB
YP09HWM	6980	MB
YP09HWN	6981	MB
YP09HWO	6982	MB
YP09HWR	6983	MB
YP09HWS	6959	MB
YP09HWT	6984	MB
YP09HWU	6985	MB
YX09FLP	SEN39	LN
YX09FLW	SEN40	LN
YX09FLZ	SEN41	LN
YX09FMU	SEN42	LN
YX09FMV	SEN43	LN
AE59AWH	418	CA
AE59AWJ	419	CA
BF59NHJ	MEC27	LN
BG59FXA	WWN24	LN
BG59FXB	WWN25	LN
BG59FXC	WWN26	LN
BG59FXD	WWN27	LN
BG59FXE	WWN28	LN
BG59FXF	WWN29	LN
BG59FXH	WWN30	LN
EU59AFF	292	HD
EU59AFJ	293	HD
EU59AYM	263	HD
EU59AYP	264	HD
HF59DMO	1406	SC
HF59DMU	1407	SC
HF59DMV	1408	SC
HF59DMX	1409	SC
HF59FAH	1501	SC
HF59FAJ	1502	SC
HF59FAK	1503	SC
HF59FAM	1504	SC
HF59FAO	1505	SC
HF59FAU	1506	SC
LK59FDE	WWN15	LN
LK59FDF	WWN16	LN
LK59FDG	WWN12	LN
LK59FDJ	WWN17	LN
LK59FDL	WWN18	LN
LK59FDM	WWN19	LN
LK59FDN	WWN20	LN
LK59FDO	WWN21	LN
LK59FDP	WWN22	LN
LK59FDU	WWN23	LN
LK59FDV	WWN4	LN
LK59FDX	WWN5	LN
LK59FDY	WWN6	LN
LK59FDZ	WWN7	LN
LK59FEF	WWN8	LN
LK59FEG	WWN9	LN
LK59FEH	WWN10	LN
LK59FEJ	WWN13	LN
LK59FEM	WWN14	LN
LK59FEO	WWN11	LN
LK59FEP	WWN1	LN
LK59FET	WWN2	LN
LK59FEU	WWN3	LN
LX59CYA	WWL303	LN
LX59CYC	WWL304	LN
LX59CYE	WWL305	LN
LX59CYF	WWL306	LN
LX59CYG	WWL307	LN
LX59CYH	WWL308	LN
LX59CYJ	WWL309	LN
LX59CYK	WWL310	LN
LX59CYL	WWL274	LN
LX59CYO	WWL275	LN
LX59CYP	WWL276	LN
LX59CYS	WWL277	LN
LX59CYT	WWL278	LN
LX59CYU	WWL279	LN
LX59CYV	WWL280	LN
LX59CYW	WWL281	LN
LX59CYY	WWL282	LN
LX59CYZ	WWL283	LN
LX59CZA	WWL284	LN
LX59CZB	WWL285	LN
LX59CZC	WWL286	LN
LX59CZD	WWL287	LN
LX59CZF	WWL288	LN
LX59CZG	WWL289	LN
LX59CZH	WWL290	LN
LX59CZJ	WWL291	LN
LX59CZK	WWL292	LN
LX59CZL	WWL293	LN
LX59CZM	WWL294	LN
LX59CZN	WWL295	LN
LX59CZO	WWL296	LN
LX59CZP	WWL297	LN
LX59CZR	WWL298	LN
LX59CZS	WWL299	LN
LX59CZT	WWL300	LN
LX59CZU	WWL301	LN
LX59CZV	WWL302	LN
LX59CZW	WWL311	LN
LX59CZY	WWL312	LN
LX59CZZ	WWL313	LN
LX59DAA	WWL314	LN
LX59DAO	WWL315	LN
LX59DAU	WWL316	LN
LX59DBO	WWL317	LN
LX59DBU	WWL318	LN
LX59DBV	WWL319	LN
LX59DBY	WWL320	LN
LX59DBZ	WWL321	LN
LX59DCE	WWL322	LN
LX59DCF	WWL323	LN
LX59DCO	WWL324	LN
LX59DCU	WWL325	LN
LX59DCV	WWL326	LN
LX59DCY	WWL327	LN
LX59DCZ	WWL328	LN
LX59DDA	WWL329	LN
LX59DDE	WWL330	LN
LX59DDF	WWL331	LN
LX59DDJ	WWL332	LN
LX59DDK	WWL333	LN
LX59DDN	WWL334	LN
LX59DDN	WWL335	LN
LX59DDO	WWL336	LN
LX59DDU	WWL337	LN
LX59DDV	WWL338	LN
LX59DDY	WWL339	LN
LX59DDZ	WWL340	LN
LX59DEU	WWL341	LN
LX59DFA	WWL342	LN
LX59DFC	WWL343	LN
LX59DFD	WWL344	LN
LX59DFE	WWL345	LN
LX59DFF	WWL346	LN
LX59DFG	WWL347	LN
LX59DFJ	WWL348	LN
LX59DFK	WWL349	LN
PO59KFW	894	LN
PO59KFX	895	LN
PO59KFY	896	LN
PO59KFZ	897	LN
PO59KGA	898	LN
PO59KGE	899	LN
SN59AWW		OX
UK59BCL	505	BH
WK59CWU	710	NE
WK59CWW	711	NE
WK59CWX	712	NE
WK59CWY	713	NE
WK59CWZ	714	NE
WX59GJF	523	SC
WX59GJG	524	SC
WX59GJJ	525	SC
WX59GJK	526	SC
WX59GJO	527	SC
WX59GJU	528	SC
YJ59NNH	697	NE
YT59DYA	958	LN
YT59DYB	959	LN
YT59DYC	960	LN
YT59DYD	961	LN
YT59DYF	962	LN
YT59DYG	963	LN
YT59DYH	964	LN
YT59DYJ	966	LN
YT59DYM	967	LN
YT59DYN	965	LN
YT59DYO	968	LN
YT59DYP	969	LN
YT59DYS	970	LN
YT59DYU	971	LN
YT59DYV	972	LN
YT59DYV	973	LN
YT59SFJ	2101	SC
AF10OXF	212	TT
BF10OXF	213	TT
BJ10VUN	5328	NE
BJ10VUO	5329	NE
BJ10VUP	5330	NE
BJ10VUR	5331	NE
BJ10VUS	5332	NE
BJ10VUT	5333	NE
BJ10VUU	5334	NE
BJ10VUV	5335	NE
BJ10VUW	5336	NE
BK10MGV	440	BH
BV10WWD	WVN31	LN
BV10WWE	WVN32	LN
BV10WWF	WVN33	LN
BV10WWG	WVN34	LN

BV10WVH	WVN35	LN	FJ60KVR	52	OX	YX60EOL	SE53	LN	HG11OXF	307	OX	NK11HJC	8332	NE
BV10WVJ	WVN36	LN	LX60DVY	WWL350	LN	YX60EOO	SE54	LN	HH11OXF	308	OX	NK11HJE	8334	NE
BV10WVK	WVN37	LN	LX60DVZ	WWL351	LN	YX60EOP	SE66	LN	HJ11OXF	309	OX	NK11HJF	8335	NE
BV10WVL	WVN38	LN	LX60DWA	WWL352	LN	YX60EPO	SE62	LN	HK11OXF	310	OX	NK11HJG	8336	NE
BV10WWA	WVN39	LN	LX60DWC	WWL353	LN	YX60EPP	SE64	LN	HL11OXF	311	OX	NK11HJV	8333	NE
BV10WWC	WVN40	LN	LX60DWD	WWL354	LN	YX60EPU	SE65	LN	HM11OXF	312	OX	NK11HJX	8331	NE
BV10WWD	WVN41	LN	LX60DWE	WWL355	LN	YX60FBU	SE69	LN	HN11OXF	313	OX	NK11HKP	8337	NE
BV10WWF	WVN42	LN	LX60DWF	WWL356	LN	YX60FBY	SE70	LN	HP11OXF	314	OX	NK11HKT	8338	NE
BV10WWO	WVN43	LN	LX60DWG	WWL357	LN	YX60FBZ	SE71	LN	HR11OXF	315	OX	SN11BTY	E151	LN
BV10WWP	WVN44	LN	LX60DWJ	WWL358	LN	YX60FCA	SE72	LN	HY11BRD	301	OX	SN11BTZ	E152	LN
BV10WWR	WVN45	LN	LX60DWK	WWL359	LN	YX60FCC	SE73	LN	HY11OXF	317	OX	SN11BUA	E153	LN
CF10OXF	214	CA	LX60DWL	WWL360	LN	YX60FCD	SE74	LN	LX11CVL	WVL386	LN	SN11BUE	E154	LN
DF10OXF	215	CA	LX60DWM	WWL361	LN	YX60FCE	SE75	LN	LX11CVM	WVL387	LN	SN11BUF	E155	LN
EF10OXF	216	CA	LX60DWN	WWL362	LN	YX60FCF	SE76	LN	LX11CVN	WVL388	LN	SN11BUH	E156	LN
EU10AOX	265	HD	LX60DWO	WWL363	LN	YX60FCG	SE77	LN	LX11CVP	WVL390	LN	SN11BUJ	E157	LN
FF10OXF	217	CA	LX60DWP	WWL364	LN	YX60FCL	SE78	LN	LX11CVR	WVL391	LN	SN11BUO	E158	LN
GF10OXF	218	CA	LX60DWU	WWL365	LN	YX60FCM	SE79	LN	LX11CVS	WVL392	LN	SN11BUP	E159	LN
HF10OXF	219	CA	LX60DWV	WWL366	LN	YX60FCO	SE80	LN	LX11CVT	WVL393	LN	SN11BUU	E160	LN
JF10OXF	220	CA	LX60DWW	WWL367	LN	YX60FCP	SE81	LN	LX11CVV	WVL395	LN	SN11BUV	E161	LN
KF10OXF	221	CA	LX60DWY	WWL368	LN	YX60FCU	SE82	LN	LX11CVW	WVL396	LN	SN11BUW	E162	LN
LF10OXF	222	CA	LX60DXF	WWL375	LN	YX60FCV	SE83	LN	LX11CVY	WVL397	LN	SN11FFZ	SE94	LN
LX10AUR	SE38	LN	LX60DXG	WWL376	LN	YX60FCY	SE84	LN	LX11CVZ	WVL398	LN	SN11FGA	SE95	LN
LX10AUT	SE39	LN	LX60DXJ	WWL378	LN	YX60FCZ	SE67	LN	LX11CWA	WVL399	LN	SN11FGC	SE96	LN
LX10AUU	SE40	LN	LX60DXK	WWL379	LN	YX60FDA	SE68	LN	LX11CWM	WVL407	LN	SN11FGD	SE97	LN
LX10AUV	SE41	LN	LX60DXM	WWL380	LN	YX60FSN	SE56	LN	LX11CWN	WVL408	LN	YT11LVE	453	KO
LX10AUW	SE42	LN	LX60DXO	WWL381	LN	YX60FSO	SE58	LN	LX11CWO	WVL409	LN	YT11LVF	454	KO
LX10AUY	SE43	LN	LX60DXP	WWL382	LN	YX60FSP	SE59	LN	LX11CWP	WVL410	LN	YX11CPE	SE85	LN
LX10AVB	SE44	LN	LX60DXR	WWL383	LN	YX60FSS	SE60	LN	LX11CWR	WVL411	LN	YX11CPF	SE86	LN
LX10AVC	SE45	LN	LX60DXS	WWL384	LN	YX60FSU	SE63	LN	LX11CWT	WVL412	LN	YX11CPK	SE87	LN
LX10AVD	SE46	LN	LX60DXT	WWL385	LN	YX60FTZ	154	LN	LX11CWU	WVL413	LN	YX11CPN	SE88	LN
MF10OXF	223	OX	RX60DLY	420	CA	YX60FUH	SEN7	LN	LX11CWV	WVL414	LN	YX11CPO	SE89	LN
NK10GNY	8310	NE	RX60DLZ	421	CA	YX60FUP	SEN11	LN	LX11CWW	WVL415	LN	YX11CPU	SE90	LN
NK10GNZ	8311	NE	RX60DME	422	CA	YX60FUT	SEN12	LN	LX11CWY	WVL416	LN	YX11CPV	SE91	LN
NK10GOA	8312	NE	RX60DMF	423	CA	YX60FUV	155	LN	LX11CWZ	WVL417	LN	YX11CPY	SE92	LN
NK10GOC	8313	NE	RX60FKF	424	CA	YX60FUW	156	LN	LX11CXA	WVL418	LN	YX11CPZ	SE93	LN
NK10GOE	8314	NE	SN60BZA	E129	LN	YX60FUY	157	LN	LX11CXB	WVL419	LN	YX11CTE	731	LN
NK10GOH	8315	NE	SN60BZB	E130	LN	YX60FVA	158	LN	LX11CXC	WVL420	LN	YX11CTF	732	LN
NK10GOJ	8316	NE	SN60BZC	E131	LN	YX60FVB	159	LN	LX11CXD	WVL421	LN	YX11CTK	733	LN
NK10GOP	8317	NE	SN60BZD	E132	LN	YX60FVC	160	LN	LX11DVA	WHY8	LN	AE61EWO	873	CA
NK10GOU	8318	NE	SN60BZE	E133	LN	YX60FVD	161	LN	LX11DVB	WHY9	LN	AE61EWP	874	CA
OF10OXF	224	OX	SN60BZF	E134	LN	YX60FVE	162	LN	LX11DVC	WHY10	LN	AE61EWR	875	CA
PF10OXF	225	OX	SN60BZG	E135	LN	AU11EPE	309	KO	LX11DVF	WHY11	LN	AF61OXF	1	OX
RF10OXF	226	OX	SN60BZH	E136	LN	AU11EPF	308	KO	LX11DVG	WHY12	LN	AN61BUS	456	KO
SF10OXF	227	OX	SN60BZJ	E137	LN	AU11ESG	307	KO	LX11DVH	WHY13	LN	AN61LAN	455	KO
SN10CCV	616	HD	SN60BZK	E138	LN	BJ11XHA	401	BH	LX11FHV	WVL422	LN	AU61AVK	457	KO
SN10CCX	295	HD	SN60BZL	E139	LN	BJ11XHB	402	BH	LX11FHW	WVL423	LN	BF61OXF	2	OX
SN10CCY	296	HD	SN60BZM	E140	LN	BJ11XHC	403	BH	LX11FHY	WVL424	LN	BG61SXS	441	BH
SN10CCZ	297	KO	SN60BZO	E141	LN	BJ11XHD	404	BH	LX11FHZ	WVL425	LN	BL61ACX	WVN47	LN
SN10CEX	604	KO	SN60BZP	E142	LN	BJ11XHE	405	BH	LX11FJA	WVL426	LN	BL61ACY	WVN46	LN
SN10CFD	600	KO	SN60BZR	E143	LN	BJ11XHF	406	BH	LX11FJC	WVL427	LN	BL61ACZ	WVN49	LN
SN10CFE	601	KO	SN60BZS	E144	LN	BJ11XHG	407	BH	LX11FJD	WVL428	LN	BL61ADO	WVN51	LN
SN10CFF	602	KO	SN60BZT	E145	LN	BJ11XHH	408	BH	LX11FJE	WVL429	LN	BL61ADU	WVN48	LN
SN10CFG	603	KO	SN60BZU	E146	LN	BJ11XHK	409	BH	LX11FJF	WVL430	LN	BL61ADV	WVN50	LN
TF10OXF	228	TT	SN60BZV	E147	LN	BJ11XHL	410	BH	LX11FJJ	WVL431	LN	BL61ADX	WVN52	LN
UF10OXF	229	TT	SN60BZW	E148	LN	BJ11XHM	411	BH	LX11FJK	WVL432	LN	BL61ADZ	WVN53	LN
VF10OXF	230	TT	SN60BZX	E149	LN	BJ11XHN	412	BH	LX11FJN	WVL433	LN	BX61DKV	318	PL
WF10OXF	231	TT	SN60BZY	E150	LN	BJ11XHO	413	BH	LX11FJO	WVL434	LN	CF61OXF	3	OX
YJ10MFA	701	NE	WX60EDL	408	SC	BJ11XHP	414	BH	NK11BGZ	6001	NE	DF61OXF	4	OX
YJ10MFE	702	NE	WX60EDO	407	SC	BJ11XHR	415	BH	NK11BHA	6002	NE	EF61OXF	5	OX
YJ10MFF	703	NE	WX60EDP	406	SC	BJ11XHS	416	BH	NK11BHD	6003	NE	FF61OXF	6	OX
YJ10MFK	704	NE	WX60EDR	405	SC	BJ11XHT	417	BH	NK11BHE	6004	NE	FJ61EVX	7051	SC
YJ10MFN	705	NE	WX60EDU	404	SC	BJ11XHU	418	BH	NK11BHF	6005	NE	FJ61EWX	7812	SC
YJ10MFO	698	NE	WX60EDV	403	SC	BJ11XHV	419	BH	NK11BHJ	6006	NE	FJ61EWY	7813	SC
YJ10MFP	699	NE	WX60EEA	402	SC	BJ11XHW	420	BH	NK11BHL	6007	NE	FJ61GZC	7103	NE
YJ10MFU	700	NE	WX60EEB	401	SC	BJ11XHX	421	BH	NK11FXB	8319	NE	FJ61GZD	7104	NE
YX10OCA	EH45	LN	YJ60GGE	MDL1	LN	BX11GVP	317	PL	NK11FXC	8320	NE	GF61OXF	7	OX
FJ60EGY	7113	NE	YJ60KGU	305	KO	FJ11GNP	7806	SC	NK11FXD	8321	NE	HF61FWL	2011	SC
FJ60EHB	7801	SC	YJ60KGV	306	KO	FJ11GNU	7807	SC	NK11FXE	8322	NE	HF61FWM	2012	SC
FJ60EHC	7802	SC	YX60DXT	SE55	LN	FJ11GNV	7808	SC	NK11FXF	8323	NE	JF61OXF	9	OX
FJ60EHD	7803	SC	YX60DXU	SE57	LN	FJ11GNX	7809	SC	NK11FXG	8324	NE	KF61OXF	81	OX
FJ60EHE	7804	SC	YX60DXW	SE61	LN	FJ11GNY	7810	SC	NK11FXH	8325	NE	LF61OXF	44	OX
FJ60EHF	7805	SC	YX60EOE	SE47	LN	FJ11GNZ	7811	SC	NK11GWX	8326	NE	LJ61GVP	WVL455	LN
FJ60HXW	7114	NE	YX60EOF	SE48	LN	HB11OXF	302	OX	NK11GWY	8327	NE	LJ61GVT	WVL456	LN
FJ60HYB	7115	NE	YX60EOG	SE49	LN	HC11OXF	303	OX	NK11HBB	625	NE	LJ61GVW	WHV1	LN
FJ60KVM	7116	NE	YX60EOH	SE50	LN	HD11OXF	304	OX	NK11HBC	8328	NE	LJ61GVX	WHV2	LN
FJ60KVO	7117	NE	YX60EOJ	SE51	LN	HE11OXF	305	OX	NK11HDN	8329	NE	LJ61GVY	WHV3	LN
FJ60KVP	51	OX	YX60EOK	SE52	LN	HF11OXF	306	OX	NK11HDO	8330	NE	LJ61GVZ	WHV4	LN

Reg	No	Area	Reg	No	Area	Reg	No	Area	Reg	No	Area	Reg	No	Area
LJ61GWA	WHV5	LN	LJ61NXD	WVL474	LN	SN61DAU	EH11	LN	YX61BYF	SE110	LN	YX61FZW	SEN37	LN
LJ61GWC	WHV6	LN	LJ61NXE	WVL475	LN	SN61DBO	EH12	LN	YX61BYG	SE111	LN	YX61FZZ	SEN29	LN
LJ61GWD	WVL445	LN	LJ61NXF	WVL476	LN	SN61DBU	EH13	LN	YX61DPF	E238	LN	BF12KWZ	425	BH
LJ61GWE	WVL446	LN	MF61OXF	41	OX	SN61DBV	EH14	LN	YX61DPK	E239	LN	BF12KXA	426	BH
LJ61GWF	WVL447	LN	NK61DBX	626	NE	SN61DBX	EH15	LN	YX61DPN	E240	LN	BF12KXB	424	BH
LJ61GWG	WVL448	LN	NK61DBY	627	NE	SN61DBY	EH16	LN	YX61DPO	E241	LN	BF12KXC	428	BH
LJ61GWK	WVL449	LN	NK61DBZ	628	NE	SN61DBZ	EH17	LN	YX61DPU	E242	LN	BF12KXD	427	BH
LJ61GWL	WVL450	LN	NK61EFY	629	NE	SN61DCE	EH18	LN	YX61DPV	E243	LN	BF12KXE	432	BH
LJ61GWM	WVL451	LN	NK61EGY	630	NE	SN61DCO	EH19	LN	YX61DPY	E244	LN	BF12KXG	431	BH
LJ61GWN	WVL452	LN	NK61FEU	631	NE	SN61DCU	EH20	LN	YX61DPZ	E245	LN	BF12KXH	429	BH
LJ61GWO	WVL453	LN	NK61FEV	632	NE	SN61DCV	E205	LN	YX61DSE	E229	LN	BF12KXJ	430	BH
LJ61GWP	WVL454	LN	NK61FEX	633	NE	SN61DCX	E206	LN	YX61DSO	E230	LN	BF12KXK	434	BH
LJ61GWU	WVL435	LN	NK61FJO	634	NE	SN61DCY	E207	LN	YX61DSU	E231	LN	BF12KXL	433	BH
LJ61GWV	WVL436	LN	NK61FJP	635	NE	SN61DCZ	E208	LN	YX61DSV	E232	LN	BF12KXM	437	BH
LJ61GWW	WVL437	LN	NK61FMD	636	NE	SN61DDA	E209	LN	YX61DSY	E233	LN	BF12KXN	435	BH
LJ61GWX	WVL438	LN	OF61OXF	42	OX	SN61DDE	E210	LN	YX61DSZ	E234	LN	BF12KXO	436	BH
LJ61GWY	WVL439	LN	PF61OXF	43	OX	SN61DDF	E211	LN	YX61DTF	E235	LN	BF12KXP	550	BH
LJ61GWZ	WVL440	LN	RF61OXF	82	OX	SN61DDJ	E212	LN	YX61DTK	E236	LN	BF12KXR	438	BH
LJ61GXA	WVL441	LN	SF61OXF	45	OX	SN61DDK	E213	LN	YX61DTN	E237	LN	BF12KXS	439	BH
LJ61GXB	WVL442	LN	SN61BGE	E173	LN	SN61DDL	E214	LN	YX61DTO	SE148	LN	BF12KXT	551	BH
LJ61GXC	WVL443	LN	SN61BGF	E163	LN	SN61DDO	E215	LN	YX61DTU	SE149	LN	BF12KYX	422	BH
LJ61GXD	WVL444	LN	SN61BGK	E164	LN	SN61DDU	E216	LN	YX61DTV	SE150	LN	BF12KYY	423	BH
LJ61GXE	WHV7	LN	SN61BGO	E165	LN	SN61DDV	E217	LN	YX61DTY	SE151	LN	HF12GVP	2251	SC
LJ61GXF	WHV8	LN	SN61BGU	E166	LN	SN61DDX	E218	LN	YX61DTZ	SE152	LN	HF12GVR	2252	SC
LJ61GXG	WHV9	LN	SN61BGV	E167	LN	SN61DDY	E219	LN	YX61DVA	SE153	LN	HF12GVT	2253	SC
LJ61GXH	WHV10	LN	SN61BGX	E168	LN	SN61DDZ	E220	LN	YX61DVB	SE154	LN	HF12GVU	2254	SC
LJ61GXK	WHV11	LN	SN61BGY	E169	LN	SN61DEU	E221	LN	YX61DVC	SE155	LN	HF12GVV	2255	SC
LJ61GXL	WHV12	LN	SN61BGZ	E170	LN	SN61DFA	E222	LN	YX61DVF	SE156	LN	HF12GVW	2256	SC
LJ61GXM	WHV13	LN	SN61BHA	E171	LN	SN61DFC	E223	LN	YX61DVG	SE157	LN	HF12GVX	2257	SC
LJ61GXN	WHV14	LN	SN61BHD	E172	LN	SN61DFD	E224	LN	YX61DVH	SE158	LN	HF12GVY	2258	SC
LJ61GXO	WHV15	LN	SN61BHE	E174	LN	SN61DFE	E225	LN	YX61DVJ	SE159	LN	HF12GVZ	2259	SC
LJ61GXP	WHV16	LN	SN61BHF	E175	LN	SN61DFF	E226	LN	YX61DVK	SE160	LN	HF12GWA	2260	SC
LJ61NUM	WVL457	LN	SN61BHJ	E176	LN	SN61DFG	E227	LN	YX61DVL	SE161	LN	HF12GWC	2261	SC
LJ61NUO	WVL458	LN	SN61BHK	E177	LN	SN61DFJ	E228	LN	YX61DVM	SE162	LN	HF12GWD	2262	SC
LJ61NUP	WVL459	LN	SN61BHL	E178	LN	TF61OXF	46	OX	YX61DVN	SE163	LN	HF12GWE	2263	SC
LJ61NUU	WVL460	LN	SN61BHO	E179	LN	UF61OXF	322	PL	YX61DVO	SE164	LN	HF12GWG	2264	SC
LJ61NUV	WVL461	LN	SN61BHP	E180	LN	YX61BVY	SE140	LN	YX61DVP	SE165	LN	HF12GWJ	2265	SC
LJ61NUW	WVL462	LN	SN61BHU	E181	LN	YX61BVZ	SE141	LN	YX61DVR	SE166	LN	HF12GWK	2266	SC
LJ61NUX	WVL463	LN	SN61BHV	E182	LN	YX61BWA	SE104	LN	YX61EKF	SE167	LN	HF12GWL	2267	SC
LJ61NUY	WVL464	LN	SN61BHW	E183	LN	YX61BWB	SE105	LN	YX61EKG	SE168	LN	HF12GWM	2268	SC
LJ61NVA	WVL465	LN	SN61BHX	E184	LN	YX61BWC	SE106	LN	YX61EKH	SE169	LN	HF12GWN	2269	SC
LJ61NVB	WVL466	LN	SN61BHY	E185	LN	YX61BWD	SE107	LN	YX61EKJ	SE170	LN	HF12GWO	2270	SC
LJ61NVC	WHV17	LN	SN61BHZ	E186	LN	YX61BWF	SE130	LN	YX61EKK	SE171	LN	HF12GWT	2271	SC
LJ61NVD	WHV18	LN	SN61BJE	E187	LN	YX61BWG	SE131	LN	YX61EKL	SE172	LN	HF12GWU	2272	SC
LJ61NVE	WHV19	LN	SN61BJF	E188	LN	YX61BWH	SE132	LN	YX61EKM	SE173	LN	HF12GWV	2273	SC
LJ61NVF	WHV20	LN	SN61BJJ	E189	LN	YX61BWJ	SE133	LN	YX61EKN	SE174	LN	HF12GWW	2274	SC
LJ61NVG	WHV21	LN	SN61BJK	E190	LN	YX61BWK	SE134	LN	YX61ENC	163	LN	HF12GWX	2275	SC
LJ61NVH	WHV22	LN	SN61BJO	E191	LN	YX61BWL	SE135	LN	YX61ENE	164	LN	HF12GWY	2276	SC
LJ61NVK	WHV23	LN	SN61BJU	E192	LN	YX61BWM	SE136	LN	YX61ENF	165	LN	HF12GWZ	2277	SC
LJ61NVL	WHV24	LN	SN61BJV	E193	LN	YX61BWN	SE137	LN	YX61ENH	166	LN	HF12GXA	2278	SC
LJ61NVM	WHV25	LN	SN61BJX	E194	LN	YX61BWO	SE138	LN	YX61ENJ	167	LN	HF12GXB	2279	SC
LJ61NVN	WHV26	LN	SN61BJY	E195	LN	YX61BWP	SE139	LN	YX61ENK	168	LN	HF12GXC	2280	SC
LJ61NVP	WHV28	LN	SN61BJZ	E196	LN	YX61BWU	SE120	LN	YX61ENL	169	LN	HF12GXD	2281	SC
LJ61NVR	WHV29	LN	SN61BKA	E197	LN	YX61BWV	SE121	LN	YX61ENM	170	LN	HF12GXE	2282	SC
LJ61NVS	WHV30	LN	SN61BKD	E198	LN	YX61BWW	SE122	LN	YX61ENN	171	LN	HF12GXG	2283	SC
LJ61NVZ	WVL487	LN	SN61BKE	E199	LN	YX61BWY	SE123	LN	YX61ENO	172	LN	HF12GXH	2284	SC
LJ61NWA	WVL488	LN	SN61BKF	E200	LN	YX61BWZ	SE124	LN	YX61ENP	173	LN	HF12GXJ	2285	SC
LJ61NWB	WVL489	LN	SN61BKG	E201	LN	YX61BXA	SE125	LN	YX61ENR	174	LN	HF12GXK	2286	SC
LJ61NWC	WVL490	LN	SN61BKJ	E202	LN	YX61BXB	SE126	LN	YX61ENT	175	LN	LJ12CGF	WS1	LN
LJ61NWD	WVL491	LN	SN61BKK	E203	LN	YX61BXC	SE127	LN	YX61ENU	176	LN	LJ12CGG	WS2	LN
LJ61NWE	WVL492	LN	SN61BKL	E204	LN	YX61BXD	SE128	LN	YX61ENV	177	LN	LJ12CGK	WS3	LN
LJ61NWF	WVL493	LN	SN61BKO	SE98	LN	YX61BXE	SE129	LN	YX61ENW	178	LN	LJ12CGO	WS4	LN
LJ61NWG	WVL494	LN	SN61BKU	SE99	LN	YX61BXK	SE142	LN	YX61FYT	SEN21	LN	LJ12CGU	WS5	LN
LJ61NWH	WVL495	LN	SN61BKV	SE100	LN	YX61BXL	SE143	LN	YX61FYU	SEN22	LN	LJ12CGV	WS6	LN
LJ61NWL	WVL477	LN	SN61BKX	SE101	LN	YX61BXM	SE144	LN	YX61FYV	SEN23	LN	LJ12CGX	WS7	LN
LJ61NWM	WVL478	LN	SN61BKY	SE102	LN	YX61BXN	SE145	LN	YX61FYW	SEN24	LN	LJ12CGY	WS8	LN
LJ61NWN	WVL479	LN	SN61BKZ	SE103	LN	YX61BXO	SE146	LN	YX61FYY	SEN25	LN	LJ12CGZ	WS9	LN
LJ61NWO	WVL480	LN	SN61BLJ	EH6	LN	YX61BXP	SE147	LN	YX61FYZ	SEN26	LN	LJ12CHC	WVL469	LN
LJ61NWR	WVL482	LN	SN61BLK	EH7	LN	YX61BXR	SE112	LN	YX61FZA	SEN27	LN	LJ12CHD	WVL481	LN
LJ61NWU	WVL485	LN	SN61BLV	EH8	LN	YX61BXS	SE113	LN	YX61FZB	SEN28	LN	LJ12CHF	WVL483	LN
LJ61NWV	WVL486	LN	SN61CZV	605	KO	YX61BXU	SE114	LN	YX61FZO	SEN30	LN	LJ12CHG	WVL484	LN
LJ61NWW	WVL467	LN	SN61CZW	606	KO	YX61BXV	SE115	LN	YX61FZP	SEN31	LN	LJ12CHH	WHV27	LN
LJ61NWX	WVL468	LN	SN61CZX	607	KO	YX61BXW	SE116	LN	YX61FZR	SEN32	LN	LJ12CHK	WHV31	LN
LJ61NWZ	WVL470	LN	SN61CZY	608	KO	YX61BXY	SE117	LN	YX61FZS	SEN33	LN	NK12GCO	6043	NE
LJ61NXA	WVL471	LN	SN61CZZ	609	KO	YX61BYA	SE119	LN	YX61FZT	SEN34	LN	NK12GCU	6044	NE
LJ61NXB	WVL472	LN	SN61DAA	EH9	LN	YX61BYD	SE109	LN	YX61FZU	SEN35	LN	NK12GCV	6045	NE
LJ61NXC	WVL473	LN	SN61DAO	EH10	LN				YX61FZV	SEN36	LN	NK12GCX	6046	NE

NK12GCY	6047	NE	BF62UXP	449	BH	NK62CZA	6069	NE	LJ13GKA	WS15	LN	YX13BKL	EH37	LN
NK12GCZ	6048	NE	BF62UXR	450	BH	NK62CZL	6070	NE	LJ13GKC	WS16	LN	YX13BKN	EH38	LN
NK12GDA	6049	NE	BF62UXS	451	BH	NK62DWY	640	NE	LJ13GKD	WS17	LN	YY13VKO	189	LN
NK12GDE	6050	NE	BF62UXT	452	BH	NK62EJF	6055	NE	LJ13GKE	WS18	LN	YY13VKP	190	LN
NK12GDF	6051	NE	HW62CAO	1518	SC	NK62EKD	6054	NE	LJ13GKF	WS19	LN	YY13VKR	191	LN
NK12GDJ	6052	NE	HW62CCD	1519	SC	NK62FAA	6071	NE	LJ13GKG	WS20	LN	YY13VKS	192	LN
NK12GDO	6053	NE	HW62CEJ	1520	SC	NK62FBA	6072	NE	LJ13GKK	WS21	LN	BF63HDE	WVL509	LN
NK12HCD	637	NE	HW62CGF	3803	SC	NK62FCC	6073	NE	LJ13GKL	WS22	LN	BF63HDG	WVL510	LN
NK12HCE	638	NE	HW62CGO	3804	SC	NK62FDM	6074	NE	LJ13GKN	WS23	LN	BF63ZPV	7105	NE
NK12HCF	639	NE	HW62CGY	3805	SC	NK62FDN	6075	NE	LJ13GKO	WS24	LN	BF63ZPW	7106	NE
SN12AAE	6734	MB	HW62CHC	3806	SC	NK62FEU	6076	NE	LJ13GKP	WS25	LN	BF63ZPY	7107	NE
SN12AAF	6735	MB	HW62CHZ	3807	SC	NK62FGJ	6077	NE	LJ13GKU	WS26	LN	BF63ZPZ	7108	NE
SN12AAJ	6736	MB	HW62CJE	3808	SC	NK62FHE	6078	NE	LJ13GKV	WS27	LN	BF63ZRA	7109	NE
SN12AAK	6737	MB	HW62CJJ	3809	SC	NK62FHY	6079	NE	LJ13GKX	WS28	LN	BF63ZRC	7110	NE
SN12AAO	6738	MB	HW62CKO	3810	SC	NK62FJE	6080	NE	LJ13GKY	WS29	LN	BF63ZRY	7111	NE
SN12AAU	6739	MB	HW62CKY	3811	SC	NK62FKG	6081	NE	LJ13GKZ	WS30	LN	BF63ZRZ	7112	NE
SN12AUM	SE175	LN	HW62CLV	1525	SC	NK62FLF	6082	NE	LJ13GLF	WS31	LN	BF63ZSO	7052	SC
SN12AUP	SE177	LN	HW62CMK	3812	SC	SN62AVG	610	KO	LJ13GLK	WS32	LN	BF63ZSP	7053	SC
SN12AUR	SE178	LN	HW62CMU	1526	SC	SN62AVO	611	KO	LK13AEJ	6101	MB	BJ63UJA	473	BH
SN12AUT	SE179	LN	HW62CMV	3813	SC	SN62AVR	612	KO	MX13AZV	105	SC	BJ63UJB	474	BH
SN12AUU	SE180	LN	HW62CMY	3814	SC	SN62AVY	613	KO	MX13BBV	106	SC	BJ63UJC	475	BH
SN12AUV	SE181	LN	HW62CMZ	1521	SC	SN62AVZ	614	KO	MX13BBZ	107	SC	BJ63UJD	476	BH
SN12AUW	SE182	LN	HW62CNA	1522	SC	SN62DDE	E261	LN	NK13EJO	6083	NE	BJ63UJE	477	BH
SN12AUX	SE183	LN	HW62CNE	1523	SC	SN62DDO	E262	LN	SN13CJE	E276	LN	BJ63UJF	478	BH
SN12AUY	SE184	LN	HW62CNJ	3815	SC	SN62DDX	E263	LN	SN13CJF	E277	LN	BJ63UJG	479	BH
SN12AVB	SE185	LN	HW62CNK	3816	SC	SN62DFL	E264	LN	SN13CJJ	E278	LN	BJ63UJH	480	BH
SN12AVC	SE186	LN	HW62CNO	3817	SC	SN62DFX	E265	LN	SN13CJO	E279	LN	BJ63UJK	481	BH
SN12AVD	SE187	LN	HW62CNU	1524	SC	SN62DGF	E266	LN	SN13CJU	E280	LN	BJ63UJL	482	BH
SN12AVE	SE188	LN	HW62CNV	3818	SC	SN62DGU	E267	LN	YJ13HNW	691	NE	BJ63UJM	483	BH
SN12AVF	SE189	LN	HW62CPK	3819	SC	SN62DHA	E268	LN	YJ13HNX	692	NE	BJ63UJN	484	BH
SN12AVG	SE190	LN	HW62CVF	1507	SC	SN62DHK	E269	LN	YJ13HNY	693	NE	BJ63UJO	485	BH
SN12AVJ	SE191	LN	HW62CVL	1508	SC	SN62DHZ	E270	LN	YJ13HNZ	694	NE	BJ63UJP	486	BH
SN12AVK	SE192	LN	HW62CVM	1509	SC	SN62DJO	E271	LN	YJ13HOA	695	NE	BJ63UJR	487	BH
SN12AVL	SE193	LN	HW62CVO	1510	SC	SN62DKJ	E272	LN	YJ13HOH	696	NE	BJ63UJS	488	BH
SN12AVO	SE176	LN	HW62CVZ	1511	SC	SN62DLY	E273	LN	YX13AFF	740	LN	BJ63UJT	489	BH
WA12ACJ	100	PL	HW62CWN	1512	SC	SN62DLZ	E274	LN	YX13AFJ	741	LN	BJ63UJU	490	BH
WA12ACO	101	PL	HW62CXK	1513	SC	SN62DMV	E275	LN	YX13AFK	742	LN	BX63BCK	5358	NE
WA12ACU	102	PL	HW62CXR	1514	SC	WX62HFU	705	PL	YX13AFN	743	LN	BX63BCO	5359	NE
WA12ACV	103	PL	HW62CYJ	1515	SC	WX62HGG	713	PL	YX13AFO	744	LN	BX63BCU	5360	NE
WA12ACX	104	PL	HW62CZO	1516	SC	WX62HGU	706	PL	YX13AFU	745	LN	BX63BCV	5361	NE
WA12ACY	105	PL	HW62CZY	1517	SC	WX62HHE	707	PL	YX13AFV	746	LN	BX63BCY	5362	NE
WA12ACZ	106	PL	LJ62KBY	6149	NE	WX62HHF	708	PL	YX13AFY	747	LN	BX63BCZ	5363	NE
WA12ADO	107	PL	LJ62KCU	6150	NE	WX62HHP	709	PL	YX13AFZ	748	LN	BX63BDE	5364	NE
WA12ADU	108	PL	LJ62KDV	6151	NE	YX62DYH	179	LN	YX13AGO	749	LN	BX63BDF	5365	NE
WA12ADV	109	PL	LJ62KDZ	6152	NE	YX62DYN	180	LN	YX13AGU	750	LN	BX63BDO	5366	NE
WX12GDO	416	SC	LJ62KFD	WHV32	LN	YX62DYS	181	LN	YX13AGV	751	LN	BX63BDU	5367	NE
WX12GDU	415	SC	LJ62KFF	WHV33	LN	YX62DZE	182	LN	YX13AGY	752	LN	BX63BDV	5368	NE
WX12GDV	414	SC	LJ62KFU	WHV34	LN	YX62DZN	183	LN	YX13AGZ	753	LN	GB63OXF	61	OX
WX12GDY	413	SC	LJ62KGF	WHV35	LN	YX62DZU	184	LN	YX13AHA	754	LN	GO63OXF	62	OX
WX12GDZ	412	SC	LJ62KGG	WHV36	LN	AU13FBJ	710	PL	YX13AHC	755	LN	HJ63JHV	1527	SC
WX12GEJ	411	SC	LJ62KGN	WHV37	LN	AU13FBK	711	PL	YX13AHD	756	LN	HJ63JHX	1528	SC
YX12FPA	E246	LN	LJ62KGY	WHV38	LN	AU13FBL	712	PL	YX13AHE	757	LN	HJ63JHY	1529	SC
YX12FPC	E248	LN	LJ62KHF	WHV39	LN	BK13NZV	453	BH	YX13AHF	758	LN	HJ63JHZ	1530	SC
YX12FPD	E249	LN	LJ62KHV	WHV40	LN	BK13NZW	454	BH	YX13AHG	759	LN	HJ63JJE	1531	SC
YX12FPE	E250	LN	LJ62KKP	WHV41	LN	BK13NZX	455	BH	YX13AHJ	760	LN	HJ63JJF	1532	SC
YX12FPF	E247	LN	LJ62KLC	6153	NE	BK13NZY	456	BH	YX13AHK	761	LN	HJ63JJK	1533	SC
YX12FPG	E251	LN	LJ62KLS	6154	NE	BK13NZZ	457	BH	YX13AHL	762	LN	HJ63JJL	1534	SC
YX12FPJ	E252	LN	LJ62KOX	6155	NE	BK13OAA	458	BH	YX13AJO	185	LN	HJ63JJO	1535	SC
YX12FPK	E253	LN	LJ62KXX	6156	NE	BK13OAB	459	BH	YX13AJU	186	LN	HJ63JJU	1536	SC
YX12FPL	E254	LN	LJ62KXZ	6157	NE	BK13OAC	460	BH	YX13AJV	187	LN	HJ63JJV	1537	SC
YX12FPN	E255	LN	LJ62KYA	6158	NE	BK13OAD	461	BH	YX13AJY	188	LN	HJ63JJX	1538	SC
YX12FPO	E256	LN	LJ62KYG	6159	NE	BK13OAE	462	BH	YX13BJE	EH21	LN	HJ63JJY	1539	SC
YX12FPP	E257	LN	LJ62KZD	6160	NE	BK13OAG	463	BH	YX13BJF	EH22	LN	HJ63JJZ	1540	SC
YX12FPT	E258	LN	LJ62KZP	6161	NE	BK13OAH	464	BH	YX13BJJ	EH23	LN	HJ63JKE	1541	SC
YX12FPU	E259	LN	NK62CBV	6056	NE	BK13OAJ	465	BH	YX13BJN	EH24	LN	HJ63JKF	1542	SC
YX12FPV	E260	LN	NK62CCV	6057	NE	BK13OAL	466	BH	YX13BJO	EH25	LN	HJ63JKK	1543	SC
AU62DWC	701	PL	NK62CCY	6058	NE	BK13OAM	467	BH	YX13BJU	EH26	LN	HJ63JKN	1544	SC
AU62DWG	702	PL	NK62CEN	6059	NE	BK13OAN	468	BH	YX13BJV	EH27	LN	HJ63JKO	1545	SC
AU62DWL	703	PL	NK62CFN	6060	NE	BK13OAO	469	BH	YX13BJY	EH28	LN	HJ63JKU	1546	SC
AU62DWN	704	PL	NK62CJE	6061	NE	BK13OAP	470	BH	YX13BJZ	EH29	LN	HJ63JKV	1547	SC
BF62UXH	442	BH	NK62CJJ	6062	NE	BK13OAS	471	BH	YX13BKA	EH30	LN	HJ63JKX	1548	SC
BF62UXJ	443	BH	NK62CKC	6063	NE	BK13OAU	472	BH	YX13BKD	EH31	LN	HJ63JKY	1549	SC
BF62UXK	444	BH	NK62CLZ	6064	NE	LJ13GJU	WS10	LN	YX13BKE	EH32	LN	HJ63JKZ	1550	SC
BF62UXL	445	BH	NK62CME	6065	NE	LJ13GJV	WS11	LN	YX13BKF	EH33	LN	HJ63JLO	1551	SC
BF62UXM	446	BH	NK62CYC	6066	NE	LJ13GJX	WS12	LN	YX13BKG	EH34	LN	HJ63JLU	1552	SC
BF62UXN	447	BH	NK62CYE	6067	NE	LJ13GJY	WS13	LN	YX13BKJ	EH35	LN	HJ63JLV	1553	SC
BF62UXO	448	BH	NK62CYF	6068	NE	LJ13GJZ	WS14	LN	YX13BKK	EH36	LN	HJ63JLX	1554	SC

HJ63JMO	1555	SC	NL63XZZ	652	NE	BN14CUG	6002	MB	HF64BTO	1600	SC	BP15OLU	WHV46	LN
HJ63JMU	1556	SC	NL63YAA	5377	NE	BN14CUH	6003	MB	HW64AWZ	2709	SC	BP15OLV	WHV45	LN
HJ63JMV	1557	SC	NL63YAD	5378	NE	BN14CUJ	6004	MB	HW64AXA	2710	SC	BP15OLW	WHV49	LN
HJ63JMX	1558	SC	NL63YAE	5379	NE	BN14CUK	6005	MB	HW64AXB	2711	SC	BP15OLX	WHV50	LN
HJ63JNF	1559	SC	NL63YAF	5380	NE	BN14CUO	6006	MB	HW64AXC	2712	SC	BP15OMA	WHV51	LN
HJ63JNK	1560	SC	NL63YAG	5381	NE	BN14CUU	6007	MB	HW64AXD	2713	SC	BP15OMB	WHV55	LN
HJ63JNL	1561	SC	NL63YAH	5382	NE	BN14CUV	6008	MB	HW64AXF	2714	SC	BP15OMC	WHV53	LN
HJ63JNN	1562	SC	NL63YAJ	5383	NE	BN14CUW	6009	MB	HW64AXG	2715	SC	BP15OMD	WHV60	LN
HJ63JNO	1563	SC	NL63YAK	5384	NE	BN14CUX	6010	MB	HW64AXH	2716	SC	BP15OME	WHV54	LN
HJ63JNU	1564	SC	NL63YAO	5385	NE	BN14CUY	6011	MB	HW64AXJ	2717	SC	BP15OMF	WHV59	LN
HJ63JNV	1565	SC	NL63YAU	5386	NE	BN14CVA	6012	MB	JG64OXF	613	OX	BP15OMJ	WHV57	LN
HJ63JNX	1566	SC	NL63YAV	5387	NE	BN14CVB	6013	MB	LM64OXF	611	OX	BP15OMK	WHV56	LN
HJ63JNZ	1567	SC	NL63YAW	5388	NE	BN14CVC	6014	MB	PK64OXF	610	OX	BP15OML	WHV58	LN
HJ63JOA	1568	SC	NL63YAX	5389	NE	BU14EFS	6015	MB	PS64OXF	609	OX	BX15OMT	921	BH
HJ63JOH	1569	SC	NL63YAY	5390	NE	BU14EFT	6016	MB	RW64OXF	608	OX	BX15OMU	922	BH
HJ63JOU	1570	SC	NL63YBA	641	NE	BU14EHK	6017	MB	SB64OXF	607	OX	BX15OMV	923	BH
HJ63JOV	2287	SC	NL63YCJ	6106	NE	BU14EHL	6018	MB	SC64OXF	606	OX	BX15OMW	924	BH
HJ63JPF	2288	SC	NL63YCK	6107	NE	BX14TJV	WHV111	LN	SM64OXF	605	OX	BX15OMY	925	BH
HW63FGM	1571	SC	NL63YCM	6108	NE	CF14OXF	23	OX	SN64CUC	WS35	LN	BX15ONA	926	BH
HW63FGN	1572	SC	NL63YCN	6109	NE	DF14OXF	24	OX	SN64CUG	WS36	LN	BX15ONB	927	BH
HW63FGO	1573	SC	NL63YCO	6110	NE	EF14OXF	25	OX	SN64CUJ	WS38	LN	BX15ONC	928	BH
HW63FGP	1574	SC	NL63YHN	6085	NE	GB14OXF	601	OX	WA64FZY	319	PL	BX15ONF	929	BH
HW63FGU	1575	SC	NL63YHO	6086	NE	GX14OXF	603	OX	YJ64DZM	9084	NE	BX15ONG	930	BH
HW63FGV	1576	SC	NL63YHP	6087	NE	SU14OXF	604	OX	YX64VOB	2701	SC	BX15ONH	931	BH
HW63FGX	1577	SC	NL63YHR	6088	NE	UK14OXF	602	OX	YX64VOC	2702	SC	BX15ONJ	932	BH
HW63FGZ	1578	SC	NL63YHS	6089	NE	YX14RTV	E281	LN	YX64VOD	2703	SC	BX15ONK	933	BH
HW63FHA	1579	SC	NL63YHT	6090	NE	YX14RTZ	E282	LN	YX64VOF	2704	SC	BX15ONL	934	BH
HW63FHB	1580	SC	NL63YHU	6091	NE	YX14RUA	E283	LN	YX64VOG	2705	SC	BX15ONM	935	BH
HW63FHC	251	TT	NL63YHV	6092	NE	YX14SFE	320	PL	YX64VOH	2706	SC	BX15ONN	936	BH
HW63FHD	252	TT	NL63YHW	6093	NE	YX14SFN	321	PL	YX64VOJ	2707	SC	BX15ONO	937	BH
HW63FHE	253	TT	NL63YHX	6094	NE	YY14WDT	SE198	LN	YX64VOK	2708	SC	BX15ONP	938	BH
HW63FHF	254	TT	NL63YHY	6095	NE	YY14WDU	SE199	LN	YY64GWZ	SE213	LN	BX15ONR	939	BH
HW63FHG	1585	SC	NL63YHZ	6096	NE	YY14WDV	SE200	LN	YY64GXA	SE214	LN	BX15ONS	940	BH
HW63FHH	1586	SC	NL63YJA	6097	NE	YY14WDW	SE201	LN	YY64GXB	SE215	LN	BX15ONT	941	BH
HW63FHJ	1587	SC	NL63YJB	6098	NE	YY14WDX	SE202	LN	YY64GXC	SE216	LN	BX15ONU	942	BH
HW63FHK	1588	SC	NL63YJC	6099	NE	YY14WDZ	SE203	LN	YY64GXD	SE217	LN	BX15ONV	943	BH
HW63FHL	1589	SC	NL63YJD	6100	NE	YY14WEA	SE204	LN	YY64GXE	SE218	LN	BX15ONW	944	BH
HW63FHM	1590	SC	NL63YJE	6101	NE	YY14WEC	SE205	LN	YY64GXF	SE219	LN	HF15BMV	3833	SC
HW63FHN	1591	SC	NL63YJF	6102	NE	YY14WEF	SE206	LN	YY64GXH	SE220	LN	HF15BMY	3834	SC
HW63FHO	1592	SC	NL63YJG	6104	NE	YY14WEH	SE207	LN	YY64GXJ	SE221	LN	HF15BMZ	3835	SC
HW63FHP	1593	SC	NL63YJH	6105	NE	YY14WEJ	SE208	LN	YY64GXK	SE222	LN	NK15EMJ	666	NE
HW63FHR	1594	SC	SK63GAA	417	SC	YY14WEK	SE209	LN	YY64TXH	SE223	LN	NK15EMV	5391	NE
NL63XAZ	5369	NE	TO63OXF	63	OX	YY14WEO	SE210	LN	YY64TXJ	SE224	LN	NK15EMV	5392	NE
NL63XBA	5370	NE	WF63LYA	501	PL	YY14WEP	SE211	LN	YY64TXK	SE225	LN	NK15ENC	5393	NE
NL63XBB	5371	NE	WF63LYB	502	PL	YY14WEU	SE212	LN	YY64TXL	SE226	LN	NK15ENE	5394	NE
NL63XBC	5372	NE	WF63LYC	503	PL	BN64CNO	2289	SC	YY64TXM	SE227	LN	NK15ENF	5395	NE
NL63XBD	5373	NE	WF63LYD	504	PL	BN64CNU	2290	SC	YY64TXN	SE228	LN	NK15ENH	5396	NE
NL63XBE	5374	NE	WF63LYO	505	PL	BN64CSV	2291	SC	YY64TXO	SE229	LN	NK15ENJ	5397	NE
NL63XBF	5375	NE	WF63LYP	506	PL	GA64OXF	612	OX	YY64TXP	SE230	LN	NK15ENL	5398	NE
NL63XBG	5376	NE	WF63LYR	507	PL	GH64OXF	614	OX	YY64TXR	SE231	LN	NK15ENM	5399	NE
NL63XBH	8339	NE	WF63LYS	508	PL	HF64BNN	3822	SC	BG15RNF	6118	NE	NK15ENN	5400	NE
NL63XBJ	8340	NE	WF63LYT	509	PL	HF64BNO	3823	SC	BG15RNJ	6119	NE	NK15ENO	5401	NE
NL63XBK	8341	NE	WF63LYU	510	PL	HF64BNU	3824	SC	BG15RNN	6120	NE	NK15ENP	5402	NE
NL63XBM	8342	NE	WF63LYV	511	PL	HF64BNX	3825	SC	BG15RNO	6121	NE	NK15ENR	5403	NE
NL63XBN	8343	NE	WF63LYW	512	PL	HF64BNY	3826	SC	BJ15TWL	EHV3	LN	NK15ENT	5404	NE
NL63XBO	8344	NE	WF63LYX	513	PL	HF64BNY	3827	SC	BJ15TWP	EHV5	LN	NK15ENU	5405	NE
NL63XBP	8345	NE	WF63LYY	514	PL	HF64BNZ	3828	SC	BJ15TWU	6019	MB	NK15ENV	5406	NE
NL63XBR	8346	NE	WF63LYZ	515	PL	HF64BOH	3829	SC	BJ15TWW	6020	MB	NK15ENW	5407	NE
NL63XBS	6084	NE	WF63LZE	516	PL	HF64BOJ	3830	SC	BK15AZR	EHV1	LN	NK15ENX	5408	NE
NL63XBT	6103	NE	WG63HHV	517	PL	HF64BOU	3831	SC	BK15AZT	EHV2	LN	NK15ENY	5409	NE
NL63XBV	6111	NE	WG63HHW	518	PL	HF64BOV	1601	SC	BL15HBJ	EHV6	LN	NK15EOA	5410	NE
NL63XBW	6112	NE	WG63HHX	519	PL	HF64BPE	1602	SC	BL15HBK	EHV4	LN	NK15EOB	5411	NE
NL63XBX	6113	NE	WG63HHY	520	PL	HF64BPK	1603	SC	BL15HBN	EHV16	LN	NK15EOC	5412	NE
NL63XBY	6114	NE	XS63OXF	65	OX	HF64BPO	1604	SC	BL15HBO	EHV7	LN	NK15EOD	5413	NE
NL63XBZ	6115	NE	YX63ZWW	6763	MB	HF64BPU	2718	SC	BL15HBP	EHV8	LN	NK15EOE	5414	NE
NL63XCA	6116	NE	YX63ZWY	6764	MB	HF64BPV	2719	SC	BL15HBU	EHV9	LN	NK15EOF	5415	NE
NL63XCB	6117	NE	YX63ZWZ	6765	MB	HF64BPX	2720	SC	BL15HBX	EHV10	LN	NK15EOG	5416	NE
NL63XZO	642	NE	YX63ZXA	6766	MB	HF64BPY	2721	SC	BL15HBY	EHV11	LN	NK15EOH	5417	NE
NL63XZP	643	NE	YX63ZXB	6767	MB	HF64BPZ	2722	SC	BL15HBZ	EHV12	LN	NK15EOJ	5418	NE
NL63XZR	644	NE	YX63ZXC	6768	MB	HF64BRV	2723	SC	BL15HCA	EHV13	LN	NK15EOL	5419	NE
NL63XZS	645	NE	YX63ZXD	6769	MB	HF64BRZ	3832	SC	BL15HCC	EHV14	LN	NK15GDE	653	NE
NL63XZT	646	NE	YX63ZXE	6770	MB	HF64BSU	2292	SC	BL15HCD	EHV15	LN	NK15GDJ	655	NE
NL63XZU	647	NE	YX63ZXF	6771	MB	HF64BSV	1595	SC	BP15OLM	WHV43	LN	NK15GDO	656	NE
NL63XZV	648	NE	YX63ZXG	6772	MB	HF64BSX	1596	SC	BP15OLN	WHV42	LN	NK15GEY	657	NE
NL63XZW	649	NE	AF14OXF	21	OX	HF64BSY	1597	SC	BP15OLR	WHV47	LN	NK15GFA	658	NE
NL63XZX	650	NE	BF14OXF	22	OX	HF64BSZ	1598	SC	BP15OLT	WHV48	LN	NK15GFE	659	NE
NL63XZY	651	NE	BN14CUC	6001	MB	HF64BTE	1599	SC						

Reg	No	Area	Reg	No	Area	Reg	No	Area	Reg	No	Area	Reg	No	Area
NK15GFG	660	NE	YY15HKD	SE253	LN	BX65WAO	53	OX	WJ65BZB	535	PL	BX16CLO	7131	NE
NK15GFJ	661	NE	YY15HKE	SE254	LN	BX65WAU	54	OX	WJ65BZC	536	PL	BX16CLU	7132	NE
NK15GFO	662	NE	YY15HKF	SE255	LN	BX65WCK	55	OX	WJ65BZD	537	PL	BX16CLV	7814	SC
NK15GFU	663	NE	YY15HKG	SE256	LN	BX65WDA	7120	NE	WJ65BZE	538	PL	BX16CLY	7815	SC
NK15GFV	664	NE	YY15HKH	SE257	LN	BX65WDC	7121	NE	WJ65HMA	147	PL	BX16CLZ	7816	SC
NK15GFX	665	NE	YY15HKJ	SE258	LN	BX65WDD	7122	NE	WJ65HMC	148	PL	HJ16HSC	1613	SC
OX15BUS	77	OX	BD65EVM	WHV83	LN	BX65WDE	7123	NE	WJ65HMD	149	PL	HJ16HSD	1614	SC
OX15LON	78	OX	BD65EVN	WHV81	LN	HF65AXY	1605	SC	WJ65HME	150	PL	HJ16HSE	1615	SC
SK15HKA	617	KO	BD65EVP	WHV85	LN	HF65AXZ	1606	SC	WJ65HMF	151	PL	HJ16HSF	1616	SC
SK15HKB	618	KO	BD65EVR	WHV84	LN	HF65AYA	1607	SC	WJ65HMG	152	PL	HJ16HSG	1617	SC
SK15HKC	619	KO	BD65EVT	WHV86	LN	HF65AYB	1608	SC	WJ65HMH	153	PL	HJ16HSK	1618	SC
SK15HKD	620	KO	BD65EVU	WHV87	LN	HF65AYC	2724	SC	WJ65HMK	154	PL	HJ16HSL	1619	SC
SK15HKE	621	KO	BD65EVV	WHV101	LN	HF65AYD	2725	SC	WJ65HMO	155	PL	HJ16HSN	1620	SC
SL15ZGC	651	OX	BD65EVW	WHV90	LN	HF65AYE	2726	SC	WJ65HMU	156	PL	HJ16HSO	1621	SC
SL15ZGD	652	OX	BD65EVX	WHV88	LN	HF65AYG	2727	SC	WJ65HMV	157	PL	HJ16HSU	1622	SC
SL15ZGE	653	OX	BD65EVY	WHV89	LN	HF65AYH	2728	SC	WJ65HMW	158	PL	HJ16HSV	1701	SC
SL15ZGF	654	OX	BD65EWA	WHV91	LN	HF65AYJ	2729	SC	WJ65HMY	159	PL	HJ16HSX	1702	SC
SL15ZGG	655	OX	BD65EWN	WHV102	LN	HF65AYK	2730	SC	YJ65EPU	9083	NE	HJ16HSY	1703	SC
SL15ZGH	656	OX	BD65EWO	WHV93	LN	HF65AYL	2731	SC	YX65RJV	SE261	LN	HJ16HSZ	1704	SC
SL15ZGJ	657	OX	BD65EWP	WHV92	LN	HF65AYM	2732	SC	YX65RJX	SE262	LN	HJ16HTA	1705	SC
SL15ZGK	658	OX	BD65EWR	WHV103	LN	HF65AYN	1609	SC	YX65RJZ	SE263	LN	HJ16HTC	1706	SC
SL15ZGM	659	OX	BD65EWS	WHV94	LN	HF65AYO	1610	SC	YX65RKA	SE264	LN	LJ16NNG	SEe3	LN
SL15ZGN	660	OX	BD65EWT	WHV110	LN	HF65AYP	1611	SC	YX65RKE	SE265	LN	LJ16NNH	SEe4	LN
SL15ZGO	661	OX	BD65EWU	WHV104	LN	HF65AYS	1612	SC	YX65RKF	SE266	LN	LJ16NNK	SEe5	LN
SM15HWC	401	CA	BD65EWW	WHV98	LN	HF65CXE	2733	SC	YX65RKJ	SE267	LN	LJ16NNL	SEe6	LN
SM15HWD	402	CA	BD65EWX	WHV100	LN	HF65CXG	2734	SC	YX65RNY	SE268	LN	LJ16NNM	SEe7	LN
SM15HWE	WS49	LN	BD65EWY	WHV95	LN	HF65CXH	2735	SC	YX65RNZ	SE269	LN	LJ16NNO	SEe8	LN
SM15HWF	WS50	LN	BD65EWZ	WHV96	LN	HF65CXJ	2736	SC	YX65ROH	SE270	LN	LJ16NNP	SEe9	LN
SM15HWG	WS51	LN	BD65EXA	WHV109	LN	HF65CXK	2737	SC	YX65ROU	SE271	LN	LJ16NNR	SEe10	LN
SM15HWH	WS52	LN	BD65JDZ	7124	NE	HF65CXL	2738	SC	YX65RPO	SE272	LN	LJ16NNT	SEe11	LN
SM15HWJ	WS53	LN	BF65HUJ	MEC51	LN	HF65CXM	2739	SC	YX65RPU	SE273	LN	LJ16NNU	SEe12	LN
SM15HWK	WS54	LN	BF65HUK	MEC53	LN	HF65CXN	2740	SC	YX65RPV	SE274	LN	NK16AZU	5439	NE
SM15VJZ	WS55	LN	BF65HUO	MEC52	LN	HF65CXO	2741	SC	YX65RPY	SE275	LN	NK16AZV	5440	NE
SM15VKA	WS56	LN	BF65HUP	MEC54	LN	HF65CXP	2742	SC	YX65RPZ	SE276	LN	NK16AZW	5441	NE
SM15VKB	WS57	LN	BF65HUU	MEC55	LN	HF65CXT	2743	SC	YX65RRO	SE277	LN	NK16BWY	5437	NE
SM15VKC	WS58	LN	BF65HUV	MEC56	LN	HF65CXU	2744	SC	YX65RRU	SE278	LN	NK16BWZ	5438	NE
SM15VKD	WS59	LN	BF65HUY	MEC57	LN	HF65CXV	2745	SC	YX65RRV	SE279	LN	NK16BXA	6301	NE
SM15VKE	WS60	LN	BF65HUZ	MEC58	LN	HF65CXW	2746	SC	YX65RRY	SE280	LN	NK16BXB	6302	NE
SM15WCK	WS61	LN	BF65HVA	MEC59	LN	HF65CXX	2747	SC	YX65RRZ	SE281	LN	NK16BXC	6303	NE
SM15WCL	WS62	LN	BF65HVB	MEC60	LN	HF65CXY	2748	SC	YX65RSO	SE282	LN	NK16BXD	6304	NE
SM15WCN	WS63	LN	BF65HVC	MEC61	LN	HF65CXZ	2749	SC	YX65RSU	SE283	LN	NK16BXE	6305	NE
SM15WCO	WS64	LN	BF65HVD	MEC62	LN	HF65CYA	2750	SC	YX65RSV	SE284	LN	NK16BXF	6306	NE
YP15NLM	EI1		BF65HVE	MEC63	LN	SM65LNE	403	CA	YX65RSY	SE285	LN	NK16BXG	6307	NE
YP15NLN	EI2		BF65HVG	MEC64	LN	SM65LNF	404	CA	YX65RSZ	SE286	LN	NK16BXH	667	NE
YX15XMK	SE232	LN	BF65HVH	MEC65	LN	SM65LNG	405	CA	YX65RTO	SE287	LN	NK16BXJ	668	NE
YX15XML	SE233	LN	BF65HVJ	MEC66	LN	SN65OAA	622	KO	BU16OYJ	MHV1	LN	NK16BXL	669	NE
YX15XMM	SE234	LN	BF65HVK	MEC67	LN	SN65OAB	623	KO	BU16OYK	MHV4	LN	NK16BXM	670	NE
YY15CNF	SE240	LN	BF65HVL	MEC68	LN	SN65OAC	624	KO	BU16OYL	MHV3	LN	NK16BXN	671	NE
YY15CNJ	SE236	LN	BF65HVM	MEC69	LN	SN65OAD	625	KO	BU16OYM	MHV2	LN	NK16BXO	672	NE
YY15CNK	SE237	LN	BF65WJA	WHV52	LN	SN65OAE	626	KO	BU16OYN	MHV5	LN	NK16BXP	673	NE
YY15CNO	SE239	LN	BF65WJC	WHV63	LN	SN65OAG	627	KO	BU16OYO	MHV6	LN	NK16BXR	674	NE
YY15CNU	SE235	LN	BF65WJD	WHV61	LN	SN65OAH	628	KO	BU16OYP	MHV7	LN	NK16BXS	675	NE
YY15CNV	SE241	LN	BF65WJE	WHV62	LN	SN65OAJ	629	KO	BU16OYR	MHV8	LN	NK16BXU	676	NE
YY15CNX	SE242	LN	BF65WJG	WHV71	LN	SN65OAL	630	KO	BU16OYS	MHV9	LN	NK16BXV	677	NE
YY15EYP	SE243	LN	BF65WJJ	WHV67	LN	SN65OAM	631	KO	BU16OYT	MHV10	LN	NK16BXW	678	NE
YY15EYR	SE244	LN	BF65WJK	WHV64	LN	SN65OAO	632	KO	BU16OYV	MHV11	LN	NK16BXX	679	NE
YY15EYS	SE245	LN	BF65WJM	WHV66	LN	SN65OAP	633	KO	BU16OYW	MHV12	LN	NK16BXY	680	NE
YY15EYT	SE246	LN	BF65WJN	WHV65	LN	SN65OAS	634	KO	BU16OYX	MHV13	LN	NK16BXZ	5436	NE
YY15EYU	SE247	LN	BF65WJO	WHV70	LN	SN65OAU	635	KO	BU16OYY	MHV14	LN	NK16BYA	5420	NE
YY15EYV	SE248	LN	BF65WJU	WHV69	LN	SN65OAV	636	KO	BU16OYZ	MHV15	LN	NK16BYB	5421	NE
YY15EYW	SE249	LN	BF65WJV	WHV68	LN	SN65OAW	637	KO	BU16OZA	MHV16	LN	NK16BYC	5422	NE
YY15GBZ	6773	MB	BF65WJX	WHV72	LN	SN65OAX	638	KO	BU16OZB	MHV20	LN	NK16BYD	5423	NE
YY15GCF	6774	MB	BF65WJY	WHV74	LN	SN65OAY	639	KO	BU16OZC	MHV18	LN	NK16BYF	5424	NE
YY15GCK	6775	MB	BF65WJZ	WHV76	LN	WJ65BYM	521	PL	BU16OZD	MHV19	LN	NK16BYG	5425	NE
YY15GCO	6776	MB	BF65WKA	WHV73	LN	WJ65BYN	522	PL	BU16OZE	MHV17	LN	NK16BYJ	5427	NE
YY15GCU	6777	MB	BF65WKB	WHV75	LN	WJ65BYO	523	PL	BW16LCL	7817	SC	NK16BYL	5428	NE
YY15GCV	6778	MB	BF65WKC	WHV79	LN	WJ65BYP	524	PL	BW16LCM	7818	SC	NK16BYM	5429	NE
YY15GCX	6779	MB	BF65WKD	WHV78	LN	WJ65BYR	525	PL	BW16LCN	7819	SC	NK16BYN	5430	NE
YY15GCZ	6780	MB	BF65WKE	WHV80	LN	WJ65BYS	526	PL	BW16LCO	7820	SC	NK16BYO	5431	NE
YY15GDA	6781	MB	BF65WKG	WHV77	LN	WJ65BYT	527	PL	BW16LCP	7821	SC	NK16BYP	5432	NE
YY15GDB	6782	MB	BF65WKH	WHV82	LN	WJ65BYU	528	PL	BW16LCT	7822	SC	NK16BYR	5433	NE
YY15GDF	SE259	LN	BT65JFZ	WHV105	LN	WJ65BYV	529	PL	BX16CKG	7125	NE	NK16BYS	5434	NE
YY15GDJ	SE260	LN	BT65JGF	WHV97	LN	WJ65BYW	530	PL	BX16CKJ	7126	NE	NK16BYT	5435	NE
YY15HKA	SE250	LN	BT65JGO	WHV106	LN	WJ65BYX	531	PL	BX16CKK	7127	NE	OY16JVK	216	SC
YY15HKB	SE251	LN	BT65JGU	WHV99	LN	WJ65BYY	532	PL	BX16CKL	7128	NE	OY16JVL	217	SC
YY15HKC	SE252	LN	BT65JGV	WHV108	LN	WJ65BYZ	533	PL	BX16CKO	7129	NE	OY16JVZ	219	SC
						WJ65BZA	534	PL	BX16CKP	7130	NE	OY16JWA	218	SC

Reg	No.	Area
SK16GWC	801	BH
SK16GWD	802	BH
SK16GWE	803	BH
SK16GWF	804	BH
SK16GWG	805	BH
SK16GWJ	806	BH
SK16GWL	807	BH
SK16GWM	808	BH
SK16GWN	809	BH
SK16GWO	810	BH
SK16GWP	811	BH
SK16GWU	812	BH
SK16GWV	813	BH
SK16GWW	814	BH
SK16GWX	815	BH
SK16GWY	816	BH
SK16GWZ	817	BH
SK16GXA	818	BH
SK16GXB	819	BH
SK16GXC	820	BH
SK16GXD	821	BH
SK16GXE	822	BH
SK16GXF	823	BH
SK16GXG	824	BH
SK16GXL	406	CA
SK16GXX	407	CA
SK16GXY	408	CA
SK16GXZ	409	CA
SL16YPK	WS65	LN
SN16OLP	SE288	LN
SN16OLR	SE289	LN
SN16OLT	SE290	LN
YX16OBT	EH39	LN
YX16OBU	EH40	LN
YX16OBV	EH41	LN
YX16OBW	EH42	LN
YX16OBY	EH43	LN
YX16OBZ	EH44	LN
YX16OCB	EH46	LN
YX16OCC	EH47	LN
YX16OCD	EH48	LN
YX16OCE	EH49	LN
YX16OCF	EH50	LN
YX16OCG	EH51	LN
YX16OCH	EH52	LN
YX16OCJ	EH53	LN
YX16OCL	EH54	LN
YX16OCM	EH55	LN
YX16OCN	EH56	LN
YX16OCO	EH57	LN
YX16OCP	EH58	LN
YX16OCR	EH59	LN
YX16OCS	EH60	LN
YX16OCX	SE291	LN
YX16OCY	SE292	LN
YY16YJE	108	SC
YY16YJF	109	SC
BG66MHX	MHV24	LN
BG66MHY	MHV29	LN
BG66MHZ	MHV31	LN
BG66MJE	MHV38	LN
BG66MJF	MHV39	LN
BG66MJJ	MHV40	LN
BG66MJO	MHV41	LN
BG66MJU	MHV43	LN
BG66MJV	MHV44	LN
BG66MJX	MHV47	LN
BG66MJY	MHV48	LN
BG66MKA	MHV34	LN
BG66MKC	MHV35	LN
BG66MKD	MHV36	LN
BT66MPE	MHV53	LN
BT66MPF	MHV54	LN
BT66MPO	MHV55	LN
BT66MPU	WHV164	LN
BT66MSO	WHV141	LN
BT66MSU	WHV142	LN
BT66MSV	WHV162	LN
BT66MSX	WHV163	LN
BT66MSY	WHV165	LN
BV66GVJ	19	OX
BV66GYJ	500	BH
BV66MHV	MHV81	LN
BV66VFT	MHV60	LN
BV66VFU	MHV63	LN
BV66VFW	MHV64	LN
BV66VFX	MHV65	LN
BV66VFY	MHV66	LN
BV66VFZ	MHV67	LN
BV66VGA	MHV68	LN
BV66VGC	MHV69	LN
BV66VGD	MHV70	LN
BV66VGE	MHV71	LN
BV66VGF	MHV72	LN
BV66VGG	MHV73	LN
BV66VGJ	MHV74	LN
BV66VGK	MHV75	LN
BV66VGL	MHV76	LN
BV66VGM	MHV77	LN
BV66VGN	MHV78	LN
BV66VGO	MHV79	LN
BV66VGP	MHV80	LN
BV66VGU	MHV49	LN
BV66VGX	MHV50	LN
BV66VGY	MHV51	LN
BV66VGZ	MHV52	LN
BV66VHA	MHV42	LN
BV66VHC	MHV45	LN
BV66VHD	MHV46	LN
BV66VHE	MHV61	LN
BV66VHG	MHV37	LN
BV66VHH	WHV139	LN
BV66VHJ	WHV135	LN
BV66VHK	WHV136	LN
BV66VHL	WHV160	LN
BV66VHN	WHV112	LN
BV66VHO	WHV113	LN
BV66VHP	WHV114	LN
BV66VHR	WHV115	LN
BV66VHT	WHV116	LN
BV66VHU	WHV117	LN
BV66VHW	WHV118	LN
BV66VHX	WHV119	LN
BV66VHY	WHV120	LN
BV66VHZ	WHV121	LN
BV66VJA	WHV143	LN
BV66VJC	WHV144	LN
BV66VJD	WHV145	LN
BV66VJE	WHV146	LN
BV66VJF	WHV147	LN
BV66VJG	WHV148	LN
BV66VJJ	WHV149	LN
BV66VJK	WHV150	LN
BV66VJL	WHV151	LN
BV66VJM	WHV152	LN
BV66VJN	WHV122	LN
BV66VJO	WHV123	LN
BV66VJP	WHV124	LN
BV66VJU	WHV125	LN
BV66VJV	WHV126	LN
BV66VJZ	WHV127	LN
BV66VKA	WHV153	LN
BV66VKB	WHV128	LN
BV66VKC	MHV83	LN
BV66VKD	MHV84	LN
BV66VKF	MHV85	LN
BV66VKG	MHV56	LN
BV66VKH	MHV57	LN
BV66VKJ	MHV58	LN
BV66VKK	MHV59	LN
BV66VKL	MHV62	LN
BV66VKM	MHV82	LN
BV66VKN	MHV21	LN
BV66VKO	MHV22	LN
BV66VKP	MHV23	LN
BV66VKR	MHV25	LN
BV66VKS	MHV26	LN
BV66VKT	MHV27	LN
BV66VKU	MHV28	LN
BV66VKW	MHV30	LN
BV66VKX	MHV32	LN
BV66VKZ	MHV33	LN
BV66VLA	WHV138	LN
BV66VLC	WHV154	LN
BV66VLD	WHV155	LN
BV66VLE	WHV129	LN
BV66VLF	WHV132	LN
BV66VLG	WHV159	LN
BV66VLH	WHV133	LN
BV66VLJ	WHV156	LN
BV66VLK	WHV131	LN
BV66VLL	WHV157	LN
BV66VLM	WHV130	LN
BV66VLN	WHV158	LN
BV66VLO	WHV166	LN
BV66VLP	WHV137	LN
BV66VLR	WHV167	LN
BV66WNX	7823	SC
BV66WNY	7824	SC
BV66WNZ	7825	SC
BV66WOA	7826	SC
BV66WOB	7827	SC
BV66WOC	7828	SC
BV66WOD	7829	SC
BV66WOH	7830	SC
BV66WOJ	7831	SC
BV66ZRY	WHV140	LN
BV66ZRZ	WHV134	LN
BV66ZSD	WHV161	LN
HF66CDY	1623	SC
HF66CDZ	1624	SC
HF66CEA	1625	SC
HF66CEJ	1626	SC
HF66CEK	1627	SC
HF66CEN	1628	SC
HF66CEO	1629	SC
HF66CEU	1630	SC
HF66CEV	1631	SC
HF66CEX	1632	SC
HF66CEY	1633	SC
HF66CFA	1634	SC
HF66CFD	1635	SC
HF66CFE	1636	SC
HF66CFG	1637	SC
HF66CFJ	1638	SC
HF66CFK	1639	SC
HF66CFL	1640	SC
HF66CFM	1641	SC
HF66CFN	1642	SC
HF66CFO	1643	SC
HF66CFP	1644	SC
HF66CFU	1645	SC
HF66CFV	1646	SC
HF66CFX	1647	SC
HF66CFY	1648	SC
HF66CFZ	1649	SC
HF66CGE	1650	SC
HF66CGG	1651	SC
HF66CGK	1652	SC
HF66CHD	1653	SC
HF66CHG	1654	SC
HF66CHH	2751	SC
HF66DOU	2759	SC
HF66DPE	2760	SC
HF66DPK	2761	SC
HF66DPN	2762	SC
HF66DPO	2763	SC
HF66DPU	2752	SC
HF66DPV	2753	SC
HF66DPX	2754	SC
HF66DPY	2755	SC
HF66DPZ	2756	SC
HF66DRO	2757	SC
HF66DRV	2758	SC
HF66DSE	1707	SC
HF66DSO	1708	SC
HF66DSU	1709	SC
HF66DSV	1710	SC
HF66DSX	1711	SC
HF66DSY	1712	SC
LJ66CFM	SEe13	LN
LJ66CFN	SEe14	LN
LJ66CFO	SEe15	LN
LJ66CFP	SEe16	LN
LJ66CFU	SEe17	LN
LJ66CFV	SEe18	LN
LJ66CFX	SEe19	LN
LJ66CFY	SEe20	LN
LJ66CFZ	SEe21	LN
LJ66CGE	SEe22	LN
LJ66CGF	SEe23	LN
LJ66CGG	SEe24	LN
LJ66CGK	SEe25	LN
LJ66CGO	SEe26	LN
LJ66CGU	SEe27	LN
LJ66CGV	SEe28	LN
LJ66CGX	SEe29	LN
LJ66CGY	SEe30	LN
LJ66CGZ	SEe31	LN
LJ66CHC	SEe32	LN
LJ66CHD	SEe33	LN
LJ66CHF	SEe34	LN
LJ66CHG	SEe35	LN
LJ66CHH	SEe36	LN
LJ66CHK	SEe37	LN
LJ66CHL	SEe38	LN
LJ66CHN	SEe39	LN
LJ66CHO	SEe40	LN
LJ66CHV	SEe41	LN
LJ66CHX	SEe42	LN
LJ66CHY	SEe43	LN
LJ66CHZ	SEe44	LN
LJ66CJE	SEe45	LN
LJ66CJF	SEe46	LN
LJ66CJO	SEe47	LN
LJ66CJU	SEe48	LN
LJ66CJV	SEe49	LN
LJ66CJX	SEe50	LN
LJ66CJY	SEe51	LN
LJ66CJZ	SEe1	LN
LJ66GYY	SEe2	LN
NK66CWW	681	NE
NK66CWX	682	NE
NK66CWY	683	NE
NK66CWZ	684	NE
NK66CXA	685	NE
NK66CXB	686	NE
NK66CXC	687	NE
NK66CXD	688	NE
NK66CXE	689	NE
NK66CXF	690	NE
NK66EVB	5442	NE
NK66EVC	5443	NE
NK66EVD	5444	NE
NK66EVF	5445	NE
NK66EVG	5446	NE
NK66EVH	5447	NE
NK66EVJ	5448	NE
NK66EVL	5449	NE
NK66EVM	5450	NE
NK66EVN	5451	NE
NK66EWA	5452	NE
NK66EWB	5453	NE
NK66EWC	5454	NE
NK66EWD	5455	NE
NK66EWE	5456	NE
NK66EWF	5457	NE
NK66EWH	5458	NE
NK66EWJ	5459	NE
NK66EWL	5460	NE
NK66EWM	5461	NE
NK66EWN	5462	NE
SK66HRN	441	TT
SK66HRO	442	TT
SK66HSC	WS66	LN
SK66HSE	WS67	LN
SK66HSF	WS68	LN
SK66HSG	WS69	LN
SK66HSJ	WS70	LN
SK66HSL	WS71	LN
SK66HSN	WS72	LN
SK66HSO	WS73	LN
SK66HSU	WS74	LN
SK66HSV	6102	MB
SK66HSX	6103	MB
SK66HSY	6104	MB
SK66HTA	6105	MB
SK66HTC	6106	MB
SK66HTD	6107	MB
SK66HTE	6108	MB
SK66HTF	6109	MB
SK66HTG	6110	MB
SK66HTJ	6111	MB
SK66HTL	6112	MB
SK66HTN	6113	MB
SK66HTO	6114	MB
SK66HTP	6115	MB
SK66HTT	6116	MB
SK66HTU	6117	MB
SK66HTV	663	OX
SK66HTX	664	OX
SK66HTY	665	OX
SK66HTZ	666	OX
SK66HUA	667	OX
SK66HUH	668	OX
SK66HUJ	669	OX
SK66HUO	670	OX
SK66HUP	671	OX
SK66HUU	672	OX
SK66HUV	673	OX
SK66HUY	674	OX
SK66HUZ	675	OX
SK66HVA	676	OX
SK66HVB	677	OX
SK66HVC	678	OX
SK66HVD	679	OX
SK66HVE	680	OX
SK66HVF	681	OX
SK66HVG	662	OX
SN66WNE	E284	LN
SN66WNF	E285	LN
SN66WNY	EH113	LN
SN66WNZ	EH114	LN
SN66WOA	EH115	LN
SN66WOB	EH116	LN
SN66WOC	EH117	LN
SN66WOD	EH118	LN
SN66WOH	EH119	LN
SN66WOJ	EH120	LN
SN66WOM	EH121	LN
SN66WOR	EH122	LN
SN66WOU	EH123	LN
SN66WOV	EH124	LN
SN66WOX	EH125	LN
SN66WOY	EH126	LN
SN66WPA	EH127	LN
SN66WPD	EH128	LN
SN66WPE	EH129	LN
SN66WPF	EH130	LN
YX66OZM	EH106	LN
YX66WHC	EH61	LN
YX66WHD	EH62	LN
YX66WHE	EH63	LN
YX66WHF	EH64	LN
YX66WHG	EH65	LN

Callsign	Code	Region
YX66WHH	EH66	LN
YX66WHJ	EH67	LN
YX66WHK	EH68	LN
YX66WHL	EH69	LN
YX66WHM	EH70	LN
YX66WHN	EH71	LN
YX66WHP	EH72	LN
YX66WHR	EH73	LN
YY66OYC	EH75	LN
YY66OYE	EH76	LN
YY66OYF	EH77	LN
YY66OYG	EH78	LN
YY66OYH	EH79	LN
YY66OYJ	EH80	LN
YY66OYK	EH81	LN
YY66OYL	EH82	LN
YY66OYM	EH83	LN
YY66OYN	EH84	LN
YY66OYO	EH85	LN
YY66OYP	EH86	LN
YY66OYR	EH87	LN
YY66OYS	EH88	LN
YY66OYT	EH89	LN
YY66OYU	EH90	LN
YY66OYV	EH91	LN
YY66OYW	EH92	LN
YY66OYX	EH93	LN
YY66OYZ	EH94	LN
YY66OZA	EH95	LN
YY66OZB	EH96	LN
YY66OZC	EH97	LN
YY66OZD	EH98	LN
YY66OZE	EH99	LN
YY66OZF	EH100	LN
YY66OZG	EH101	LN
YY66OZH	EH102	LN
YY66OZJ	EH103	LN
YY66OZK	EH104	LN
YY66OZL	EH105	LN
YY66OZO	EH107	LN
YY66OZP	EH108	LN
YY66OZR	EH109	LN
YY66OZS	EH110	LN
YY66OZT	EH111	LN
YY66OZU	EH112	LN
BN17JXY		CA
BV17CKF	6022	MB
BV17CKG	6021	MB
BV17GVD	7133	NE
BV17GVE	7134	NE
BV17GVF	7135	NE
BV17GVG	7136	NE
BV17GVJ	7137	NE
FJ17PVY	7400	SC
HF17AZA	1	SC
HF17AZB	2	SC
HF17AZC	3	SC
HF17AZD	4	SC
LJ17THF	WES1	LN
NK17GHO	5463	NE
NK17GHU	5464	NE
NK17GHV	5465	NE
NK17GHX	5466	NE
NK17GHY	5467	NE
NK17GHZ	5468	NE
NK17GJE	5469	NE
NK17GJF	5470	NE
NK17GJG	5471	NE
NK17GJJ	5472	NE
NK17GJO	5473	NE
NK17GJU	5474	NE
NK17GJV	5475	NE
NK17GJX	5476	NE
NK17GJY	5477	NE
NK17GJZ	5478	NE
NK17GKA	5479	NE
NK17GKC	5480	NE
SK17HFU	WS75	LN
SK17HFV	WS76	LN
SK17HFW	WS77	LN
SK17HFX	WS78	LN
SK17HHE	WS79	LN
SK17HHF	WS80	LN
SK17HHN	683	OX
SK17HHO	684	OX
SK17HHP	685	OX
SK17HHR	686	OX
SK17HHS	687	OX
SK17HHT	688	OX
SK17HHU	689	OX
SK17HHV	690	OX
SK17HHW	691	OX
SK17HJA	825	BH
SK17HJC	826	BH
SK17HJD	827	BH
SK17HJE	828	BH
SK17HKA	WS81	LN
SK17HKB	WS82	LN
SK17HKC	WS83	LN
SK17HKD	WS84	LN
SK17HKE	WS85	LN
SK17HKF	WS86	LN
SK17HKG	WS87	LN
SK17HKH	WS88	LN
SK17HKJ	WS89	LN
SK17HKL	WS90	LN
WA17FSU	550	PL
WA17FSV	551	PL
WA17FSX	552	PL
WA17FSY	553	PL
WA17FSZ	554	PL
WA17FTC	555	PL
WA17FTD	556	PL
WA17FTE	557	PL
WA17FTF	558	PL
WA17FTP	559	PL
WA17FTT	560	PL
WA17FTU	561	PL
WA17FTV	562	PL
WA17FTX	563	PL
WA17FTY	564	PL
WA17FTZ	565	PL
YJ17FXX	MD1	LN
YW17JTV	EH131	LN
YW17JTX	EH132	LN
YW17JTY	EH133	LN
YW17JTZ	EH134	LN
YW17JUA	EH135	LN
YW17JUC	EH136	LN
YW17JUE	EH137	LN
YW17JUF	EH138	LN
YW17JUH	EH139	LN
YW17JUJ	EH140	LN
YW17JUK	EH141	LN
YW17JUO	EH142	LN
YW17JUT	EH143	LN
YW17JUU	EH144	LN
YW17JUV	EH145	LN
YW17JUX	EH146	LN
YW17JUY	EH147	LN
YW17JVA	EH148	LN
YW17JVC	EH149	LN
YW17JVD	EH150	LN
YW17JVE	EH151	LN
YW17JVF	EH152	LN
YW17JVG	EH153	LN
YW17JVH	EH154	LN
YW17JVJ	EH155	LN
YW17JVK	EH156	LN
YW17JVL	EH157	LN
YW17JVM	EH158	LN
YW17JVN	EH159	LN
YW17JVO	EH160	LN
YW17JVP	EH161	LN
YX17NHP	2764	SC
YX17NHT	2765	SC
YX17NHU	2766	SC
YX17NHV	2767	SC
YX17NHY	2768	SC
YX17NHZ	2769	SC
YX17NJE	2770	SC
YX17NJF	2771	SC
YY17GRX	2700	SC
BV67JYR	56	OX
BV67JYS	57	OX
EJ67KNM	7965	SC
EN67OBW	7983	SC
EN67WLD	7984	SC
EX67CWA	7966	SC
EY67ZDD	7964	SC
HF67ATN	2772	SC
HF67ATO	2773	SC
HF67ATU	2774	SC
HF67ATV	2775	SC
HF67ATX	2776	SC
HF67ATY	2777	SC
HF67ATZ	2778	SC
HF67AUA	2779	SC
HF67AUC	2780	SC
HF67AUE	2781	SC
HF67AUH	2782	SC
HF67AUJ	2783	SC
HF67AUK	2784	SC
HF67AUL	2785	SC
HF67AUM	2786	SC
HF67AUN	2787	SC
HF67AUO	2788	SC
HF67AUP	2789	SC
HF67AUR	2790	SC
HF67EUA	220	SC
HF67EUB	221	SC
HF67EUC	222	SC
HF67EUD	223	SC
HF67EUE	224	SC
HF67EUH	225	SC
HF67EUJ	226	SC
HF67EUK	227	SC
HF67EUL	228	SC
HF67EUM	229	SC
HF67EUN	230	SC
HW67AHO	1655	SC
HW67AHP	1656	SC
HW67AHU	1657	SC
HW67AHV	1658	SC
HW67AHX	1659	SC
HW67AHY	1660	SC
HW67AHZ	1661	SC
HW67AJO	1662	SC
HW67AJU	1663	SC
HW67AJV	1664	SC
HW67AJY	1665	SC
HW67AKF	1666	SC
HW67AKG	1667	SC
HW67AKJ	1668	SC
HW67AKK	1669	SC
HW67AKN	1670	SC
HW67AKO		SC
LF67EWK	MHV86	LN
LF67EWL	MHV87	LN
LF67EWM	MHV88	LN
LF67EWN	MHV89	LN
LF67EWO	MHV90	LN
LF67EWP	MHV91	LN
LF67EWR	MHV92	LN
LF67EWS	MHV93	LN
LF67EWT	MHV94	LN
LF67EWU	MHV95	LN
LF67EWV	MHV96	LN
LF67EWW	MHV97	LN
LF67EWX	MHV98	LN
LF67EWY	MHV99	LN
LF67EXA	WHV168	LN
LF67EXB	WHV169	LN
LF67EXC	WHV170	LN
LF67EXD	WHV171	LN
LF67EXE	WHV172	LN
LF67EXG	WHV173	LN
LF67EXH	WHV174	LN
LF67EXJ	WHV175	LN
LF67EXK	WHV176	LN
LF67EXL	WHV177	LN
LF67EXM	WHV178	LN
LF67EXN	WHV188	LN
LF67EXO	WHV180	LN
LF67EXP	WHV181	LN
LF67EXR	WHV182	LN
LF67EXS	WHV183	LN
LF67EXT	WHV184	LN
LF67EXU	WHV185	LN
LF67EXV	WHV186	LN
LF67EXW	WHV187	LN
LF67EXX	WHV179	LN
LF67EXZ	WHV189	LN
LF67EYA	WHV190	LN
LF67EYB	WHV191	LN
LF67EYC	WHV192	LN
LF67EYD	WHV193	LN
LF67EYG	WHV194	LN
LF67EYH	WHV195	LN
LF67EYJ	WHV196	LN
LJ67DJD	SEe52	LN
LJ67DJE	SEe53	LN
LJ67DJF	SEe54	LN
LJ67DJK	SEe55	LN
LJ67DJO	SEe56	LN
LJ67DJU	SEe57	LN
LJ67DJV	SEe58	LN
LJ67DJX	SEe59	LN
LJ67DKA	SEe60	LN
LJ67DKD	SEe61	LN
LJ67DKE	SEe62	LN
LJ67DKF	SEe63	LN
LJ67DKK	SEe64	LN
LJ67DKL	SEe65	LN
LJ67DKN	SEe66	LN
LJ67DKO	SEe67	
LJ67DKU	SEe68	LN
LJ67DKV	SEe69	LN
LJ67DKY	SEe70	LN
LJ67DKY	SEe71	LN
LJ67DLD	SEe72	LN
LJ67DLE	SEe73	LN
LJ67DLF	SEe74	LN
LJ67DLK	SEe75	LN
LJ67DLN	SEe76	LN
NK67EBC	6310	NE
NK67EBD	6311	NE
NK67EBF	6312	NE
NK67EBG	6313	NE
NK67EBJ	6314	NE
NK67ECD	6308	NE
NK67ECE	6309	NE
NK67GMG	6315	NE
NK67GMO	6316	NE
NK67GMU	6317	NE
NK67GMV	6318	NE
NK67GMX	6319	NE
NK67GMY	6320	NE
NK67GMZ	6321	NE
NK67GNF	6322	NE
NK67GNJ	6323	NE
NK67GNN	6324	NE
NK67GNO	6325	NE
NK67GNP	6326	NE
NK67GNU	6327	NE
NK67GNV	6328	NE
NK67GNX	6329	NE
NK67GNY	6330	NE
NK67GNZ	6331	NE
NK67GOA	6332	NE
NK67GOC	6333	NE
SK67FJD	945	BH
SK67FJE	946	BH
SK67FJF	947	BH
SK67FJJ	829	BH
SK67FJN	830	BH
SK67FJO	831	BH
SK67FJP	832	BH
SK67FJU	833	BH
SK67FJV	834	BH
SK67FJX	835	BH
SK67FJY	836	BH
SK67FJZ	837	BH
SK67FKA	WS91	LN
SK67FKB	WS92	LN
SK67FKE	WS93	LN
SK67FKF	WS94	LN
SK67FKG	WS95	LN
SK67FKH	WS96	LN
SK67FKJ	WS97	LN
SK67FKL	WS98	LN
SK67FKM	WS99	LN
SK67FKN	WS100	LN
SK67FKO	WS101	LN
SK67FKP	WS102	LN
SK67FKS	WS103	LN
SK67FKT	838	BH
SK67FKU	839	BH
SK67FKV	840	BH
SK67FKW	841	BH
SK67FKX	842	BH
SK67FKY	843	BH
SK67FKZ	844	BH
SK67FLA	845	BH
SK67FLJ	846	BH
SK67FLL	847	BH
SK67FLM	848	BH
SK67FLN	849	BH
SK67FLP	850	BH
SK67FLR	851	BH
SK67FLV	852	BH
SK67FLW	853	BH
SK67FLX	854	BH
SK67FLZ	855	BH
SK67FMA	WS104	LN
SK67FMC	WS105	LN
SK67FMD	WS106	LN
SK67FME	WS107	LN
SK67FMF	WS108	LN
SK67FMJ	WS109	LN
SK67FML	WS110	LN
SK67FMM	WS111	LN
SK67FMO	WS112	LN
SK67FMP	WS113	LN
SK67FMU	WS114	LN
SK67FMV	WS115	LN
SK67FMX	WS116	LN
YX67VFG	EH162	LN
YX67VFH	EH163	LN
YX67VFJ	EH164	LN
YX67VFK	EH165	LN
YX67VFL	EH166	LN
YX67VFM	EH167	LN
YX67VFN	EH168	LN
YX67VFO	EH169	LN
YX67VFP	EH170	LN
YY67UPX	EH171	LN
YY67UPZ	EH172	LN
YY67URA	EH173	LN
YY67URB	EH174	LN
YY67URC	EH175	LN
YY67URE	EH176	LN
YY67URF	EH177	LN
YY67URG	EH178	LN
YY67URH	EH179	LN

Code	Number	Suffix
YY67URJ	EH180	LN
YY67URK	EH181	LN
YY67URL	EH182	LN
YY67URM	EH183	LN
YY67URN	EH184	LN
YY67URO	EH185	LN
YY67URP	EH186	LN
YY67URR	EH187	LN
YY67URS	EH188	LN
YY67URT	EH189	LN
YY67URU	EH190	LN
YY67URV	EH191	LN
YY67URW	EH192	LN
YY67URX	EH193	LN
YY67URZ	EH194	LN
YY67USS	EH195	LN
YY67UST	EH196	LN
YY67USU	EH197	LN
YY67USV	EH198	LN
YY67USW	EH199	LN
YY67USX	EH200	LN
YY67USZ	EH201	LN
YY67UTA	EH202	LN
YY67UTB	EH203	LN
YY67UTC	EH204	LN
YY67UTE	EH205	LN
YY67UTF	EH206	LN
YY67UTG	EH207	LN
YY67UTH	EH208	LN
YY67UTJ	EH209	LN
YY67UTK	EH210	LN
YY67UTL	EH211	LN
YY67UTM	EH212	LN
YY67UTN	EH213	LN
YY67UTO	EH214	LN
BV18YBH	530	BH
HF18CGV	231	SC
HF18CGX	232	SC
HF18CGY	233	SC
HF18CGZ	234	SC
HF18CHC	235	SC
HF18CHD	236	SC
HF18CHG	237	SC
HF18CHH	238	SC
HF18CHJ	239	SC
HF18CHK	240	SC
HF18CHL	241	SC
HF18CHN	242	SC
HF18CHO	243	SC
HF18CHV	244	SC
HF18CHX	245	SC
HF18CHY	246	SC
HF18CHZ	247	SC
HF18CJE	248	SC
HF18CJJ	249	SC
HF18CJO	250	SC
HF18CJU	251	SC
HF18CJV	252	SC
HF18CJX	253	SC
HF18CJY	254	SC
HF18CJZ	255	SC
HF18CKA	256	SC
HF18CKC	257	SC
HF18CKD	258	SC
HF18CKE	259	SC
HF18CKG	260	SC
SN18KLU	EH264	LN
SN18KLV	EH265	LN
SN18KLX	EH266	LN
SN18KLZ	EH267	LN
SN18KMA	EH268	LN
SN18KME	EH269	LN
SN18KMF	EH270	LN
SN18KMG	EH271	LN
SN18KMJ	EH272	LN
SN18KMK	EH273	LN
SN18KMO	EH275	LN
SN18KMU	EH276	LN
SN18KMV	EH277	LN
SN18KMX	EH278	LN
SN18KMY	EH279	LN
SN18KMZ	EH280	LN
SN18KNA	EH281	LN
SN18KNB	EH282	LN
SN18KNC	EH283	LN
SN18KND	EH284	LN
SN18XYV	WSD3	LN
SN18XYW	WSD4	LN
SN18XYX	WSD5	LN
SN18XYY	WSD6	LN
SN18XYZ	WSD7	LN
SN18XZB	WSD8	LN
SN18XZC	WSD9	LN
SN18XZD	WSD10	LN
SN18XZE	WSD11	LN
SN18XZF	WSD12	LN
SN18XZG	WSD13	LN
SN18XZH	WSD14	LN
SN18XZJ	WSD15	LN
SN18XZK	WSD16	LN
SN18XZL	WSD17	LN
SN18XZM	WSD18	LN
SN18XZO	WSD19	LN
SN18XZP	WSD20	LN
SN18XZR	WSD21	LN
SN18XZS	WSD22	LN
SN18XZT	WSD23	LN
SN18XZV	WS117	LN
YX18KPA	EH215	LN
YX18KPE	EH216	LN
YX18KPF	EH217	LN
YX18KPG	EH218	LN
YX18KPJ	EH219	LN
YX18KPK	EH220	LN
YX18KPL	EH221	LN
YX18KPN	EH222	LN
YX18KPO	EH223	LN
YX18KPP	EH224	LN
YX18KPR	EH226	LN
YX18KPT	EH227	LN
YX18KPU	EH228	LN
YX18KPV	EH229	LN
YX18KPY	EH230	LN
YX18KPZ	EH231	LN
YX18KRD	EH232	LN
YX18KRE	EH233	LN
YX18KRF	EH234	LN
YX18KRG	EH235	LN
YX18KRJ	EH236	LN
YX18KRK	EH237	LN
YX18KRN	EH238	LN
YX18KRO	EH239	LN
YX18KRU	EH240	LN
YX18KRV	EH241	LN
YX18KRZ	EH242	LN
YX18KSE	EH243	LN
YX18KSF	EH244	LN
YX18KSJ	EH245	LN
YX18KSK	EH246	LN
YX18KSN	EH247	LN
YX18KSO	EH248	LN
YX18KSU	EH249	LN
YX18KSV	EH250	LN
YX18KSY	EH251	LN
YX18KSZ	EH252	LN
YX18KTA	EH253	LN
YX18KTC	EH254	LN
YX18KTD	EH255	LN
YX18KTE	EH256	LN
YX18KTF	EH257	LN
YX18KTG	EH258	LN
YX18KTJ	EH259	LN
YX18KTK	EH260	LN
YX18KTL	EH261	LN
YX18KTN	EH262	LN
YX18KTO	EH263	LN
YX18KWW	EH285	LN
YX18KWY	EH286	LN
YX18KWZ	EH287	LN
YX18KXA	EH288	LN
YX18KXB	EH289	LN
YX18KXC	EH290	LN
YX18KXD	EH291	LN
YX18KXE	EH292	LN
YX18KXF	EH293	LN
YX18KXG	EH294	LN
YX18KXH	EH295	LN
YX18KXJ	EH296	LN
YX18KXK	EH297	LN
YX18KXL	EH298	LN
YX18KXM	EH299	LN
YX18KXN	EH300	LN
YX18KXO	EH301	LN
YX18KXP	EH302	LN
YX18KXR	EH303	LN
YX18KXS	EH304	LN
YX18KXT	EH305	LN
YX18KXU	EH306	LN
YX18KXV	EH307	LN
YX18KXW	EH308	LN
YX18KXY	EH309	LN
YX18KXZ	EH310	LN

Brighton & Hove – vehicle names

A majority of the vehicles in the Brighton & Hove fleet carry names. Detailed in this section is a full listing of the names carried by those named vehicles.

51	Ron Cunningham	443	Levi Emanuel Cohen
52	Kenneth Fines	444	Chris Copset
53	Helena Normanton	445	Antony Dale
54	John Peckham	446	Reg Moores
55	Lis Solkhon	447	Fred Perry
56	Maurice Tate	448	Paul Plumb
57	Ralph Vaughan Williams	449	Harold Poster
401	King Charles II	450	Wendy Richard
402	Prince Regent	451	Peter Stockbridge
403	Jack Arlidge	452	Ray Evison
404	Sir Charles Barry	453	George Basevi
405	Sir Samuel Brown	454	Don Bath
406	Sir Herbert Carden	455	Pauline Benjamin
407	King Edward VII	456	Charles Busby
408	Maria Fitzherbert	457	Dr Julius Carlebach
409	Norman Freedman	458	Hewitt Cobb
410	Martha Gunn	459	Countess of Rothes
411	Mother Riccarda	460	Harry Cowley
412	Phoebe Hessel	461	Henry Venn Elliott
413	Tony Hewison	462	Frank Furlong
414	Thomas Kemp	463	David Gray
415	Tommy Loates	464	John Bailey Haynes
416	Cardinal Newman	465	Maggie King
417	Sir Harry Preston	466	Robin McNair
418	Eugenis Birch	467	Andrew Melville
419	Sir Harry Ricardo	468	Herbert Menges
420	Dr Richard Russell	469	Lew Norris
421	Aubrey Beardsley	470	Dr Reginald Saxton
422	Queen Adelaide	471	Hubert Scott-Paine
423	William Ainsworth	472	Sir Arthur Pearson
424	Havergal Brian	473	Peter Avis
425	Edward Booth	474	Georgiana Burne-Jones
426	Janet Brown	475	Roy Chuter
427	Sir Arthur Conan Doyle	476	George Haines
428	Stanley Deason	477	Bernard Holden
429	S B Fry	478	Derek Jameson
430	Sir Jack Hobbs	479	Jeff Keen
431	Sir John Howard	480	Theodore Wright
432	Paul Millmore	481	Pat Moorman
433	John Nash	482	Chris Ogden
434	Elisabeth Howard	483	Cecil Pashley
435	Lord Oliver	484	Wilfred Pickles
436	Cap Nicholas Tettersell	485	Margaret Powell
437	Sir Charles Thomas-Stanford	486	Alan Randall
438	Dr Trevor Mann	487	William Stroudley
439	Phil Starr	488	Stanley Theobold
440	Lord Cohen	489	Andy Durr
441	Magnus Volk	490	Herbert Toms
442	Ronnie Ablett	550	Sir Winston Churchill

551	Charles Dickens		685	Donald Peers
616	Henry Allingham		686	Chris Moyes
623	Matthew Grimstone		687	Dr William Stone
629	George Humphrey		688	Elsie and Doris Waters
630	Harry Leader		801	Jessica-Jade Allen
631	Bobby Lee		802	John Heward
632	Ida Lupino		803	Martin Langfried
633	Henry Solomon		804	Doreen Valiente
634	Dorothy Stringer		805	William Moon
635	Angela Thirkell		806	Ernest F Beal
636	Grace Eyre Woodhead		807	Chris Cooke
637	Kenneth Bredon		808	William Henry Volkins
638	Sir Anton Dolin		809	Thomas Tilling
639	Raymond Francis		810	Ann Quin
640	Graham Greene		811	Mabel Pratt
641	John Jackson		812	Eva Moore
642	Howard Johnson		813	Jack Jenkins
643	Victoria Lidiard		814	George Albert Smith
644	K S Ranjitsinhji		815	James Williamson
645	Paul Stonor		816	Janet Turner
646	Herbert Wilcox		817	Mary Merrifield
647	Lord Fulton of Falmer		818	Elaine Baird
648	Jimmy Edwards		819	Harry Vowles
649	Adam Faith		820	Amon Wilds
650	Prince Petr Kropotkin		821	Minnie Turner
652	Sir William Nicholson		822	Sake Dean Mahomed
655	Elizabeth Allan		823	Tommy Cook
656	Dame Henrietta Barnett		824	John James Crowe
657	Wynne Baxter		825	Peter Stocker
658	Clementina Black		826	Dame Dicely Saunders
659	Helen Boyle		827	Johnny West
660	Sir Lindsay Bryson		828	Richard Addinsell
662	Bernard Jordan		829	John Carcass
663	Eric Gill		830	Alan Weeks
665	Jacob Schilt		831	John Johnson
666	Eleanor Marx		832	Baron Goldsmid
667	Dame Clara Butt		833	Charlie Jordan
668	Bob Copper		834	Ellen Nye Chart
669	Sir Edward Sassoon		835	Ernie Johnstone
670	Dr Herzl Sless		836	Phyllis Pearsall
671	Vanessa Bell		837	Eddie Whalley
672	Mike Bamber		838	Dusty Springfield
673	Isambard Kingdom Brunel		839	William Wheeler
674	John Constable		840	Robert Metcalfe
675	Edward Carpenter		841	Thomas Attree
676	David Lane		842	Kitty O'Shea
677	Charles Neville		843	Sir John Cordy Burrows
678	Jack Howe		844	Caroline of Brunswick
679	Dr William King		845	Virginia Woolf
680	George Larner		846	Capt Frederick Collins
681	Sir George Lewis		847	Jessica-Jayde Allen
682	Samuel Lewis		848	Sir George Everest
683	Terence Morgan		849	Jim Howell
684	Rev Frederick Robertson		850	Margaret Bondfield

851	John Rastrick		923	Zoe Bridgen
852	Ivy Compton-Burnett		924	Dora Bryan
853	Patricia Harding		925	Adrian Bunting
854	Enid Bagnold		926	Brian Cobby
855	William Marsh		927	Henry Cozwell
901	Charles Burt Brill		928	Jonathan Darby
902	Fanny Burney		929	Dr Jan De Winter
903	Douglas Byng		930	Tirzah Garwood
904	Sir John Clements		931	Ian Gow
905	Rev Richard Enraght		932	George Holkham
906	James Gray		933	Jamie Jones
907	Patrick Hamilton		934	Richard Jones
908	Thomas Harrington		935	Rudyard Kipling
909	Trevor Kaye		936	The Lawrence Sisters
910	Thomas Lainson		937	John Nathan-Turner
911	William Lillywhite		938	Dame Anna Neagle
912	Dame Anita Roddick		939	Edith Nesbit
913	Pete McCarthy		940	Don Partridge
914	Daisy Noakes		941	Eric Ravilious
915	Dr William Parker		942	Ralph Reader
916	Ben Sherman		943	Alfred Richardson
917	Sir Hans Singer		944	Eric Slater
918	Rex Whistler		945	Ref Alfred Evans
919	Max Miller		946	Dame Gracie Fields
920	Dame Flora Robson		947	James Hurdis
921	Bill Axcell		7951	Ian Mills
922	Frank Bridge		RML2317	Colin Curtis

Thamesdown – vehicle names

A majority of the vehicles in the Thamesdown (part of Go South Coast) fleet carry names. Detailed in this section is a full listing of the names carried by those named vehicles.

103	Seagull		501	Brunel
104	Skylark		502	Iron Duke
105	Blackbird		503	Great Britain
106	Bullfinch		504	Lightning
107	Starling		505	Emperor
108	Peacock		506	Sulton
109	Nightingale		507	Lord of the Isles
201	Salzgitter		508	Royal Sovereign
202	Ocotal		509	Tornado
203	Pontorson		511	Pasha
204	Grenville		512	Courier
207	Hermes		513	Tartar
208	Highflyer		514	Warlock
209	Intrepid		515	Wizard
210	Jupiter		516	Rougemont
212	Kelly		517	Hirondelle
213	Magpie		518	Swallow
214	Majestic		519	Timour
216	Isambard Kingdom Brunel		520	Prometheus
217	Sir Daniel Gooch		521	Perseus
218	Sudeley Castle		522	Estaffete
219	Sarum Castle		523	Rover
363	Alexandra		524	Amazon
365	Achilles		525	Alma
366	Thunderbolt		526	Balaklava
371	Earl of Devon		527	Inkermann
372	Earl of Dartmouth		528	Kertch
373	Earl of Plymouth		2764	King George V
374	City of Exeter		2765	King Edward II
375	River Tamar		2766	King Charles II
376	Duke of Cornwall		2767	King James I
377	Earl of St Germans		2768	King Henry VIII
378	Earl of Mount Edgcumbe		2769	King John
379	City of Truro		2770	King Richard I
401	Queen Elizabeth		2771	King William
402	King George VI		2772	Western Enterprise
403	King Edward VIII		2773	Western Pathfinder
404	King George V		2774	Western Explorer
405	King Edward VII		2775	Western Pioneer
406	Queen Victoria		2776	Western Crusader
407	King William IV		2777	Western Venturer
408	King George IV		2778	Western Stalwart
411	Queen Berengaria		2779	Western Talisman
412	Queen Boadicea		2780	Western Harrier
413	The Prince of Wales		2781	Western Invader
414	Prince Albert		2782	Western Campaigner
415	Princess Mary		2783	Western Thunderer
416	Princess Patricia		2784	Western Firebrand
417	Princess Eugenie			